Evaluation is for making it work.

If it works . . .
Notice and nurture.

If it doesn't work . . .
Notice and change.

Sourcebook

Program Evaluation

A PRACTITIONER'S GUIDE FOR TRAINERS AND EDUCATORS

ROBERT O. BRINKERHOFF

DALE M. BRETHOWER

TERRY HLUCHYJ

JERI RIDINGS NOWAKOWSKI

Kluwer-Nijhoff Publishing
Boston   The Hague   Dordrecht   Lancaster
a member of the Kluwer Academic Publishers Group

Distributors for North America:
Kluwer·Nijhoff Publishing
Kluwer Boston, Inc.
190 Old Derby Street
Hingham, Massachusetts 02043, U.S.A.

Distributors outside North America:
Kluwer Academic Publishers Group
Distribution Centre
P.O. Box 322
3300 AH Dordrecht, The Netherlands

Library of Congress Cataloging in Publication Data
Main entry under title:

Program evaluation: a practitioner's guide for trainers and
educators: sourcebook and casebook

(Evaluation in education and human services)
1. Educational accountability. 2. Educational
accountability—United States—Case studies.
I. Brinkerhoff, Robert O. II. Series.
LB2806.P77 1983   379.1'54   81-14913
ISBN 0-89838-121-5

Program evaluation: a practitioner's guide for trainers and
educators: A sourcebook.

(Evaluation in education and human services)
1. Evaluation research (Social action programs)—
Handbooks, manuals, etc. 2. Educational accountability
—Handbooks, manuals, etc. I. Brinkerhoff, Robert O.
II. Series
HV11.P739 1983   361.6'1   82-16213
ISBN 0-89838-120-7

Printed in the United States of America.

Contents

About these Materials

Introduction to the Package

Program Evaluation: A Practitioner's Guide was developed by the Evaluation Training Consortium (ETC) project at the Evaluation Center, Western Michigan University. The ETC project was funded by the U.S. Office of Special Education from 1972 to 1982; it has developed program evaluation procedures for use by teacher educators and delivered training to thousands of professionals across the United States. The mission of the ETC has been to improve the evaluation capabilities of projects and programs engaged in preparing personnel to work with special and regular education clients and pupils. This package of materials is intended to carry forward that mission, and help educators to help themselves improve educational practice.

This set of materials is for use in training, teacher education, and other professional development programs and projects in private and public agencies, public schools and colleges and universities. They are designed to help individuals or groups in their own work, and they can be used to train others.

The package has the following parts:

(1) Sourcebook, which contains chapters of guidelines, resources and references for each of 7 key evaluation functions.
(2) Casebook (bound together with Sourcebook), which is a collection of twelve stories about evaluation applied to real-life projects and programs in different settings. These show people planning, conducting and using evaluation.
(3) Design Manual, which contains a programmed set of directions, worksheets, examples, and checklists to help you design an evaluation for a particular use.

Conceptual Basis

These materials are about designing, conducting, and using evaluation, but their underlying assumption is that evaluation should be useful for improving current and/or future training efforts. While these materials are meant to help you do evaluation well, we believe that evaluation is not worth doing at all unless you can use it to make training better, or to better invest training resources.

Good training, whether preservice or inservice, must satisfy four conditions:

(1) Training must be directed toward worthwhile goals.

(2) Training strategies must be theoretically sound, reflect good practice, be feasible, and make optimum use of available resources.

(3) Implementation of training must be efficiently managed and responsive to emerging problems and changing conditions.

(4) Recycling decisions (i.e., to terminate, continue, curtail or expand training) should be based on knowledge of impacts of training, the extent to which training outcomes are in use, and the worth of training. These decisions should be responsive to continuing and emerging needs and problems.

These criteria are not independent, and each is important to another. Training designs must be not only potent but they must be directed toward worthwhile goals; good designs can serve as guides to implementation, and implementation is facilitated by good design; and, well-implemented training is most likely to have positive outcomes. Also, these criteria are functionally related in a cycle which repeats as training programs grow and develop:

Cycle of Training Functions

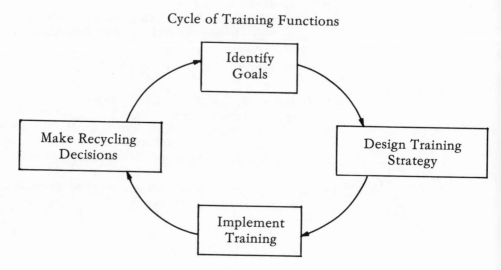

Evaluation activities are what tie these training functions together. Different kinds of evaluations are done during each of these training function stages to ensure that the function is carried out as well as it can be.

Table 1 shows the different kinds of evaluation we have defined and portrayed in these materials. The *Casebook* provides examples of these different uses; the *Sourcebook* will help you learn about options and guidelines for doing these different kinds of evaluation. The *Design Manual* can help you design an evaluation to serve one or more of these evaluation purposes.

Evaluation Purposes Related to the Key Training Program Functions

Key Training Function	Evaluation Purposes and Uses
1. Identify worthwhile training goals	Assess needs, validate goals, prioritize goals, identify constraints and problems related to goals for training
2. Design effective training strategies	Assess alternative strategies, compare training designs, identify criteria to judge designs, determine feasibility and potential for success
3. Effectively implement training	Monitor and control program operation, identify problems and revision needs, determine whether objectives are achieved, document costs and activities
4. Decide whether to terminate, continue, curtail or expand training	Determine usage and application, identify emerging and continuing needs, determine benefits of training, identify problems and revision needs to enhance training usage

How the Materials Are Organized

The *Sourcebook* is organized by major evaluation function:

(1) focusing an evaluation and clarifying its purpose
(2) designing an evaluation
(3) collecting information
(4) analyzing information
(5) reporting: interpreting and using evaluation findings
(6) managing evaluation activities
(7) evaluating evaluation efforts

Each function is defined, then the several key decisions needed to complete the function are explained. The *Sourcebook* contains examples, guidelines, criteria and checklists you can use to do more effective evaluation. It also includes references to other books and resources that can be useful in evaluating training programs.

The *Casebook* contains twelve case-examples. Each is a story about evaluation within a particular training program. The case examples, designed to portray evaluation applications of different types in different settings, were contributed by field practitioners and written in conjunction with ETC staff. They are fictional accounts but based on actual programs and uses of evaluation. Each case-example is annotated to highlight the seven major evaluation functions as set forth in the *Sourcebook*. This is done to show how these functions differ according to particular program needs and settings. Following each case is a set of review and discussion questions to help extend the lessons available in the case-example.

The *Design Manual* contains worksheets, directions, and guidelines for designing an evaluation. Its organization is similar to the *Sourcebook,* as it helps you produce different parts of an overall evaluation design. Each section presents an example of the design product needed; gives you worksheets, directions, and aids for producing that document; and provides a checklist for assessing your work.

You can use the *Design Manual* to produce:

(1) an evaluation overview
(2) an outline of evaluation questions
(3) an information collection plan
(4) an analysis and interpretation plan
(5) a management plan
(6) a report plan
(7) a plan for evaluating your evaluation

Suggestions for Using the Materials

There is no one particular order in which these materials are meant to be used. You could begin in any of the three parts, using them alone or in combination. Where you begin and how you use the materials depends on what you want to use them for. We'll suggest some possible options and applications here. You could follow one or more of these, or simply look through the materials and make up your own way of using them.

Remember that you can use these materials by yourself or in conjunction with a group. Or, you could use these materials to train other people in evaluation.

Some Options

1. To learn about how evaluation could be used to help with particular problems, you could read some of the case-examples. Use the guide below to see which cases relate to certain problems.

some common uses/problems	relevant case-examples (numbers listed are from Casebook Table of Contents)
–putting together an inservice workshop or program	–L-1, L-2, C-2
–designing, conducting a needs assessment	–L-1, C-1, C-5
–looking at child-change as a result of inservice (worth of training)	–L-4
–managing a new project	–C-2
–evaluating services provided from an agency	–S-3

some common uses/problems	relevant case-examples (numbers listed are from Casebook Table of Contents)
–improving curriculum and courses	–C-1, C-5
–proposal evaluation	–S-2
–monitoring programs, improving services	–S-1, S-3, L-3
–looking for evidence of impact and worth	–L-4, S-3, C-3, L-2
–improving an evaluation	–C-4

2. To learn more about evaluation applications in your setting: read the case-examples for your setting (state agency, local school, college).
3. To learn more about evaluation in general and how it fits in with training: read the *Sourcebook* and discuss a few cases with yourself or others.
4. To complete some evaluation design work for a program you're working on: use the *Design Manual*.
5. To become more knowledgeable and proficient in evaluation: read the *Sourcebook* (then try some more evaluation work!).
6. To train others:
    (1) Read the *Sourcebook* yourself and use it as the basis for training.
    (2) Select some case-examples from the *Casebook* for participants to read and discuss.
    (3) Have participants work on evaluation designs using the *Design Manual*.

Acknowledgments

The ideas and procedures described in this package of materials have evolved in ways too circuitous and interwoven to be accurately described. For us the "authors" to attach our names to them is as brazen perhaps as the fixing of a zoologist's name to a newly discovered snail; the zoologist, at least, makes no claim to creation.

We can quite clearly dedicate this work to Malcolm M. Provus, creator of the Discrepancy Evaluation Model, who initiated the project from which these materials came. His vision and impetus enabled the Evaluation Training Consortium (ETC) to survive beyond his untimely death in 1975. We can quite clearly, too, state that the work of dozens of ETC staff members from years past, advisors and friends is reflected in virtually every page. And finally, the several thousand teacher educators who labored in ETC workshops have inspired and shaped all that is between these covers.

With this labyrinthian progenesis recognized, let us humbly but more precisely try to point out credit and blame.

The four whose names appear on the books' covers stand jointly responsible for the materials. We worked together on all parts, though leadership was partitioned among us on the several pieces. Jeri Ridings Nowakowski brought forth the *Sourcebook*, as well as editing a section of the *Casebook*. Terry Hluchyj and Dale Brethower collaborated on the *Design Manual*. Bob Brinkerhoff, Director of ETC since 1975, wrote parts of and edited all of the books, kibitzed, harassed and midwived the entire effort.

Working closely with the primary authors during the last two years of the project were ETC staff members Ann Hallawell and Bob Olsen, who edited each a Casebook section and assisted with many other parts as well. Also ably assisting were graduate assistants Dick Frisbie and Laurie Rudolph.

Dan Stufflebeam, Director of the College of Education's Evaluation Center at Western Michigan University, provided critical reviews and administrative guidance throughout the project. Jim Sanders and Bob Rodosky played similar roles, reviewing draft after draft.

Becky Fitch, ETC project secretary, typed more drafts than she or any of us care to remember before being lured from Michigan's fiscal wastelands to booming Texas. Amy Leftwich saved us. We are indebted to Becky and Amy for their cheerful patience and sure skills.

Since its inception in 1972, the ETC project has been blessed with the support of an especially able Advisory Board. Bruce Balow, now at the University of Minnesota but once a USOE official, helped begin the project and has given invaluable leadership and counsel for eleven years. Hanging in with Bruce for the full eleven also was Vic Baldwin. Rounding out this current board, all of whom guided our work on the materials, are Helen

Almanza, Jeanie Crosby, Egon Guba, Bruce Irons and John Johnson. Past board members of noteworthy long service since 1972 are: Roger Kroth, Marty Martinson, Hugh McKenzie, and Dick Whelan.

There are many others whose help we acknowledge.

Early in this work's development, we visited several training sites to learn and be told about current needs and problems. Persons who graciously arranged for and hosted these visits were: Margaret Arbuckle, Ed Blackhurst, Phil Burke, Larry Carmichael, Stan Fagen, John Mathey, Herb Prehm, Hugh Watson, Daun Dickie, Deane Crowell, Rose Hicks, Vicki LaBrie and Mike Wilhelm.

Abe Nicolaou and Stacia Farrell conducted literature reviews and context studies early in the material's development. Ariah Lewy from Israel, during a visit to Michigan reviewed our plans and provided helpful development guidance. Providing a crucial panel review in January 1981 were:

College and university	Local school	State agency
Dwight Allen	Margaret Arbuckle	Vic Baldwin
Bruce Balow	Paula Tissot	Cy Freston
Ed Blackhurst	Kathy Byers	Dee John
Egon Guba	Phil Cartwright	Carol Lacey
Steve Lilly	Steve Checkon	Alex Law
Glen Vergason	Jim Collins	Bill Schipper
	Bruce Irons	

Jay Millman and Wayne Welch joined Jim Sanders and Dan Stufflebeam in a marathon review of cases which dramatically shaped their revision.

The next-to-final draft of the materials were reviewed by Fred Baars, Egon Guba, John Hansen, John McLaughlin, Nancy Zimpher and Tom Ryan in early 1982.

The entire package was submitted to an extensive field test in November 1981 and again in January 1982, coordinated by Vic Dotson of the ETC. Field testers were:

Fred Appelman	James Impara	Nancy Spinner
Kathleen Bolland	David Kazen	Sandra K. Squires
Jane R. Braden	Cynthia L. Knorr	Diane Treadway
Ruth V. Burgess	William Lee	Diana Trehary
Janice R. Duncan	Marvin Lew	Elaine M. Walsh
Kathryn Dunn	George Madaus	Miriam O. Williams
Robert Flexer	Kenneth R. Olson	
Janet Freese	Michael Plog	

Finally, we should acknowledge the institutional support provided to the ETC from 1972–1978 at the University of Virginia and 1978 to 1982 at Western Michigan University. The Division of Personnel Preparation of the U.S. Office of Special Education provided funding for the project, ably overseen by project officer Jim Siantz.

EVALUATION: WHAT IS IT?

David Nevo

Different people mean different things when they use the word "evaluation." They might also "do" evaluation in different ways, use it for different purposes, or even use different standards to decide what a good evaluation should look like. If you want to pinpoint what someone means, you have to find out a number of things.

Here are ten questions that will help you summarize what is mean when someone talks about evaluation. You can use the ten questions to find out what others have in mind when they talk about or ask you to do evaluation. Most important, these ten questions will help you clarify what *you* mean when you use the word "evaluation," or how you will define it the next time you use it.

1. *How is evaluation defined?* What are the unique features of an evaluation? How do you know when you see one? How does it differ from things such as "measurement" or "research?"

Is evaluation administering tests and questionnaires? Providing information for decision makers? Determining whether goals have been achieved? Assessment of merit? Or something else?

2. *What is evaluation for?* Why do evaluation? What is the purpose of evaluation? What functions does it serve? Is it done to serve decision making? To demonstrate accountability? For accreditation or certification? To motivate people? To change and improve programs? Or for some other reason?

3. *What are the objects of evaluation?* What could or should be evaluated? Are the "things" that are to be evaluated students, teachers, projects, programs, institutions or something else?

4. *What aspects and dimensions of an object should evaluation investigate?* What questions should be addressed about whatever is being evaluated? What types of information should be gathered? Are the aspects of the object that should be evaluated resources, impacts or outcomes, processes or implementation, staff and client transactions, goals and plans, costs and benefits, needs, organizational characteristics, or something else?

5. *What criteria should be used to judge an object?* How are you going to interpret the findings? How should value meaning be assigned to collected information? How will you decide if the object is "good" or "bad?" Should the criterion be achievement of stated goals, adherence to plans, responding to identified needs, achievement of social goals or ideals, comparison with alternative objects, adherence to laws and guidelines, conformity with audience expectations, or something else?

6. *Who should be served by an evaluation?* Who is the client? Who is the audience for the evaluation? Whose information needs does it serve? Is it done for yourself, your students, the staff, the funding agency, the general public, or someone else?

7. *What steps and procedures are involved in doing an evaluation?* How do you start an evaluation and how do you proceed? What are the major stages of an evaluation project? Is there a "best" sequence for conducting an evaluation?

8. *What methods of inquiry should be used in evaluation?* How do you collect information? What kind of inquiry design should be used in evaluation? Is the "best" methodology for evaluation tests and questionnaires, panels of experts, experimental design, surveys and correlational studies, ethnographies and case studies, "jury" trials, naturalistic approaches, or some other approach?

9. Who should do evaluation? What kind of evaluator should you employ? What kind of skills should an evaluator have? What should be the authority and responsibilities of an evaluator? Should the evaluation be done by a professional evaluator, an internal or external evaluator, an evaluation specialist or an expert in the field to be evaluated, regular staff, or someone else?

10. By what standards should evaluation be judged? How do you know what is a good evaluation? What are the characteristics of a well-done evaluation? How do you evaluate an evaluation? Should evaluation be practical and useful, provide accurate and reliable information, be realistic, prudent and frugal, be conducted legally and ethically, be objective and scientific, or should it be something else?

As mentioned earlier in this section, the ten questions can be used for various purposes, but there are two ways in which the ten questions can be particularly useful:
· *Use them to organize your own perception of what evaluation is.*
· *Use them to understand what others mean when they refer to evaluation.*

SOME ANSWERS TO THE TEN QUESTIONS FROM THE EVALUATION LITERATURE

Your acquaintance with some major evaluation approaches will help you to develop your own perception of evaluation and its main concerns.

1. How is evaluation defined? Many definitions of evaluation can be found in the literature. One well-known definition, originated by Ralph Tyler, perceives evaluation as *the process of determining to what extent the educational objectives are actually being realized* (Tyler, 1950, p. 69). Another widely accepted definition of evaluation has been that of *providing information for decision making* suggested by various leading evaluators, such as Lee Cronbach (1963), Dan Stufflebeam (*Stufflebeam, et al., 1971) or Marvin Alkin (1969). Malcolm Provus, the originator of Discrepancy Evaluation (1971), defined evaluation as *the comparison of performance to some standards to determine whether discrepancies existed.* In recent years, a considerable amount of consensus has been reached among evaluators regarding the definition of evaluation as *the assessment of merit or worth* (Scriven, 1967; Glass, 1969; Stufflebeam, 1974). A joint committee on standards for evaluation, comprised of seventeen members representing twelve organizations associated with educational evaluation, published their definition of evaluation as *the systematic investigation of the worth or merit of some object* (Joint Committee, 1981, p. 12). Such a definition, which points to the judgmental character of evaluation might create a considerable amount of anxiety among potential evaluees and raise resistance among opponents of evaluation. Obviously, a nonjudgmental definition of evaluation might be accepted in a more favorable way by evaluees and clients. However, it may be unrealistic to create positive attitudes towards evaluation by ignoring the fact of judgment as its major and inevitable feature. Another approach intended to develop positive attitudes towards evaluation might be to demonstrate its constructive functions within the various domains of education.

2. What is evaluation for? Scriven (1967) was the first to suggest the distinction between *formative evaluation* and *summative evaluation*, referring to two major roles or functions of evaluation, although he was probably not the first one to realize the importance of such a distinction. Later on, referring to the same two functions, Stufflebeam (1971) suggested the distinction between *proactive evaluation intended to serve decision making* and *retroactive evaluation to serve accountability.* Thus, evaluation can serve two functions. In its formative function, evaluation is used for the improvement and development of an ongoing activity (or program, person, product, etc.). In its summative function, evaluation is used for accountability, certification, selection or continuation.

A third function of evaluation, which has been less often treated by evaluation literature, should also be considered. This is the *psychological or socio-political* function of evaluation. In many cases it is apparent that evaluation is not serving only formative purposes nor is it being used solely for accountability or other summative purposes. However, it may have a major use to increase awareness of special activities, motivate desired behavior of evaluees, or promote public relations. Regardless of our personal feelings about the use (or misuse) of evaluation for this purpose, we cannot ignore it.

Obviously, there are no "right" or "wrong" functions of evaluation, and more than one function can be served by an evaluation. There also might be more than these three evaluation functions. However, different functions can be served by different evaluation methods.

3. What are the objects of evaluation? Almost any training entity can serve as an object of evaluation. While some, like students or faculty, have always been popular objects of evaluation in education, others, like projects, programs, curricular materials, or educational institutions, have presently become favorite objects of educational evaluation. Two major conclusions can be drawn from the review of evaluation literature:

(a) almost anything can be an object of evaluation and evaluation should not be limited to the evaluation of students or faculty;
(b) the clear identification and delineation of the evaluation object is an important part of the development of any evaluation design.

It is very important that you determine what is "the thing" that you want to evaluate. This will help you decide what kind of information you should collect, and how you should analyze it. It helps keep an evaluation focused. And, clear object identification helps clarify and resolve value conflicts and potential threat among stakeholders and others likely to be affected.

4. What aspects and dimensions of an object should evaluation investigate? After an evaluation object has been chosen, a decision has to be made regarding the various aspects of the object that should be evaluated. Earlier approaches to evaluation focused mainly on results or outcomes. Thus, to evaluate an educational object (e.g., a workshop) would mean to evaluate the quality of the results of its functioning (e.g., participant's achievements). In recent years, some interesting attempts have been made to extend the scope of evaluation variables in various evaluation models (Stake, 1967; Stufflebeam, 1969, 1974; Stufflebeam, et al., 1971; Alkin, 1969; Provus, 1971). Stufflebeam's CIPP Model, for example, suggests that evaluation focus on four aspects of an evaluation object: (1) its *goals*; (2) its *design*; (3) its *process of implementation*; and (4) its *outcomes*. According to this approach a complete evaluation of an educational project, for example, would be an assessment of (a) the merit of its goals, (b) the quality of its plans, (c) the extent to which those plans are being carried out, and (d) the worth of its outcomes.

You should not *confuse "outcome evaluation" with "summative evaluation" nor "process evaluation" with "formative evaluation." "Outcome evaluation" is an evaluation focused on outcomes; "process evaluation" is one focused on process rather than outcomes—both of them could be either formative or summative.*

5. What criteria should be used to judge an object? To choose the criteria to be used to judge an evaluation object or any of its aspects is one of the most difficult tasks in educational evaluation. Those who think that evaluation should only attempt to determine whether goals have been achieved make this task easy for themselves by ignoring partially the issue of evaluation criteria. What they do is use "goal achievement" as the evaluation criterion without necessarily having justified or investigated the intrinsic worth of the goals. What about trivial goals or all kinds of "stated objectives" that may not be worth achieving? Should they be used as evaluation criteria?

Nonetheless, the *achievement of (important!) goals* is one possible basis for evaluation criteria. Alternative bases for evaluation criteria might be: *identified needs* of actual and potential clients, *ideals or social values,* known *standards* set by experts or other relevant groups, or the *quality or efficiency in comparison to alternative objects.*

There seems to be agreement among most evaluation experts that the criterion (or criteria) to be used for the assessment of a specific object must be determined within the specific context of the object and the function of its evaluation. While in many cases the evaluators do not or should not have the authority to choose among the various alternative criteria, *it is the evaluators' responsibility that such a choice be made, and they should be able to provide a sound justification for the choice,* made by them or by somebody else.

6. *Who should be served by an evaluation?* If evaluation is to be useful at all, it has to be useful to some specific *client* or *audience.* Most evaluation literature does not suggest which is the "most appropriate" audience for evaluation, but three important propositions can be found in writings regarding this issue. They are:

(1) An evaluation can have more than one client or audience.
(2) Different evaluation audiences might have different evaluation needs.
(3) The specific audiences for an evaluation and their evaluation needs have to be clearly identified at the early stages of planning an evaluation.

Differences in evaluation needs might be reflected in many ways: by the kind of information to be collected, the level of data analysis to be used, or the form of reporting the evaluation results. Sometimes it is impossible to serve all identified evaluation needs, and a decision has to be made regarding the specific evaluation needs to which the evaluation will respond.

7. *What steps and procedures are involved in doing an evaluation?* The process of doing an evaluation might differ according to the theoretical perception guiding the evalua-tion. A theoretical approach perceiving evaluation as an activity intended to determine whether goals have been achieved (Tyler, 1950) might recommend the following evaluation process:

(1) Stating goals in behavioral terms
(2) Developing measurement instruments
(3) Collecting data
(4) Interpreting findings
(5) Making recommendations

Another approach, perceiving evaluation as providing information for decision making (Stufflebeam, et al., 1971) might use an evaluation process including:

(1) Identification of information needs of decision makers
(2) Collection of relevant information
(3) Providing evaluative information to decision makers

Or, an evaluation aiming to build staff awareness, commitment and knowledge might proceed through many cycles of:

(1) Identifying problem areas
(2) Defining staff expectations and value positions
(3) Collecting performance information
(4) Providing discrepancy reports to staff and helping resolve conflicts

While there seems to be no agreement among evaluation experts regarding the "best" process to follow when conducting an evaluation, most of them would agree that all evaluations should include a certain amount of interaction between evaluators and their audiences at the outset of the evaluation, to identify evaluation needs, and at its conclusion, to communicate its findings. *Evaluation cannot be limited to the technical activities of data collection and analysis.*

8. What methods of inquiry should be used in evaluation? While challenging the usefulness of various research methods for evaluation studies (Provus, 1971, Stufflebeam, et al., 1971), recent years have also introduced a variety of methods of inquiry into the field of evaluation. In addition to traditional experimental and quasi-experimental designs (Campbell and Stanley, 1963) naturalistic methods (Guba and Lincoln, 1981; Patton, 1980), jury trials (Wolf, 1975), system analysis, and many others became legitimate methods for the conduct of evaluation. Some methodologists still advocate the superiority of certain methods, but overall there seems to be more support among evaluators for a more eclectic approach to evaluation methodology. Such an approach seeks to find the best method or set of methods for meeting a particular evaluation purpose, rather than assume that one method is best for all purposes.

9. Who should do evaluation? Becoming a professional group, evaluators devoted a lot of attention to identifying the characteristics of "good" evaluators and appropriate ways to train them. To be a competent and trustworthy evaluator one needs to have a combination of a wide variety of characteristics. These include: technical competence in the area of measurement and research methods, understanding of the social context and the substance of the evaluation object, human relations skills, personal integrity, and objectivity as well as characteristics related to organizational authority and responsibility. Since it is difficult to find one person possessing all those qualifications, it often becomes necessary to conduct an evaluation by a team, or choose the person with the most appropriate characteristics for a specific evaluation task.

The evaluation literature suggests two important distinctions that should be taken into account when deciding who should do an evaluation. The first is the distinction between an *internal evaluator* and an *external evaluator*. An internal evaluator of a project is usually one who is employed by the project and reports directly to its management. Obviously, the internal evaluator's objectivity as well as external credibility might be different from those of an external evaluator who is not directly employed by the project and/or enjoys a higher degree of independence.

The second distinction is between a *professional evaluator* and an *amateur evaluator*. This distinction, suggested by Scriven (1967), refers to two different foci of training and expertise rather than to a value judgment regarding the quality of an evaluator. An amateur evaluator is usually one whose major professional training is not in evaluation and whose involvement in evaluation represents only part of the job description. A professional evaluator is one with extensive training in evaluation and whose major (or even only) responsibility is the conducting of evaluation. While the amateur evaluator's technical evaluation skills might be less than those of a professional evaluator, the amateur might have a better understanding of the project's unique evaluation needs and be able to develop better rapport with the members of the evaluated project.

These two distinctions are independent; there may be an internal-amateur evaluator, an external-amateur, an internal-professional evaluator, etc.

10. By what standards should evaluation be judged? Several attempts have been made during the recent years to develop standards for evaluation of educational activities. Boruch and Cordray (1980) analyzed six sets of such standards and reached the conclusion that there has been a a large degree of overlap and similarity among them. The most elaborate and comprehensive set of standards and the one based on the largest amount of consensus is probably the set developed and published by the Joint Committee on Standards for Educational Evaluation (Joint Committee, 1981). These standards have been developed by a committee of seventeen members, chaired by Dr. Daniel Stufflebeam, which represented twelve professional organizations associated with educational evaluation. Thirty standards divided into four major groups have been suggested by the committee: *utility* standards (to ensure that evaluation serves practical information needs); *feasibility* standards (to ensure that evaluation be realistic and prudent); *propriety* standards (to ensure that evaluation be conducted legally and ethically); and *accuracy* standards (to ensure that evaluation reveal and convey technically adequate information). Table 1 lists the 30 standards.

No single evaluation is expected to meet all of the standards, and the degree of agreement among evaluators regarding the relative importance of the various standards is still to be determined. However, the comprehensive set of standards and the rationale on which they have been developed provide an invaluable source for major issues ato be considered in developing an evaluation and assessing its quality.

Lee J. Cronbach (1980) raises the consideration that standards related to the conduct of the evaluation may not be as important as those related to its consequences. This viewpoint suggests that the "best" evaluation is that which has a positive effect on program improvement.

Table 1 Thirty Standards for Evaluation

A. *Utility Standards*	C. *Propriety Standards*
1. Audience identification	1. Formal obligation
2. Evaluator credibility	2. Conflict of interest
3. Information scope and selection	3. Full and frank disclosure
4. Valuational interpretation	4. Public's right to know
5. Report clarity	5. Rights of human subjects
6. Report dissemination	6. Human interaction
7. Report timeliness	7. Balanced reporting
8. Evaluation impact	8. Fiscal responsibility
B. *Feasibility Standards*	D. *Accuracy Standards*
1. Practical procedures	1. Object identification
2. Political viability	2. Context analysis
3. Cost effectiveness	3. Described purposes and procedures
	4. Defensible information sources
	5. Valid measurement
	6. Reliable measurement
	7. Systematic data control
	8. Analysis of quantitative information
	9. Analysis of qualitative information
	10. Justified conclusions
	11. Objective reporting

THE PERCEPTION OF EVALUATION YOU FIND IN THESE MATERIALS

This introductory chapter has intended to help you think about evaluation and understand more about what others—and *you*—mean by evaluation. It has presented several different views and definitions that demonstrate a fairly broad range of expressed and potential opinion. But, this doesn't mean we don't have a more unified approach to evaluation to which we subscribe. This perception is a combination of our interpretations of several conceptualizations of evaluation and our experience in helping others conduct evaluations of training and development programs. We do not consider our perception as being the "right" perception of evaluation or even the best possible one. However, *we* find it logically sound and very useful.

In general, we believe that evaluation should be part and parcel of any training or professional preparation effort. You can't do training well without doing some evaluation of needs and goals, designs, implementation activities, and immediate and longer term effects of training. We see evaluation as functional. It is done for a reason, and that reason is to serve training efforts. Above all else, evaluation should be useful, and it should be used to make better decisions about key aspects of training programs. Here, then, is how we would respond to the ten questions in light of these materials.

1. How is evaluation defined? Evaluation is systematic investigation of various aspects of professional development and training programs to assess their merit or worth.

2. What is evaluation for? Evaluation should serve the development, implementation and recycling needs of training programs. It should be used for one or more purposes; to improve a particular program (formative); for accountability or selection (summative); to motivate, increase knowledge and gain support of staff and others (psychological).

3. What are the objects of evaluation? While we think most any entity can be an evaluation object, in these materials, the objects and training programs and/or their component parts.

4. What aspects and dimensions of an object should evaluation investigate? To best serve training programs, evaluation should focus on goals and needs, training designs, implementation and transactions, and effects of training.

5. What criteria should be used to judge an object? The following criteria should be considered when evaluating training efforts: (a) a responsiveness to needs, ideals and values; (b) optimal use of available resources and opportunities, (c) adherence to effective training practices, and (d) achievement of intended and other (important!) objectives and goals. Multiple criteria should most often be used.

6. Who should be served by an evaluation? Evaluation should serve the information needs of actual and potential stakeholders in the evaluation object. Evaluation should carefully identify these stakeholders and determine their needs and interests.

7. What steps and procedures are invovled in doing an evaluation? Evaluation must include decisions and action in regard to seven (7) functions: (1) focusing the evaluation; (2) designing the evaluation; (3) collecting information; (4) analyzing information; (5) reporting information from and about the evaluation; (6) managing the evaluation; and (7) evaluating the evaluation. They are not necessarily pursued in the order shown, and one often recycles among them. The *Sourcebook* is devoted to guidelines and options for doing these seven functions.

8. What methods of inquiry should be used in evaluation? We think an eclectic approach is best. Evaluation should use inquiry methods from the behavioral sciences and related fields as they are appropriate to a particular setting and evaluating purpose. At the present state of art an a priori preference for any specific method of inquiry is not warranted.

9. *Who should do evaluation?* Evaluation should be conducted by individuals or teams possessing: (a) extensive competencies in research methodology and data analysis techniques; (b) understanding of the social context and the unique substance of the evaluation object; (c) the ability to maintain correct human relations and develop rapport with individuals and groups involved in the evaluation; and (d) a conceptual framework to integrate all the abovementioned capabilities.

10. *By what standards should evaluation be judged?* Evaluation should strike for an optimal balance in meeting standards of: (a) utility (to be useful and practical); (b) accuracy (to be technically adequate); (c) feasibility (to be realistic and prudent); and (d) propriety (to be conducted legally and ethically). An evaluation not worth doing is not worth doing well.

REFERENCES

Alkin, M.C. "Evaluation Theory Development." Evaluation Comment 2, 1969: 2-7.

Alkin, M.C. quoted in *Educational Research & Development Report*, Volume 3, Number 1, Winter 1980, pp. 8-12.

Boruch, F.R. and Cordray, D.S. *An Appraisal of Educational Program Evaluations: Federal, State and Local Agencies.* Evanston, IL: Northwestern University, 1980.

Brinkerhoff, R.O. Evaluation of Inservice Programs. *Teacher Education and Special Education.* Vol. III, No. 3, Summer, 1980. pp. 27-38.

Campbell, D.T. and Stanley, J.C. "Experimental and Quasi-Experimental Designs for Research of Teaching." In N.L. Gage (Ed.), *Handbook of Research on Teaching.* Chicago: Rand McNally, 1963.

Cronbach, L.J. "Course Improvement through Evaluation." *Teachers College Record 64,* May 1963: 672-683.

Cronbach, L.J., Ambron, S.R., Dornbusch, S.M., Hess, R.D., Hornik, R.C., Phillips, D.C., Walker, D.E., and Weiner, S.S. *Toward Reform of Program Evaluation.* San Francisco: Jossey-Bass, 1980.

Dornbusch, S.M. and Scott, W.R. *Evaluation and the Exercise of Authority.* San Francisco: Jossey-Bass, 1975.

Glass, G.V. *The Growth of Evaluation Methodology.* Research paper no. 27. Boulder, CO: Laboratory of Educational Research, University of Colorado, 1969 (mimeo).

Guba, E.G. and Lincoln, Y.S. *Effective Evaluation.* San Francisco: Jossey-Bass, 1981.

Joint Committee on Standards fo Educational Evaluation, *Standards for Evaluations of Educational Programs, Projects and Materials.* New York: McGraw-Hill, 1981.

Nevo, D. "The Evaluation of a Multi-Dimensional Project." In A. Lewy *et al., Decision Oriented Evaluation in Education: The Case of Israel.* Philadelphia: International Science Services, 1981.

Patton, M.Q. Qualitative Evaluation Methods. Beverly Hills, CA: Sage Publications, 1980.

Provus, M.M. *Discrepancy Evaluation.* Berkeley, CA: McCutchan, 1971.

Scriven, M. "The Methodology of Evaluation" in R.E. Stake (Ed.), *Curriculum Evaluation,* AERA Monograph Series on Evaluation, No. 1. Chicago: Rand McNally, 1967.

Stufflebeam, D.L., Foley, W.J., Gephart, W.J., Guba, E.G., Hammond, R.L., Merriman, H.O., and Provus, M.M. *Educational Evaluation and Decision-Making.* Itasca, IL: Peacock, 1971.

Stufflebeam, D.L. *Meta-Evaluation.* Occasional Paper Series, The Evaluation Center, Western Michigan University, December 1974.

Tyler, R.W. *Basic Principles of Curriculum and Instruction.* Chicago, IL: University of Chicago Press, 1950.

Wolf, R.L. "The Use of Judicial Evaluation Methods in the Formation of Educational Policy." *Educational Evaluation and Policy Analysis*, 1, 1979: 19-28.

Worthen, B.R. and Sanders, J.R. *Educational Evaluation: Theory and Practice.* Belmont, CA: Wadsworth Publishing Co., 1973.

INFLUENCES ON SPECIAL EDUCATION EVALUATION

Bruce Balow and *Robert Brinkerhoff*

The history of special education in the United States is much like that of many of its clients: an outsider attempting to move into the mainstream. Education of handicapped children has had to prove its value time and again, to the children it teaches, and more difficult, to the larger educational system, and more difficult yet, to society.

Much of what makes special education special in some measure influences the nature and purpose of the evaluation programs relating to the handicapped. Special education is more often oriented to basic life skills than is education for others: its procedures are highly individualized and resource intensive, and more recently, highly data based. Handicapped education can move painfully slowly, and since results are sometimes marginal at best, special education is emotionally costly and frustrating. The influences these and other characteristics of special education have on evaluation go beyond evaluation of direct intervention programs. These influences extend in an unbroken line to activities and programs that prepare professionals who provide educational services.

In this brief chapter, we explore the specialness of special education, and show how evaluation of programs that prepare personnel who may work with the handicapped should attend to special needs. First, the history of special education is briefly reviewed; then, we move to consider consequences for evaluation.

HISTORY

It can be argued that the history of education is the history of society. That is, it is part and parcel of the culture, occasionally influencing but more often being influenced by larger events in society. The placement, care, and education of handicapped children is reflected in and by those larger events.

In the late 1800's an agrarian nation found productive uses for the mentally handicapped without taking particular note of them as deviant, disabled or different. Severely handicapped persons were placed in residential schools that were categorical in nature and limited in availability, and there was little optimism about curing handicaps.

Through the early 1900's institutions increased in size and in number, segregation of the handicapped increased in popularity, and the protection of society came on strongly as social policy. By 1926, 29 states had sterilization laws covering the mentally retarded, the mentally ill, and epileptics.

Perhaps 25% of the population graduated from high school in the period around the 1920's, and while there continued to be a few noteworthy programs of special classes in public schools, handicapped children and others who were poor achievers in the schools were not well accommodated. The vast majority of the population attained no more than a grade school education, and many of the handicapped were simply excluded from school.

The great depression and World War II kept the United States preoccupied for fifteen years, and there is little evidence of particular progress in the education; of handicapped children during those years. However, the 1940's and that war established a launching pad in this country for the greatest and longest sustained economic boom in history. It entirely changed the outlook and the educational status of most of our people. People learned other ways of thinking, other life styles, other ideas; in short, we became better educated. And following that war, millions of young people, who had never previously considered vistas beyond high school graduation and employment in their home town, went on to post-high-school education and personal-social and geographic mobility with opportunity and unprecedented prosperity.

Concurrently, there was an enormous expansion of special education programs in the public schools, for the most part following a "special class" model. But many handicapped children, especially those most severely handicapped, continued to be excluded from school. With society in general becoming more open, more sophisticated, more involved in the political process, and more increased belief in the power of education, parents of handicapped children and their allies began to press effectively for legislation mandating the inclusion of handicapped children in public schools.

A strong belief in the power of education to lead to individual and group prosperity and to solve the social welfare ills of the nation increased through the 1950's and the 1960's. In the 1960's, in a period of enormous prosperity, the United States government under President Johnson turned markedly toward attempts to improve social welfare through education. Mr. Johnson obtained from the Congress more federal appropriations for education than had been true in the previous 100 years together. Similarly, for children's welfare and public health activities, he obtained record increases and expenditures. The Civil Rights Movement was strong and moving rapidly at that time, the youth movement was strong and gaining strength, and the contemporary movement for equal rights for women was in its early beginnings. Improvements in circumstances for the handicapped were beginning to come as well, but only in small amounts with limited visibility. However, local school board decisions, local community decisions, and state and federal legislation began to include handicapped, and colleges and universities responded with increased attention to teacher education for handicapped children. From a very few training programs attending to the needs of teachers of handicapped in the 1940's, there were 40 personnel preparation programs by the 1950's and 400 such programs by the 1970's. Many of the teacher education programs were a direct result of specific federal financing aid for preparation of teachers of handicapped children.

By 1965 the United States had enjoyed for some years an economic paradise believed by many at that time to be essentially permanent. There was steady growth, low unemployment, and a low rate of inflation. The president had set a principal goal of abolishing poverty and, at the same time, many people believed that American free enterprise and American democracy would be able to do so, not only in this country, but around the world. We are now a nation of urban sophisticates, yet naive enought to hold such a belief. That belief disintegrated in the late 1970's.

The 1970's was a decade of litigation and legislation. Integration of handicapped children in regular public schools and in regular classes to the extent possible, zero rejection, thus including the serverely handicapped in the public schools, the development of due process procedures, IEP's, a range of service provisions for handicapped children, nondiscriminatory assessment, parental participation in decision processes and similar requirements of the schools all came about as a result of federal and state legislation and numerous actions in state and federal courts. The society was receptive, parents led, and professionals began to fulfill on the expectations promulgated.

The 1970's may well have been the watershed of widely shared economic prosperity in the United States and, with that economic change, a similar parallel watershed in the provision of free, appropriate public education to the handicapped. While much of the evidence to support or deny such a concern will likely become clear in the immediate future, the early portents are troublesome.

An apparent change of social values in the 1980's, reflected by political decisions, which have the effect of reducing requirements for inclusion of handicapped persons in the mainstream of society and which tend to reduce their claim on educational resources, are more than a cause for concern. They are that, to be sure, but they are also a reason for increased attention to the collection and distribution of evidence that the education of handicapped children is neither charity nor a holding tank, but an investment with remarkable payoff in social and economic value.

There is a strong expectation that the education of handicapped children must constantly prove itself in order to be accepted as a normal part of schooling and society. This is due to several factors: (1) special education curriculum is sometimes different and more labor intensive; (2) regular education colleges are often skeptical; (3) special education requires a lengthy political process to obtain significant amounts of money over and beyond what is required for educating pupils who are not handicapped; and (4) special educators' own expectations for children's growth and progress is limited.

Limited resources may be provided on the basis of charity, but substantial resources come about only on the basis of investment. In a growing, expanding and prosperous economy there is far greater willingness to expend resources on problematic or "unproven" areas of social welfare but, in a contracting economy and inward turning culture, the danger is that without extraordinarily strong evidence as to the effectiveness of activities for marginal contributors, the decision makers will cut back on those resources and those commitments. The early portents from the current political leadership in this country show a very strong move in the direction of financial retrenchment for expenditures to educate the handicapped and show also a considerable willingness to reduce the regulatory requirements for inclusion and education of such persons.

Possibly more important even than that area of concern, is that the long history of involvement of parents and others in the development and financing of programs for handicapped children has rightly led to strongly held expectations about the use of resources allocated to such programs, the progress of children included in those programs and the overall effectiveness of the program. Those expectations, together with our own enlightened self-interest, strongly call for information routinely obtained through evaluation procedures.

The outcomes and expectations for handicapped children have often been less global, more specific, more narrowly task oriented and detailed than is true for nonhandicapped children. When expectations are relatively limited, it is important to note small changes, often difficult to observe, in order to understand whether progress is occurring.

The audiences interested in the education of handicapped children are oftentimes more actively concerned than are the audiences concerned with the education of nonhandicapped. Parents and handicapped persons have had to work quite hard to obtain special programs and therefore they maintain a strong interest and concern for what occurs in those programs. Legislators oftentimes take an active interest in handicapped children because they frequently allocate special sums of money for the purpose. Accountability demands in special education tend to be high, not only for those reasons, but because not all allied professionals are convinced, a priori, that specific programs for handicapped children are likely to be successful.

Special education is more similar to regular education than it is different. Nonetheless, differences are significant and by their nature often call for information about resource allocation, program procedures, and results. Because handicapped children frequently make very slow progress, teachers and other direct service persons need data to help them make daily decisions. Because the content of special education programs is often the skills learned by normal children in the normal course of growing up, decision makers need evidence demonstrating that those life functions are effectively taught.

EVALUATION OF PREPARATION PROGRAMS FOR TEACHERS OF THE HANDICAPPED

It can be argued that it is no more necessary to evaluate programs for teachers of handicapped children than for any other aspect of teacher education. If professional competence were the only criterion, that would be true, but educating handicapped children is more difficult, costly, and controversial than general education—and the audiences, our critics, are more active, better informed, and more watchful. Among these critics are the financing agencies that, on occasion, give off signals that they regard special education as outside of the normal responsibility of the public educational system. Clearly, it is in the best interest of teacher-educators engaged in preparation of special education personnel to analyze program designs, identify program deficiencies, establish accountability information, measure the competence of program graduates, and estimate cost-benefit results of our programs.

Professional competence is, of itself, sufficient reason for careful, detailed evaluation of professional preparation programs in special education. While it can be argued (though questionably) that teachers of normal children do not particularly need to be highly skilled because the children will learn in any event, surely no one would argue that case with respect to handicapped children. If handicapped children are to learn effectively or as effectively as they are capable of learning, the teacher is responsible for a degree of skill in managing the learning process. That skill will only come about if the teacher preparation program is comprehensive and highly effective. Those outcomes in turn will only be true if the program staff knows the effect of program components on student attitude, knowledge, and skill. The idea that knowledge is power is as true in teacher education as it is anywhere else. A key source for this knowledge is evaluation of our teacher education programs.

No one in or near public education today is unaware of recent litigation in which the school's provision of education and services to children has been legally challenged. A prevailing interpretation of laws has been that the school may not be legally accountable for the outcomes of education, but that it certainly is responsible to assure that persons providing services (e.g., teachers, clinicians) are qualified to do so. This has sometimes resulted in court-ordered inservice training. While this legal aspect is probably not a wholly sufficient reason for evaluating personnel training, evaluation of personnel training seems a prerequisite to a defensible argument that the staff is qualified; this would apply to the evaluation of preservice as well as inservice education of personnel.

The current state-of-the-art of evaluation is not sufficiently well developed that one can present much in the way of a ironclad case that recipients of professional training are, in fact, competent. But, one can certainly present data about what and how much training has been delivered and received, logical and empirical rationale for training content, and data about training effects (e.g., knowledge acquired) and perceptions of trainees as to skills practiced and mastered. In short, one can construct a dramatically more defensible argument for professional competence with, rather than without, training evaluation information.

EVALUATION AND STAFF DEVELOPMENT

Finally, the special nature of special education requires evaluation as part and parcel of preservice and inservice education efforts. In fact, when evaluation comes full circle and provides information about effects and outcomes of teaching or clinical intervention, evaluation *is* professional development.

Special education is, like all other kinds of education, an imperfect art. While there is much we know about teaching and learning, there remains much we do not know. And, what we do is always less than we know. Practice inevitably lags behind knowledge, because knowledge dissemination is incomplete and because the facts of our daily work-life are such that we hurry, are harried, forget, and act impulsively more often than we like. We know more about how to swim with grace and power and certainly want to, but keeping our heads about water is a demanding concern and can take nearly all our time.

When evaluation becomes a more regular and systematic part of educational endeavors, knowledge becomes greater. We learn more about the effects we have and are better able to change, to try, and then to improve what gets done. When such information is regularly provided to program staff, practice almost inevitably improves as a sort of biofeedback process. And as staff are provided with more information about results—particularly in a field like special education where results are slow and hard to come by—work becomes more satisfying.

Good professional development does not just transfer professional knowledge from sellers to buyers, it creates professional knowledge and competence from everyday professional experience. Evaluation is a necessary ingredient in this process.

The Sourcebook

READER'S GUIDE TO THE SOURCEBOOK

The Sourcebook that follows divides evaluation into seven functional areas:

1. Focusing the Evaluation
2. Designing the Evaluation
3. Collecting Information
4. Analyzing & Interpreting Information
5. Reporting Information
6. Managing Evaluation
7. Evaluating Evaluation

Within these seven major functions, the Sourcebook identifies 35 critical questions and tasks.

The Sourcebook is intended to be a supplement to the Casebook and the Design Manual. It focuses on decisions evaluators commonly need to make and provides options and procedural suggestions to guide evaluation performance. References are included so that you can study any topic in further detail.

To use the Sourcebook, turn to the *Contents Grid* that follows. This grid summarizes the major functions, critical questions, and evaluation tasks discussed in the Sourcebook. Page numbers are provided to locate the discussion within the Sourcebook. An abbreviated guide precedes each functional area in the Sourcebook. It summarizes critical questions found in the section and topics discussed within them.

Each question addressed in the Sourcebook proposes some options for the evaluator in dealing with a question or issue, provides alternative procedures available to accomplish the evaluation tasks related to the issue, and finally, provides guidelines and criteria that help the evaluator determine whether the job has been done adequately.

A number of tables and figures have been included to efficiently summarize information, examples have been provided, and each major functional area concludes with a reference section.

Function	Key Issues	Tasks	Page Numbers
Focusing the Evaluation	1. What will be evaluated?	1. Investigate what is to be evaluated	7-15
	2. What is the purpose for evaluating?	2. Identify and justify purpose(s)	16-19
	3. Who will be affected by or involved in the evaluation?	3. Identify audiences	20-22
	4. What elements in the setting are likely to influence the evaluation?	4. Study setting	23-26
	5. What are the crucial evaluation questions?	5. Identify major questions	27-30
	6. Does the evaluation have the potential for successful implementation?	6. Decide whether to go on with evaluation	31-36
Designing Evaluation	1. What are some alternative ways to design an evaluation?	1. Determine the amount of planning, general purpose, and degree of control	37-42
	2. What does a design include?	2. Overview evaluation decisions, tasks, and products	43-58
	3. How do you go about constructing a design?	3. Determine general procedures for the evaluation	59-63
	4. How do you recognize a good design?	4. Assess the quality of the design	64-71

Function	Key Issues	Tasks	Page Numbers
Collecting Information	1. What kinds of information should you collect?	1. Determine the information sources you will use	77-83
	2. What procedures should you use to collect needed information?	2. Decide how you'll collect information	84-88
	3. How much information should you collect?	3. Decide whether you need to sample and, if so, how	89-94
	4. Will you select or develop instruments?	4. Determine how precise your information must be and design a means to collect it	95-99
	5. How do you establish reliable and valid instrumentation?	5. Establish procedures to maximize validity and reliability	100-107
	6. How do you plan the information collection effort to get the most information at the lowest cost?	6. Plan the logistics for an economical information collection procedure	108-115
Analyzing and Interpreting (Evaluation)	1. How will you handle returned data?	1. Aggregate and code data if necessary	119-122
	2. Are data worth analyzing?	2. Verify completeness and quality of raw data	123-126
	3. How will you analyze the information?	3. Select & run defensible analyses	127-144
	4. How will you interpret the results of analyses?	4. Interpret the data using prespecified and alternative sets of criteria	145-147
Reporting	1. Who should get an evaluation report?	1. Identify who you will report to	151-153
	2. What content should be included in a report?	2. Outline the content to be included	154-158

Function	Key Issues	Tasks	Page Numbers
	3. How will reports be delivered?	3. Decide whether reports will be written, oral, etc.	159-164
	4. What is the appropriate style and structure for the report?	4. Select a format for the report	165-167
	5. How can you help audiences interpret and use reports?	5. Plan post-report discussions, consultation, follow-up activities	168-169
	6. When should reports be scheduled?	6. Map out the report schedule	170-173
Managing	1. Who should run the evaluation?	1. Select, hire, and/ or train the evaluator	176-180
	2. How should evaluation responsibilities be formalized?	2. Draw up a contract or letter of agreement	181-186
	3. How much should the evaluation cost?	3. Draft the budget	187-190
	4. How should evaluation tasks be organized and scheduled?	4. Draft a time/task strategy	191-196
	5. What kinds of problems can be expected?	5. Monitor the evaluation and anticipate problems	197-200
Evaluating Evaluation (Meta-evaluation)	1. What are some good uses of meta-evaluation?	1. Determine whether you need to meta evaluate; if so, when	205-207
	2. Who should do the meta evaluation?	2. Select a meta evaluator	208-209
	3. What criteria or standard should you use to evaluate the evaluation?	3. Select or negotiate standards	210-217
	4. How do you apply a set of meta-evaluation criteria?	4. Rank order standards, determine compliance	218-220

Focusing the Evaluation

Focusing evaluation is the progressive specification of what and how you are going to evaluate. Like focusing a camera, focusing an evaluation demands that a number of variables be considered simultaneously. This section provides information about which variables to consider in order to focus your evaluation. Generally, these variables include: the "object" being evaluated (what your camera will be focused upon); the purpose for evaluating; the people who should be considered; the background or setting and its effect on the evaluation; and the important questions the evaluation must answer to serve its purpose.

Remember that focusing involves progressive attempts; expect initial drafts and discussions to be general—even vague. And, as sequential plans become more and more detailed, continue to ask whether the evaluation is still worth the effort and cost. Not every evaluation that is contemplated should be undertaken.

WHEN FOCUSING DECISIONS GET MADE
Focusing marks the beginning of the evaluation process and design. The decisions outlined in this chapter must be reviewed regularly to accommodate changes in the object being evaluated, its setting, and the people involved. You need to consider these decisions for any kind of evaluation, whether it's to meet an external funding requirement, to improve a program, or for some other purpose.

WHAT WILL BE EVALUATED?

The object of an evaluation is whatever you are investigating—it can be a program, a project, a three-day inservice, materials, or even another evaluation. In short, anything can be the "object" of an evaluation. In this book, the objects of evaluation are related to training and include curriculum programs, inservice workshops, and demonstration projects.

The task of identifying and describing the object to be evaluated seems simple and straightforward; it is often neither. In fact it is one of the most difficult and important evaluation responsibilities you will face. This is true for two reasons: (1) the object (e.g., a program) is not static—it grows, is affected by external and internal events, and, in short, constantly changes; and (2) the object looks different depending upon perspective (e.g., an administrator would see a program in one way, a client in another). It is necessary to describe and get agreement about what is being evaluated in order to design an evaluation. And if there is little agreement about what an object is or does, it might be premature to evaluate unless the purpose of the evaluation is to better describe and understand the object.

SOME KINDS OF TRAINING OBJECTS THAT CAN BE EVALUATED

- course
- workshop
- workshop series
- curriculum
- management system
- trainer selection
- certification system
- self-instructional materials
- logistic system
- degree program
- service provision
- texts, materials
- information management system
- needs assessment process
- consultant services
- proposal solicitation and funding process
- staff retreat
- staff development program
- seminar
- filing and record keeping system
- evaluations of training
- training clearinghouse functions
- conferences
- meetings
- symposia

FEATURES TO INCLUDE IN DESCRIBING AN OBJECT OF EVALUATION

WHO	Actors	Who's involved? Who are the key decision makers and leaders, the funders, the personnel implementing the program and being served by the program; who are the advocates and adversaries, interested luminaries?
WHY	Goals	What goals and objectives are intended, or appear to be pursued? Are there conflicting goals? What needs are being addressed?
WHAT	Components	Is there a model or description of the object; how many separate components are included and do they interact?
	Activities	What kinds of activities are included; what services are being provided; how many maintenance or internal administrative services are provided?

	Resources	What are the available benefits and opportunities? Consider budget, manpower, facilities, use of volunteer time, expert review or guidance, use of materials, machinery, communication systems, personnel, etc.
	Problems	Generally, what appears to be the biggest constraint in the eyes of key stakeholders (dept. chair, faculty, students, dean)? Would you concur?
WHEN	Timeline	How long has the object been around? What does its history look like, and what kind of future is it anticipating? How long does it have to accomplish short and long range goals?
WHERE	Setting	What in the setting influences the object? Where does it fit into the larger organization, the political network? What and who can it be influenced by?

WHERE TO GO TO FIND OUT ABOUT AN OBJECT

TO DOCUMENTS

Letters of commendation or criticism
Presentations by staff
Attitude surveys
Existing performance data
Staffing profile
Materials produced (pamphlets, syllabi, guidelines, manuals)
Request for Proposal (RFP)
Proposal
Audit reports
Mission/goals statement
Budget
Organizational chart
Management plan
Reports
Communications between project and funding agency
Job descriptions
Minutes of advisory or management groups
Evaluations (accrediting reports)
Public relations releases
Media coverage

TO RELEVANT AUDIENCES

Sponsors

Policy Makers

Staff

Clients

Professional

Taxpayers
Funding agents
Federal agents
State education departments
Accrediting groups
Central administrations
University cabinets
Boards of education
Program planners
Present and past staff
Students
Parents
General public
Community agencies
Professional associations
Professional journals
Other educational agencies

WAYS TO DESCRIBE OBJECTS One or more of the following strategies can be used to describe what you are evaluating.

STRATEGY Pert charts

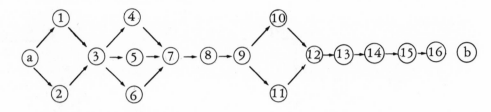

Activity or Procedure	Subgoal or Event
1. Search literature for attitude scales	a. Start scale development
2. Review attitude scaling procedures	1. Complete search
3. Select procedure to be used	2. Complete review
4. Construct scale items	3. Complete selection
5. Assemble prototype scale	4. Complete item construction
6. Arrange field test of prototype scale	5. Complete scale assembly
	6. Complete arrangements

WHAT IT TELLS YOU program activities, sequencing of tasks

STRATEGY Management Plan (And Budget)

Activity	Personnel Responsible	Person Days	October 1 2 3 4	November 1 2 3 4	December 1 2 3 4
OBJECTIVE 1: 1. Develop research questions	Schmidt Simon Trumper	14	├────┤		
2. Determine data collection procedures (includes development of instrumentation)	Simon Schmidt Feldt	15 7		├──────────────────┤ ├──────────┤	
3. Develop analysis plan					

WHAT IT TELLS YOU chain of responsibility, schedule, planned use of resources

STRATEGY   Existing Evaluation Approaches

Countenance by Robert Stake: Gathering a full range of descriptive and judgmental information about an object.

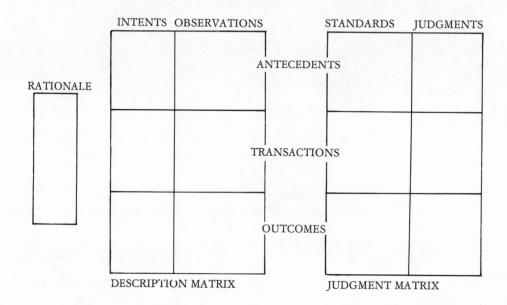

WHAT IT
TELLS YOU

When you use Countenance to describe an object, you might look at the following:

- **rationale**–for the training program
- **antecedents**–conditions that exist prior to training (willingness, skill level, interest)
- **transactions**–the instructional/delivery process
- **outcomes**–consequences of training (e.g., knowledge, transfer, relearning)
- **judgments**–of training approach, of trainer, of materials
- **intents**–what trainers or educators intended the program to do
- **observations**–what observers perceive to be happening
- **standards**–what stakeholders expect
- **judgments**–how valuable the program is in the eyes of judges and other audiences

STRATEGY   *CIPP* by Daniel Stufflebeam: Describing the context, input, process, and products of a program

	CONTEXT EVALUATION	INPUT EVALUATION	PROCESS EVALUATION	PRODUCT EVALUATION
OBJECTIVE	To define the institutional context, to identify the target population and assess their needs, to identify opportunities for addressing the needs, to diagnose *problems* underlying the *needs* & to judge whether proposed objectives are sufficiently responsive to the assessed needs.	To identify & assess *system capabilities*, alternative program *strategies*, procedural designs for implementing the strategies, budgets, & schedules, programs.	To identify or predict, in process, *defects* in the procedural design or its implementation, to provide information for the preprogrammed decisions, and to record & judge procedural events & activities.	To collect descriptions & judgments of outcomes & to relate them to objectives & to context, input, & process information, & to interpret their worth & merit.
METHOD	By using such methods as system analysis, survey, document review, hearings, interviews, diagnostic tests, & the Delplir technique.	By inventorying & analyzing available human & material resources, solution strategies, & procedural designs for relevance, feasibility & economy. And by using such methods as literature search, visits to "misicle workers," advocate teams, & pilot trials.	By monitoring the activity's potential procedural barriers & remaining alert to unanticipated ones, by obtaining specified information for programmed decisions, by describing the actual process, & by continually interacting with & observing the activities of project staff.	By defining operationally & measuring outcomes criteria, by collecting judgments of outcomes from stakeholders, & by performing both qualitative & quantitative analyses.
RELATION TO DECISION-MAKING IN THE CHANGE PROCESS	For deciding upon the *setting* to be served, the *goals* associated with meeting needs or using opportunities, & the *objectives* associated with solving problems, i.e., for *planning* needed changes. And to provide a basis for judging outcomes.	For selecting *sources of support*, solution *strategies* & procedural *designs*, i.e., for *structuring* change activities. And to provide a basis for judging implementation.	For *implementing* and *refining the program design and procedure*, i.e., for effecting *process control*. And to provide a log of the actual process for later use in interpreting outcomes.	For deciding to *continue, terminate, modify, or refocus* a change activity, & present a clear record of effects (intended & unintended, positive & negative).

WHAT IT TELLS YOU   If using CIPP as an organizer to approach a training program, you might study the following.

· the context
· needs/opportunities
· problems underlying needs

· human and material resources
· alternative service strategies
· system capabilities
· barriers to service delivery
· delivery process
· programmed decisions
· program outcomes
· outcomes in light of objectives
· objectives in light of standards or comparisons
· outcomes in light of context, input, and process information

STRATEGY   *Program Goals or Objectives*

For example, here is a set of objectives for a training program.

TRAINING RECIPIENT CHANGE VARIABLE ANALYSIS FORM

Recipient	Immediate Objectives	Job/Usage Objectives	Ultimate Outcomes
Who will receive training?	What skills, knowledge or attitudes will be changed as a result of training?	What use will be made of the training on the job?	What person, product, or organizational change will eventually result?
Special Education Teachers	Awareness of problems and concerns of regular teachers in teaching handicapped students	Increased planning with regular teachers for implementing individual educational plans	Exceptional children receiving more appropriate educational experiences in the least restrictive environment
	Increased skills in the interpretation and utilization of strategies for individual planning	Improved implementation of individual educational plans	
Building Teams	Knowledge of: - Consultation process	Improved coordination of resources used within the schools	Exceptional children receiving more appropriate educational experiences in the least restrictive environment
	Skills in: - Problem solving and diagnostic procedures	Provision of building-level technical assistance and consultation upon request	

STRATEGY   Systems Analyses

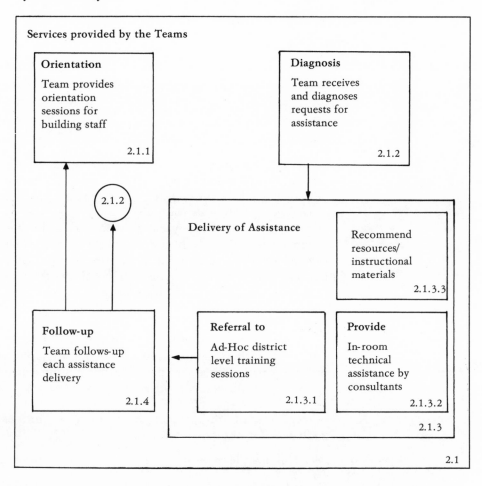

WHAT IT TELLS YOU   components of project, functional relationships among components, inter-relationships, key decision points

STRATEGY   Organizational Charts

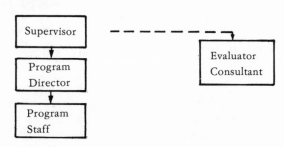

WHAT IT TELLS YOU   staff responsibilities, chain of command, unit and sub-unit organization

STRATEGY   ● *Personal Viewpoints, Observations, Histories*

Log   4/7/82
             9:15 a.m.

Today was the third and final day of training. W. was noticeably tired and it took almost an hour for the group to get started into their concluding activities.

3:30 p.m.

. . . as evaluation forms were being collected, a spontaneous conversation among trainees indicated a real sense of accomplishment (e.g., "my chairman won't believe I'm coming back with a set of specific training objectives and an evaluation plan"; and "I've never been to a more valuable workshop . . . in fifteen years this has been the best.") However, as the group leader officially began the evaluation discussion, trainees got side-tracked on their disappointment with the simulation exercise earlier. In particular, they didn't like the person walking them through the simulation. Unfortunately, W. did not hear the positive comments made earlier.

5:30 p.m.

. . . three trainees asked if they could purchase extra sets of the materials. Every set, including the extras on the supply table, were taken. A list was begun by one trainee and passed around; nine persons requested that the training be offered again within the next year.

WHAT IT TELLS YOU   perceptions of the object from experts, interested or experienced audiences, or objective observers

TIPS FOR
MAINTAINING
A GOOD
DESCRIPTION
OF THE OBJECT

Seek Multiple Viewpoints	Try to get multiple perspectives and descriptions of the object.
Use Independent Observers	Confirm what you are finding by an objective observer (one-day visit by an evaluation or content specialist).
Plan for Direct Observation	Directly observe the program or make use of other outside observers.
Listen for Repetition	Pay attention to issues brought up repeatedly across information sources and audiences.
Plan Ongoing Review	Keep a log to continue to note changes in the object throughout the evaluation.

EXAMPLE OF
AN OBJECT
DESCRIPTION

See "What Does a Design Include?" for the complete evaluation design of this workshop.

The object of the evaluation is a workshop developed and delivered by the ETC Project. It is a three-day workshop which gives participants intensive training in evaluation and time to work on their own evaluation designs. Participants are from professional development and teacher preparation programs in colleges and universities and local and state educational agencies. The Project received funding from the federal Office of Special Education to develop the materials used in the workshop, but must rely on registration fees to cover some delivery costs. The Project is based at a University Evaluation Center which is interested in insuring quality and coordinating the Project with its other activities.

How the Workshop Works

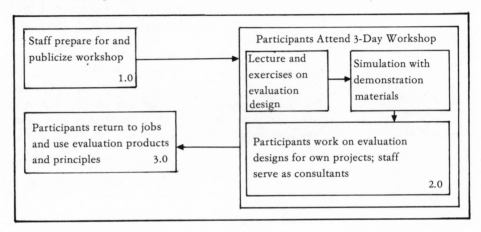

WORKSHOP AGENDA

Day One	Day Two	Day Three
9:00– 9:30 Introduction	9:00– 9:30 Introduction to the Design Manual	9:00–10:00 Lecture and demonstration: Reporting
9:30–10:30 Evaluation design exercise	9:30–12:00 Participants (each with own Design Manual) complete Products #1 and #2	10:00–11:00 Participants complete Product #5
10:30–12:00 Discussion: Review of Decision Areas from *Sourcebook*		11:00–12:00 Panel discussion: Management
12:00– 1:00 Lunch	12:00– 1:00 Lunch	12:00– 1:00 Lunch
1:00– 2:30 Participants read selected case	1:00– 2:30 Exercise and lecture: Measurement Planning	1:00– 3:30 Participants complete Products #6 and #7
2:30– 3:30 Small group exercise: Participants analyze case using Decision Areas	2:30– 4:30 Participants complete Products #3 and #4	3:30– 4:00 Wrap-up
3:30–4:30 Summary Review		

WHAT IS THE PURPOSE FOR EVALUATING?

The general purpose for evaluating should be clear. To determine the most appropriate evaluator and evaluation strategy, it's important to know why the evaluation is taking place. Will the evaluation be used to find a problem, solve a problem, provide ongoing information, or judge the success of the program? Knowing the general reason for evaluating will help you determine the strategy for generating specific evaluation questions.

Deciding on the purpose for an evaluation is probably the single most important decision initially made about the evaluation. And while there is generally one overriding or central purpose to be served by evaluation, you will find that different audiences will have different reasons for wanting the same evaluation. Accordingly, audiences will intend to use the results differently.

Multiple purposes and hidden or conflicting agendas should be investigated and negotiated openly at the outset so that useful information can be provided to key stakeholders. You can promote this by doing some of the following:

· clearly define, document and disseminate the general purpose
· determine whether there are other purposes or objectives
· rank order purposes and objectives
· determine whether there are resources to meet multiple purposes and, if so, which ones will be met

GENERAL EVALUATION PURPOSES RELATED TO TRAINING PROGRAMS		Purposes for objects being planned, developed, or recently implemented	Purposes for objects that have been around through several rounds of revision
	Goals or needs	· to establish goals or needs · to evaluate the soundness of goals or validate needs · to rank goals or needs · to seek opportunities	· to determine whether goals and needs have been met · to evaluate the soundness of goals · to identify the goals and needs that guided the object · to seek unused opportunities
	Design	· to assess a system and its resources · to select a design · to clarify roles or resolve conflicts related to the design · to compare alternative designs · to locate problems that are keeping the design from working	· to determine the adequacy of the design that was used · to assess how well the design was developed and implemented · to compare the design to alternatives not used

GENERAL EVALUATION PURPOSES RELATED TO TRAINING PROGRAMS (continued)		Purposes for objects being planned, developed, or recently implemented	Purposes for objects that have been around through several rounds of revision
	Implementation and process	· to determine the adequacy of a given design · to help staff implement the program · to help staff make incremental improvements · to identify strengths and opportunities · to diagnose problems · to assure that the design is operating as planned	· to determine whether program was run as planned and, if so, if it was worthwhile · to identify and describe problems that developed · to examine the relationship of what occurred to observed outcomes · to identify the effective or durable relationships involved in program delivery
	Products and Outcomes	· to determine immediate outcomes and initial effects · to determine what outcomes are appropriate to expect · to determine the quality of intermediate products · to monitor resources and impact	· to assess the quality of outcomes · to determine what outcomes were achieved · to determine whether intended outcomes were achieved · to determine cost effectiveness · to uncover side effects · to determine utility of the program
	Recycling	· to improve the object for future implementation · to determine how worthwhile it is · to determine whether it is what it intended to be · to determine whether it is worth the resources it will consume	· to determine whether it was worthwhile to consumers and other key audiences · to determine whether it did what it intended to do · to compare actual outcomes to needs · to determine whether it was worth the resources it consumed · to determine if the program is a viable competitor

---

CRITERIA FOR DEFENSIBLE PURPOSES

A defensible purpose is:

Clear — the purpose is understood by key audiences

Accessible — the evaluation purpose has been documented and disseminated to those who might be affected by the evaluation or have a right to know about it

CRITERIA FOR DEFENSIBLE PURPOSES *(continued)*		
	Useful	the commitment to use the evaluation information is real and the action to be taken anticipated
	Relevant	the information need the evaluation is meeting has been identified and could serve the program
	Humane	given the political and fiscal support, it is realistic to believe that evaluation can be successfully implemented without harming people involved or affected
	Compatible	evaluation seems to be congruent with the principal goals of the program, its staff, the larger institutional setting, and the target audience
	Worthwhile	the potential benefits of the evaluation justify its likely costs

COMMON PITFALLS THAT CAN UNDERMINE EVALUATION OF TRAINING

Not every evaluation conceived should be undertaken; and sometimes there is little reason to evaluate. For example:

· when the evaluation will be designed to justify a decision that has already been made
· when the evaluation information cannot be ready until after key decisions are made about the program
· when there is no clear explanation of how and by whom the evaluation information will be used
· when someone (or some group) is likely to be seriously and unjustifiably hurt through the evaluation process
· when information like that which is to be gathered already exists and is not being used
· when the normal growth process of a new program might be stifled by premature evaluation
· when control over writing and editing of the evaluation report cannot be established and nonindependence is likely
· when it is apparent that the evaluation will use resources (time, personnel, money) without providing commensurate help or benefits
· when the evaluation will alienate or polarize staff at a time when cohesion is imperative
· when it is likely that the evaluation information will not be technically accurate or credible to key audiences

EXAMPLE OF EVALUATION PURPOSES IN THE CASEBOOK

Evaluation Purposes and Uses	Case-example from Casebook
Assess needs, validate goals, prioritize goals, identify constraints and problems related to goals for training	Case L1 Case S2 Case S1
Assess alternative strategies, compare training designs, identify criteria to judge designs, determine feasibility and potential for success	Case C1 Case C4 Case S2 Case L2

EXAMPLE OF EVALUATION PURPOSES IN THE CASEBOOK *(continued)*	Evaluation Purposes and Uses	Case-example from Casebook
	Monitor and control program operation, identify problems and revision needs, determine whether objectives are achieved	Case C5 Case L3 Case S3 Case C2
	Determine usage and application, identify emerging and continuing needs, determine benefits of training, identify problems and revision needs to enhance training usage.	Case C3 Case L4 Case S3

L = local school
C = college or university
S = state agency

WHO WILL BE AFFECTED BY OR INVOLVED IN THE EVALUATION?

Evaluation affects both the object and all those who have a stake in the object. Because this is true, multiple groups are going to be interested in the evaluation. It is important to identify these "stakeholders" in the evaluation as they will provide the basis for some of the evaluation questions generated later. Evaluators cannot meet relevant needs unless they know who will use the evaluation and how.

It's usually not possible to accommodate all the identified audiences for an evaluation. It soon becomes necessary to think about whose information needs can be reasonably accommodated. This makes it necessary to rank order audiences and their concerns. A measure of how adequately you have identified audiences is the degree to which the needs of key stakeholders are reflected in your design.

Don't be fooled into thinking that audience issues are completed after you have determined the initial evaluation questions. To keep an evaluation useful and relevant, evaluators return to audiences, literally and figuratively, throughout the life of an evaluation.

TYPES OF EVALUATION AUDIENCES TO CONSIDER

Persons sponsoring or commissioning the evaluation.
Persons who will make decisions based upon the results of the evaluation.
Persons in the target group from whom information is being gathered.
Persons involved in planning or creating the program being evaluated.
Persons involved in running the program or project (the object) being evaluated.
Persons interested in the evaluation object (advocates and critics).
Persons who have a right to the information (in evaluations funded with public dollars, this can include everyone. Especially it refers to legislators, taxpayers, parents, and stakeholders who should know about the evaluation because of their responsibility for the target group.)
Persons whose roles might be affected by evaluation results and decisions.

WAYS OF IDENTIFYING RELEVANT AUDIENCES

Conversations with key program staff to identify:

program advocates
program critics
influential decision makers

Conversations with those outside the program to identify:

support for the program (economical, political)
special interest groups
controversial issues and stakeholders

Observations of program activities to identify:

formal and informal leaders
personnel responsible for work
personnel with authority to make decisions

Analysis of documents that define audiences and describe their stake in the program:

organizational charts
budget allocations
program materials

WAYS OF RANK-ORDERING AUDIENCES

By Degree of Involvement

The more directly affected the audience is by the evaluation, the more defensible their request for information, and the more important their involvement.

By Commitment and Ability to Use

The greater the potential that there is a commitment and ability to use the information, the more defensible the request.

By Request of Key Decision Maker/Sponsor

The information requests of the audiences identified by sponsors and key decision makers are ranked high because of expected follow through.

Interest in the Evaluation

Information requests of interested audiences often should be met. The greater the interest, the greater the attempt to service information needs through the evaluation.

WAYS OF INVOLVING AUDIENCES THROUGHOUT EACH STAGE OF THE EVALUATION

Focusing Evaluation

· audiences help identify key stakeholders
· audiences' perspectives of object documented
· audiences generate questions
· audiences educated about evaluation process and use
· evaluation questions reviewed by key audiences

Designing Evaluation

· audience needs are responded to in the design and choice of evaluator
· audiences identified in the design are appropriate (e.g., to give information, collect information, interpret results)

Information Collection

· audiences' information requirements considered
· audiences' information requests rank ordered
· audiences' role in information collection negotiated and practical
· key audiences are used as information sources

Information Analysis

· audience issues are key to determining level and type of analysis
· analyses are shared with key audiences
· interpretations are made in light of multiple perspectives
· audiences are given the opportunity to discuss and react to findings

**WAYS OF
INVOLVING
AUDIENCES
THROUGHOUT
EACH STAGE OF
THE EVALUATION**
(continued)

Reporting Information

· dates for audience information needs are identified
· ongoing evaluation activities are shared with key audiences
· audiences suggest in advance information that would be of interest to them; areas for recommendations; and displays and graphs that would be useful
· reports are delivered to relevant audiences in time for their use
· follow-through activities are planned based upon audience needs (e.g., post-report discussions, press releases, training)

Managing Evaluation

· audiences are treated humanely and kept informed throughout
· interruptions of regular activities are kept to a minimum for key audiences

Meta-evaluation

· audiences interested in the evaluation of the evaluation are identified and the report is shared with them

WHAT ELEMENTS IN THE SETTING ARE LIKELY TO INFLUENCE THE EVALUATION?

It is important to pay attention to the general setting of an evaluation. Generally, you want to know if the setting is stable and conducive to evaluation. Especially, you want to find out if evaluation is likely to be sabotaged or if it will be expected to function in a non-supportive environment. Understanding and describing key elements in the setting promotes a realistic design and productive coexistence between evaluation and setting.

In addition to influencing the evaluation, the setting also influences the object you are evaluating. It will be important to find out how elements in the setting (e.g., politics, economics, social patterns) impact the object in order later to interpret the evaluation.

When the success or failure of a program is reported, one piece of crucial information is the degree to which events in the setting were responsible. Others who want to adapt and use the findings of the evaluation must determine the effect the setting had on overall results and then judge how similar or dissimilar that setting is to their own.

In a small-scale evaluation, the program director/evaluator might spend only a few hours thinking about influences in the setting and how to attend to them in the design. In larger-scale evaluations, the object being evaluated and its setting might be thoroughly investigated to decide whether the evaluation should be undertaken. There is both reason and time in any evaluation to investigate the setting well enough to prevent front-end problems in the design.

A practical and ethical concern is determining how evaluation will affect the setting. If the costs are too great, it is possible that the evaluation should be reconsidered, rescheduled, or relocated. If these are not options, then certainly the evaluation will have to be sensitively designed to respond to a hostile or unstable setting.

EVENTS TO LOOK FOR IN THE SETTING	INFLUENCES	EVALUATION IMPLICATIONS
	Organizational Politics Program Leadership	Is there political support for the evaluation? Are there opponents? How secure is the object within the organization? Who has control over the program, formally and informally; what goals do they have for the program's future? How does the evaluation fit those goals?
	Professional Influences	How supportive are professional groups of the evaluation? Will you need to deal with union representatives? What will their agenda be?
	History	How mature and stable is the object to be evaluated? Has there been a tradition of self-appraisal and evaluation use? Is the object stable enough to withstand evaluation? What information already exists?

IMPLICATIONS OF SETTING FOR THE EVALUATION DESIGN (continued)	INFLUENCES	EVALUATION IMPLICATIONS
	Organizational Setting	Where does the program fit into the larger organizational network? Which decision makers can impact it? What kind of information could jeopardize the object?
	Economics	How secure is the fiscal support system for the program and the evaluation? Have funds been allocated? Will a written commitment of fiscal support be forthcoming?
	Communication and Social Patterns	How much disaffection (interpersonal conflict) is likely to result? Is the evaluation controversial to staff; are there apparent factions emerging as a result of its being discussed? What does the "normal" social pattern look like?
	Legal Guidelines	Are there legal restrictions (rights of human subjects) that will limit collection of desired information? Are there professional or institutional rulings that affect evaluation procedures? Will the object be affected by pending legislation?
	Resources	Will there be available resources to support the evaluation: e.g., skilled personnel, facilities, time, supportive climate, access to support services, access to personnel? Is there likely to be a change in resources that will affect the program?

WAYS OF INVESTIGATING THE SETTING	Conversations with key audiences	key authority figures formal/informal leaders program advocates program critics target audiences influential members persons responsible for target audience persons servicing target audience evaluation clients
	Conversations with specialists	legal consultants district/university lawyer legislators professional evaluator independent observer internal evaluator administative/political consultant union leader state department personnel dean
	Observations of the setting	social interactions climate or general atmosphere attitudes of specific personnel professional practices protocol followed efficiency and cooperation political camps existing resources facilities available and their quality support services provided budget allocations

Analysis of documents	management documents organization charts budgets funding guidelines programmatic materials proposal management plan materials used/produced historical data minutes of meetings media coverage memos and program communiques	
Interaction with existing groups	policy groups advisors client group management team staff group	

PROBES FOR INTERVIEWING KEY AUDIENCES	Probe about the object (e.g., program or project)	How well do you think things are going? Are most people supportive? Do you have the resources you need? Have things changed much over the past? (staff, goals, outcomes, support) What problems have you run into? How do you see the program's future?
	Probe about the evaluation	Do you think the evaluation will be useful? Who will use it? Will it cause problems? For whom? What do you think will be done with the results? What will happen to the program without the evaluation?

IMPLICATIONS OF SETTING FOR THE EVALUATION DESIGN	DESIGN DECISION	IMPLICATIONS OF THE SETTING
	Evaluator	Could an internal evaluator stay independent in this setting? Would an external evaluator be accepted or believed? Would a team be preferable?
	Information Collection	Is the setting conducive to close evaluator/audience interaction? Will it be possible to collect information to answer key evaluation questions? Is there more than one information source? What kinds of resources can be counted on?
	Information Sources	Are there influences in the setting that are likely to prevent access to information sources (people, documents, meetings, etc.)? What sources will be available? How much relevant information already exists?
	Information Analysis	What kind of evidence is likely to make a difference in this setting? Traditionally, what information has been produced and how? Who will be influential in interpreting data?

IMPLICATIONS OF SETTING FOR THE EVALUATION DESIGN *(continued)*	DESIGN DECISION	IMPLICATIONS OF THE SETTING
	Reporting	Is there a "no-win" situation for the report? Who will read the report; who will use it; who will be affected by it; when will it be needed to be of use? Who might want to edit it and can editing be prevented if necessary?
	Managing	What kinds of resources will be available? Who will help, be available for help? Who should receive a contract agreement? How much time will be spent in managing events related to the setting, such as political infighting or administrative protocol.
	Evaluating the Evaluation	Can outside evaluators be brought in at any time? Should they be? How credible will the evaluation be if it is not evaluated? Who is likely to insist that it isn't? What kind of evaluator would be credible in the setting?

WHAT ARE THE CRUCIAL QUESTIONS THE EVALUATION MUST ADDRESS TO ACHIEVE ITS PURPOSE?

It is important to establish the general questions the evaluation will address. As the evaluation design matures, you will carefully rethink and refine the questions to make sure you have the best set. When you finally collect information you can return to update, add, and revise these questions depending on timeline and resources.

Evaluation questions are the basic building blocks for the evaluation. The questions stakeholders would like to see answered by the evaluation influence the kind of information that should be gathered, and the type of information gathered and the means of gathering it, in turn, determine analysis options. Evaluation questions, then, are key to the whole information process.

Evaluations are apt to suffer from too many rather than too few questions. Much worse than too many questions are insignificant questions. Evaluators are responsible for identifying or helping audiences identify the crucial questions related to the evaluation purpose. If, for instance, the purpose of an evaluation is to "*assess the effectiveness of the newly installed training program in order to make improvements*," the evaluation questions might include:

1. Does the new program cost more or less per trainee?
2. Has trainee performance improved with the new training?
3. Is the new training program getting necessary administrative support?
4. How do trainers feel about the new training program?
5. How do trainees like it?
6. How valid are the competencies being taught?
7. Are some parts of the training more effective than others?

Initial evaluation questions can be gathered from audiences through conversations, interviews, surveys, and group meetings. (See also Audiences in this chapter.) Different audiences will be interested in different questions. "Training effectiveness," for instance, may translate into cost effectiveness to an administrator, positive trainee reactions to training staff, relevant information to a trainee, and better skills to a supervisor. Some audiences will find certain questions far more relevant to achieving the purpose of the evaluation than others.

To generate specific evaluation questions you must understand the general evaluation purpose and have some agreement about what is to be evaluated. For example, when you evaluate training are you evaluating its goals, the workshop, staff, outcomes, or all of these? And, you must know who will need to be involved so that their questions can be answered.

METHODS FOR DEFINING EVALUATION QUESTIONS

METHODS

1. *Analysis of the Object*: Identify key functions in the object and their critical interdependencies to highlight critical paths, major milestones, dependencies, etc. Evaluation questions are keyed to critical junctures, potential weak points, areas of staff concern, points of critical function, or key objectives and goals.

2. *Use of Theoretical Frameworks*: The object of evaluation is interpreted in light of a particular theoretical model, such as a change model, an evaluation model, learning theory, etc. Evaluation questions are derived from the model's key points and assumptions.

3. *External Expertise and Experience*: Experts in the area of the evaluation object identify evaluation questions of importance; literature review of similar evaluation; review of similar programs.

4. *Interaction with Key Audiences*: Discuss the evaluation with audience members. Ask what questions they want answered or what they believe is most important to investigate.

5. *Definition of the Purpose for Evaluation:* Do a logical, definitional analysis of the purposes for the evaluation. Identify the set of questions

EXAMPLE
(based on a hypothetical workshop)

1. The evaluator did a systems analysis of the workshop, defining components in terms of their inputs, process, and outputs. The staff reviewed this analysis, then generated evaluation questions in 3 categories:
   a. Where are breakdowns most likely to occur?
   b. Where is there the most disagreement as to the soundness of the design?
   c. What are the most important objectives?

2. A review of training and evaluation literature turned up two "models" that seemed especially relevant. Rummler's* posed 4 major questions:
   a. Did the participants like it?
   b. Did they learn it?
   c. Did they use what they learned?
   d. Did using what they learned make a difference?
   Stufflebeam's CIPP model** suggested a different set of concerns:
   a. Are the goals valid?
   b. Is the design a good one?
   c. Is the design well implemented?
   d. Were the goals achieved?
   Using these models, the evaluation came up with evaluation questions pertinent to the 2 day workshop.

3. The evaluator called a consultant friend who recommended 3 evaluation reports from similar workshops. These were reviewed, and they suggested some good evaluation questions.

4. The evaluator interviewed several key audience members: the training director, the superintendant, a school board member, and a few potential participants. Based on their interests and needs, some key evaluation questions were defined.

5. A staff meeting was held to brainstorm evaluation questions that seemed related to the purposes for the evaluation. This list was then synthesized to remove overlap and duplica-

METHODS FOR DEFINING EVALUATION QUESTIONS *(continued)*

METHODS

which, if addressed, would meet each purpose.

6. *"Bonus" Questions*: Given that you're going to do an evaluation anyway, are there some questions you can pursue that will be worthwhile, perhaps for research, public relations, marketing, etc.?

EXAMPLE
(based on a hypothetical workshop)

tion. Then a Q-sort technique was used to assemble a set of questions that most agreed defined the purpose of the evaluation.

6. The evaluator and project director discussed some opportunities presented by the evaluation. They decided it might be useful to explore whether participants who enrolled in order to meet recertification requirements were more or less successful than "volunteer" attendees, as these requirements were currently under state scrutiny.

* Brethower, K.S., & Rummler, G.A., "Evaluating Training," *Improving Human Performance Quarterly*, 1977, 5 pp. 107–120.
** Stufflebeam, Daniel L. in Worthen & Sanders Educational Evaluation: Theory and Practice, Jones Publishing, Ohio, 1973, pp. 128–150.

ASSESSING EVALUATION QUESTIONS IN LIGHT OF THE INFORMATION THEY WILL PRODUCE

Evaluation questions generate information and so should be assessed in light of the quality and type of information they will produce. To assess questions in light of their information yield, it is necessary to forecast or think ahead toward some other evaluation decisions.

Evaluation Questions
1. identified
2. rank ordered
3. as a set, they are relevant, important, comprehensive, balanced, and realistic.

Information that could be gathered
1. What information sources are available to answer these questions (e.g., people, test scores, documents)?
2. What methods might be used to gather information from these sources (e.g., interviews, testing, document review)?
3. What instruments or tools might be used (e.g., interview protocols, achievement test, checklist)?

What will be reported back to audiences
1. How might the information gathered be displayed, interpreted, and reported to answer questions?
2. What kind of report(s) might be necessary for different audiences?
3. When do audiences need information to answer questions?

How information could be analyzed
1. Would information to answer questions be qualitative or quantitative, or both?
2. What methods are available to analyze these kinds of data?
3. What or whose criteria would be used to judge the results?

EXAMPLES OF EVALUATION QUESTIONS FOR A 2-DAY INSERVICE WORKSHOP ABOUT SCHWARTZIAN THEORY

Questions related to aspects of the object	Questions for a "new" object (i.e., being planned or recently implemented)	Questions for an "old" object (i.e., been around awhile perhaps through several rounds of revision)
Goals or Needs	What problems are teachers having with handicapped children? What kinds of training do teachers want? What time and other constraints exist among the target population? To what extent do teachers value the planned workshop objectives?	Are the identified needs still valid? Did the workshop address the 3 goals intended? What needs do attendees have?
Program Design	Is Design A more practical than Design B? Is Design C any good? Are there sufficient resources for the chosen design? Are these exercises needed to meet the learning goals? What do teachers think of the design?	Is the design specific and practical enough for replication by satellite sites? What elements of the workshop are least productive? Is the new shorter design feasible? potent? Why don't other teachers attend the sessions?
Implementation or Processes	Did trainers use Schwartzian Methods correctly? Who attended the session? Were Day 1 objectives met? What problems did trainers encounter? How many people attended optional sessions?	What problems are being encountered by new training staff? Who attends? Are attendance rates consistent across times and locations? Does the Day 2 afternoon session help with problem solving?
Products or Outcomes	Did teachers' knowledge of Schwartz's Theory increase? How well can teachers use Schwartz techniques? Are graduates using Schwartz Techniques in their classrooms?	What are effects on pupils of teachers' use of new methods? What other uses or misuses are being made of workshop acquired methods? Do people who receive less workshop training perform less well than others?
Recycling Decisions	How much did the session cost? Do graduates consider the session worthwhile? Are Principals supporting graduates' efforts to use new methods?	What are the costs and benefits to attendees of using the new methods? To what extent is the workshop reaching the population? What continuing needs and problems exist despite the workshop benefits?

ANALYZING AND RANK ORDERING EVALUATION QUESTIONS Many times you generate more evaluation questions than you can answer. So, it becomes important to decide how you'll spend your resources and which questions you will answer. To do this, you can list a set of criteria that may be important in the rank-ordering process (like the key considerations listed across the grid). This allows you to illustrate not only which questions are being asked, but also to indicate the feasibility and importance of answering them. Such a display helps key audiences or the evaluator select the critical and practical evaluation questions.

General purpose: Assess the effectiveness of a two day inservice training.

Key Considerations

The Evaluation Questions	Who wants to know (nature/number)	Could you make good use of information? (decision to be made)	How much would it cost to evaluate?	Are there existing procedures /info. available? (quality/amount)	Can this information have impact on target audience?	How much time would be necessary to gather data?
Increased cost?						
Improved performance?						
Attitudes?						
Valid competencies?						
Some elements more effective than others?						
Well implemented?						
Graduates more effective?						

EVALUATE THE
QUESTIONS
AS A SET

· Questions are relevant to the purpose and will likely bring useful information.
· Questions are important, and they merit answering.
· Questions are comprehensive and cover core issues related to purpose.
· Questions are balanced and do not focus on a single program element.
· Questions are realistic and there are resources and means available to answer them.

Crucial evaluation questions can emerge throughout an evaluation, so it is important to regularly return to the evaluation questions to assess their appropriateness.

ANOTHER
EXAMPLE OF
EVALUATION
QUESTIONS

EXCERPTED FROM CASE C-3 BY DALE BRETHOWER *

Course Design	Course Delivery	Course Outcomes
Are instructional procedures consistent with the relevant learning processes?	Are logistics well managed?	Are the course objectives being met?
Subquestions:	Subquestions:	Subquestions:
Are procedures relevant to cognitive domain? objectives consistent with principles and research findings? relevant to cognitive learning? Are procedures relevant to affective domain? objectives consistent with principles and research relevant to affective learning?	Are there systematic procedures for: scheduling faculties advertising the course preparing, producing, and/or ordering materials scheduling media, etc. scheduling out-of-class meetings, etc. prompt return of student work managing production of tests, surveys, etc. managing student records etc.	Do students like the course? Do they achieve the objectives? Do they use what they learn?

*See Casebook

DOES THE
EVALUATION
STAND A GOOD
CHANCE OF BEING
IMPLEMENTED
SUCCESSFULLY?

Not every evaluation conceived should be undertaken so you must consider whether evaluation is worth the resources. Anticipating problems increases the evaluation's potential for success. This chapter provides a checklist to help you rethink issues previously introduced and to anticipate issues that lie ahead. It also provides you with a listing of products that might be useful in responding to relevant items on the checklist.

CHECKLIST OF EVALUATION CONCERNS RELATED TO POTENTIAL FOR SUCCESS	Questions to consider	Sources of evidence
	Can the evaluation object be identified?	description using existing information (proposal, organizational or management plan) and further discussions and observation using relevant audiences
	Has the object been described from a number of different value perspectives?	
	Is the evaluation object relatively stable and mature? What kind of evaluation can it withstand?	
	Are there criteria available to interpret evaluation information?	established criteria, e.g., program objectives, comparison to like programs, needs assessment data, staff judgments
	Is the evaluation purpose clear and defensible, and has it been shared with key stakeholders?	statement of evaluation purpose and rationale disseminated
	Have the events in the setting that are likely to influence the evaluation been identified?	description of setting including interviews with those in organization who can affect program
	Is the setting conducive to or supportive of evaluation (e.g., political support)?	
	Would disruptions caused by the evaluation be tolerable?	
	Have audiences who will be affected or involved been identified?	list of primary and secondary audiences
	Have key stakeholders' needs and questions been identified?	list of key evaluation questions
	Are questions for the evaluation important and worth answering?	
	Is someone available to do the evaluation who has some basic skills in conducting evaluations?	criteria for selection of evaluator documented
	Will the evaluation's credibility be jeopardized by evaluator bias?	
	Is there economic support for the evaluation?	draft of budget
	Are there procedures available to answer the evaluation questions?	lists of possible information collection procedures
	Are there criteria to interpret answers?	list of criteria to be used to interpret answers to questions has been drafted
	Is it feasible to complete the evaluation in the allotted time?	draft management plan (personnel, timeline, tasks)
	Is there a commitment to implement sound evaluation?	
	Is there some agreement about criteria to judge the success of the evaluation?	choice of evaluation criteria (e.g., Joint Committee *Standards*) specified
	Can a written agreement (memo or contract) be negotiated to document the considerations about evaluation goals, responsibilities, resources, and criteria?	draft of contract

REFERENCES

Guba, E.G. & Lincoln, Y.S. *Effective Evaluation: Improving the Usefulness of Evaluation Results Through Responsive and Naturalistic Approaches*. San Francisco: Jossey-Bass, 1981.

Joint Committee on Standards for Educational Evaluation. *Standards for Evaluation of Educational Programs, Projects, & Materials*. New York: McGraw-Hill, 1981.

Martin, Marilyn A. A framework for identifying information needs for evaluation planning, *Instructional Aids Series*, No. 4, Evaluation Center, College of Education, Western Michigan University, Kalamazoo, Michigan 49008, April, 1976.

Smith, Nick L. Evaluability assessment: a retrospective illustration and review, *Educational Evaluation and Policy Analysis, 3*, January–February, 1981.

Yavorsky, Diane K. *Discrepancy Evaluation: A Practitioner's Guide*. Evaluation Research Center, University of Virginia, 1978.

Designing Evaluation

WHAT IT IS

Evaluation design is both a process and a set of written products or plans. An evaluation design can be a loosely constructed emerging plan or a predetermined and fairly rigid blueprint for the evaluation. Whether the evaluation is planned "as it goes" or is carefully choreographed in advance, it includes: progressive focusing; collecting information; analyzing information; reporting information; managing and, often, evaluating evaluation.

Even though evaluations are essentially made of the same elements, some are distinctly better than others. In this chapter differences in approaching evaluation design are described and criteria for judging designs discussed. It is important to note at the outset that there are a number of perspectives about the best way to evaluate, and not infrequently they are at odds. This chapter provides you with some alternative ways to think about and to plan evaluation.

WHEN DESIGN DECISIONS ARE MADE

A number of important decisions often have been made before evaluators sit down to draft a design document for an evaluation. These decisions, covered in Focusing the Evaluation, are actually the beginning of the design. They are the decisions that help evaluators progressively focus their attention on what audiences want evaluated and why. (To review the checklist of concerns related to focusing, turn back to p. 32–33.) Any evaluation design typically must be readjusted over time. As problems arise and changes take place in the object being evaluated, the design must stay responsive to new needs.

To design evaluation using this sourcebook, you should remember that designing entails collection, analysis, and reporting of evaluation information. This means you will need to use other chapters in the Sourcebook to flesh out your evaluation design in detail. Also, consider using the **Design Manual**, the companion piece constructed to help readers complete their own evaluation design.

WHAT ARE SOME ALTERNATIVE WAYS TO DESIGN EVALUATION?

While every evaluation design is essentially made of similar elements, there are many ways to put those elements together. Below are three major decisions that determine the general approach to evaluation that you will be taking.

Fixed vs. Emergent Evaluation Design: Can the evaluation questions and criteria be finalized at the outset? If so, should they be?

Formative vs. Summative Evaluation: Is the evaluation to be used for improvement or to report on the worth of a program... or both?

Experimental and Quasi-Experimental Designs vs. Unobtrusive Inquiry: Is the evaluation going to include intervening into events (trying to manipulate environment, persons getting treatment, variables affected, etc.), or will it just "watch" events... or a little of both?

Answers to the questions listed above initially may not be clear cut. (For instance, you might attempt a quasi-experimental design that includes the use of unobtrusive inquiry.) Nonetheless, the categories represented by these broad decision areas reflect the amount and kind of front-end planning, the general purpose for evaluating, and the amount of control you'll want during the evaluation process. Deciding where you stand, even generally, on these issues will help you establish some preliminary benchmarks to help explain, guide, and judge evaluation tasks.

FIXED VS. EMERGENT EVALUATION DESIGNS

A fixed design is determined and systematically planned prior to the evaluation's implementation. The design likely is built around program goals and objectives and poses specific evaluation questions; it specifies information sources and collection and analysis plans and decides in advance which audiences will receive information for what purpose. While more structured than emergent evaluation, fixed or preordinate evaluation can also be readjusted to meet changing needs. Most formal evaluations in personnel preparation have been based upon preordained designs because program objectives were carefully fixed in advance by grants and proposals.

An emergent evaluation design readily responds to ongoing influences, evolving as it accommodates changing audiences, problems, and program activities. Emergent evaluation designs devote a good deal of time at the front end of the evaluation to *seeking* purposes and issues, as these are not initially specified or assumed.

FIXED DESIGNS	EMERGENT DESIGNS
greatest expenditure of evaluation resources in the design revolves around activities to specify questions, prepare and administer instruments, analyze the results, and formally report results to audiences	greatest expenditure of evaluation resources in the design is invested in observing the program and focusing further inquiry
evaluator uses program goals and objectives to identify evaluation questions for the design and stimulates relevant audiences to expand and refine these questions	evaluator does not stimulate audiences to think about program or evaluation issues as much as respond to what they say. Audiences determine the important issues and information needs for the "design."
communications between evaluator and audiences regarding the design are at regular intervals but typically formal and often written	communication between evaluator and audiences is formal and ongoing
information collection strategies specified typically involve formal instrumentation (tests, surveys, questionnaires, and rating scales) and can include research methods. Research criteria such as internal and external validity are considered important. The data gathered are often quantitative.	observation, case study, advocate team reports are examples of methods. Less "objective" and less obtrusive measures are taken and the responsive evaluator will sacrifice some precision in measurement for usefulness. Qualitative information is often gathered.
the design is usually drafted and shared with key stakeholders. While it can change, an attempt is made to adhere to initial objectives and plans.	the design continues to grow, change, and react to the setting. In a sense, it is never really finished.

FORMATIVE VS. SUMMATIVE EVALUATION

Formative evaluation is used to glean information to help improve a project, a curriculum, or inservice. It is structured for staff use and may sacrifice external credibility for usefulness. There are many who think the most defensible evaluation is formative evaluation.

Summative evaluation is designed to assess the worth of an object. It is often requested by funding agents, sponsors or administrators who must make fiscal cuts. Summative evaluation is used to make judgments about how worthwhile a program is in order to determine whether to keep it or license it; hence, the evaluation must have credibility for a number of audiences who will be affected by that decision. In funded areas of personnel preparation summative evaluation has been more common than formative evaluation. While less popular with program staff, summative evaluation does bring data to "go/no-go" decisions that must be made. How it is used, or whether it is used, depends upon the decision maker.

It is possible to build evaluations to provide ongoing information for improvement and information for judgments of worth. However, often formative and summative evaluation have conflicting purposes and cannot easily be reconciled in the same design. For example, if a program will stay or go based on an evaluation, few staff will be interested in improving as they anticipate the final report.

FORMATIVE	SUMMATIVE
evaluation resources expended on need areas identified by program staff	evaluation focuses on "success" variables considered important by sponsor or decision makers
evaluator is often part of program and works closely with program staff	external evaluator or review team frequently used, as internal evaluator is more likely to have a conflict of interest
any information collection strategy might be used but emphasis will be on turning over useful information quickly to make improvements	information collection strategy will maximize external and internal validity and might be gathered over a longer period of time
the evaluation design (fixed or emergent) is drawn up with staff and revised to meet their needs	the evaluation design (could be emergent but probably will be fixed) is drawn up to meet the needs of sponsors/key decision makers

EXPERIMENTAL AND QUASI-EXPERIMENTAL DESIGNS VS. UNOBTRUSIVE INQUIRY

Some evaluations use classic research methodology. In such cases, subjects are randomly selected or assigned, treatments are given, and measures of impact are taken. The purpose, if it's evaluation, is still to make a judgment about the worth of the object, e.g., a demonstration program or an early intervention strategy. When students or programs are randomly selected, it is possible to make generalizations to a larger population. It is, however, difficult and sometimes not ethical to intervene in an educational setting by selecting or sorting subjects or by giving or withholding treatments. Thus, the degree to which the setting can be manipulated and the degree to which such a strategy is considered sound is a major consideration at the outset of the evaluation.

In some cases, intervention is neither possible nor desirable. If events have already happened, evaluators must look at historical documents, study test scores, or analyze existing research. If it is important to evaluate a setting or a program so as to improve it, evaluators might choose to watch, talk with people, and keep a low profile so that the program they evaluate is not unduly threatened or changed by their appearance. Many methodologies (including observation, survey, meta analysis, case study and even interview) can be used in such a way as to minimize the evaluation's impact on people and events and maximize its reporting on the "what is."

RESEARCH DESIGN	NATURAL "UNOBTRUSIVE" INQUIRY
a good deal of resources go into the preparation for and administering of instruments to assess treatments; quantitative data typically gathered and statistical criteria used	evaluators spend more time on-site watching and talking to relevant audiences; multiple evaluation strategies and sources are used to increase the reliability of information gathered
statistical criteria focused on program outcomes are established at the outset and the design is formalized and left intact throughout	evaluator discusses issues with audiences; the degree to which evaluator issues are discussed depends on evaluator style
interaction with audiences is to formulate plan, gather information and report it back	interaction with audience is ongoing and informal
information collection strategies specified typically involve formal instrumentation (tests, surveys, questionnaires and rating scales) and can include research methods. Research criteria such as internal and external validity are considered important. The data gathered are often quantitative.	observation, case study, advocate team reports are examples of methods. Less "objective" and less obtrusive measures are taken and the responsive evaluator will sacrifice some precision in measurement for usefulness.
the design is usually drafted and shared with key stakeholders. While it can change, an attempt is made to adhere to initial objectives and plans.	the design may be finalized at the outset if program objectives are clear or it might be emergent and work toward identifying program goals

---

SOME EXISTING APPROACHES USEFUL IN TRAINING EVALUATION

It's possible to shop around for an existing evaluation model rather than attempt to invent your own. Since 1965 a number of evaluation approaches have been described and applied in varied settings. Below some of these approaches are briefly described. Remember that any existing approach or design must be thoughtfully retailored to fit a specific context.

GENERAL APPROACH	PURPOSES	RELEVANT MODELS AND REFERENCES
CONGRUENCY AND COMPLIANCE		
Actual program progress and activities are charted and compared to plans (designs, intentions) or to some external standards or criteria.	helping management keep a program on track documenting that plans and proposals were adhered to gaining accreditation,	Discrepancy Evaluation Model (DEM) Program Evaluation and Review Technique (PERT) Management by Objectives (MBO)

SOME EXISTING
APPROACHES
USEFUL IN
TRAINING
EVALUATION
(continued)

GENERAL APPROACH	PURPOSES	RELEVANT MODELS AND REFERENCES
CONGRUENCY AND COMPLIANCE	demonstrating compliance	Program Analysis of Service Systems (PASS) State Audits
DECISION-MAKING		
Information is collected pertinent to key developmental stages and steps (e.g., goal setting, program design) to help choose a course of action or see how well a program is progressing at any given point.	providing a data base for forecasted key decision points helping a program progress through certain developmental stages explaining or justifying why certain actions were taken	CIPP Evaluation Model Concerns-Based Adoption Model (CBAM) Discrepancy Evaluation Model (DEM) Impact Evaluation Model (IEM) NIN Child Change "Steps" Model
RESPONSIVE		
This identifies the critical audiences and stakeholders of a program, then helps get the information they need or want to use, judge, or benefit from the program.	enhancing support for and involvement in a program demonstrating good intentions and concern for audiences providing the worth of a program to its key stakeholders	R. Stake's "Responsive Evaluation" Guba & Lincoln, *Effective Evaluation*
OBJECTIVES-BASED		
Specific objectives are defined for each activity, then data are collected that will measure their achievement.	seeing whether activities produce what they're supposed to forcing specificity and clarity on program outcomes demonstrating performance	Goal Attainment Scaling ✗ R. Mager's *Preparing Instructional Objectives* R. Tyler's *Defining Educational Objectives*
ORGANIZATIONAL DEVELOPMENT		
Information about staff and project problems, expectations and progress are regularly collected, then fed back to staff.	help bring increasing knowledge and certainty about what's taking place, what's working and why help staff become more effective, productive, and satisfied identify staff development and organization development needs facilitate staff and project growth	Provus, *Discrepancy Evaluation* Brinkerhoff, "Training Evaluation" Shumsky, *Action Research*

SOME EXISTING APPROACHES USEFUL IN TRAINING EVALUATION *(continued)*	GENERAL APPROACH	PURPOSES	RELEVANT MODELS AND REFERENCES
	NATURALISTIC		
	Open, emergent inquiry into program activities and outcomes. Begins with little preconceived plan about evaluation questions, procedures, data collection, etc.	to determine what's really happening identify actual effects and consequences whether planned or not better understand the context of a program and the forces acting on it	Guba & Lincoln, *Effective Evaluation* Patton, *Qualitative Evaluation Methods*
	EXPERT-JUDGMENT		
	Information about program activities, resources, etc. is collected, then given to one or more "judges" who draw conclusions, make recommendations, etc.	get new ideas and perspectives on how to operate a program gain acceptance, credibility interpret and place a value on program outcomes	E. Eisner's Connoiseurship Judicial Evaluation Model Goal-free Evaluation
	EXPERIMENTAL		
	Outcome data are carefully specified and measured under controlled treatment conditions, after using control groups or statistical methods to assess and control error.	compare effects of one approach to another demonstrate cause-effect relationships; provide evidence that program is cause of outcomes identify correlates and relationships among key program variables gain validation from JDRP	Campbell and Stanley Cook and Campbell Joint Dissemination and Review Panel (JDRP)
	COST ANALYSIS		
	Program costs are defined and analyzed to determine how much was spent on what activities, and with what effects.	relate increments of outcomes to increments of cost document expenditures and costs facilitate replication efforts	Levin's "Cost Effectiveness Analysis"

WHAT DOES A DESIGN INCLUDE?

It is important to keep in mind that evaluation designs are comprised of the same elements or, as we refer to them, functions. These functions include focusing, collecting, analyzing, and reporting information, managing and evaluating the evaluation. Whether the design emerges or is fixed at the outset, it will contain these functions in one form or another. Adapted existing models and designs will also be constructed of these same basic functions, but they will put them together using different perspectives.

What makes evaluation designs different, or better, or more appropriate is how well these same basic functions are integrated and operationalized. Like a book with a well-blended plot, theme and setting, the sound evaluation design puts all the parts together well. Moreover, the sound evaluation design is useful for improving training.

There are a number of important decisions and corresponding tasks that must be resolved during the process of evaluation. Design decisions as well as design products that form an audit trail are described in this section. Remember, each evaluation design tells its own unique story; you do not need to include all considerations listed in this section, but you should have considered their influence on your design.

DESIGN DECISIONS AND TASKS In this book seven major evaluation activities have been described and 35 key decisions and tasks relating to these functions have been identified. Whether you choose to design your own evaluation or adapt an existing design, we recommend that you consider each decision listed in the following grid:

Function	Key Issues	Tasks	Page Numbers
Focusing the Evaluation	1. What will be evaluated?	1. Investigate what is to be evaluated	7–15
	2. What is the purpose for evaluating?	2. Identify and justify purpose(s)	16–19
	3. Who will be affected by or involved in the evaluation?	3. Identify audiences	20–22
	4. What elements in the setting are likely to influence the evaluation?	4. Study setting	23–26
	5. What are the critical evaluation questions?	5. Identify major questions	27–31
	6. Does the evaluation have the potential for success?	6. Decide whether to go on with evaluation	32–34

DESIGN DECISIONS AND TASKS *(continued)*	Function	Key Issues	Tasks	Page Numbers
	Designing Evaluation	1. What are some alternative ways to design an evaluation?	1. Determine the amount of planning, general purpose, and degree of control	37–42
		2. What does a design include?	2. Overview evaluation decisions, tasks, and products	43–58
		3. How do you go about constructing a design?	3. Determine general procedures for the evaluation	59–63
		4. How do you recognize a good design?	4. Assess the quality of the design	64–71
	Collecting Information	1. What kinds of information should you collect?	1. Determine the information sources you will use	77–83
		2. What procedures should you use to collect needed information?	2. Decide how you'll collect information	84–88
		3. How much information should you collect?	3. Decide whether you need to sample and, if so, how	89–94
		4. Will you select or develop instruments?	4. Determine how precise your information must be and design a means to collect it.	95–99
		How do you establish reliable and valid instrumentation?	Establish procedures to maximize validity and reliability	100–107
		5. How do you plan the information collection effort to get the most information at the lowest cost?	5. Plan the logistics for an economical information collection procedure	108–115
	Analyzing and Interpreting (Evaluation)	1. How will you handle returned data?	1. Aggregate and code data if necessary	119–122
		2. Are data worth analyzing?	2. Verify completeness and quality of raw data	123–126
		3. How will you analyze the information?	3. Select & run defensible analyses	127–144
		4. How will you interpret the results of analyses?	4. Interpret the data using prespecified and alternative sets of criteria	145–147
	Reporting	1. Who should get an evaluation report?	1. Identify who you will report to	151–153
		2. What content should	2. Outline the	154–158

DESIGN DECISIONS AND TASKS *(continued)*	Function	Key Issues	Tasks	Page Numbers
		be included in a report?	content to be included	
		3. How will reports be delivered?	3. Decide whether reports will be written, oral, etc.	159–164
		4. What is the appropriate style and structure for the report?	4. Select a format for the report	165–167
		5. How can you help audiences interpret and use reports?	5. Plan post-report discussions, consultation, follow-up activities	168–169
		6. When should reports be scheduled?	6. Map out the report schedule	170–173
	Managing	1. Who should run the evaluation?	1. Select, hire, and/or train the evaluator	176–180
		2. How should evaluation responsibilities be formalized?	2. Draw up a contract or letter of agreement	181–186
		3. How much should the evaluation cost?	3. Draft the budget	187–190
		4. How should evaluation tasks be organized and scheduled?	4. Draft a time/task strategy	191–196
		5. What kinds of problems can be expected?	5. Monitor the evaluation and anticipate problems	197–200
	Evaluating Evaluation (Meta Evaluation)	1. What are some good uses of meta-evaluation?	1. Determine whether you need to meta evaluate; if so, when	205–207
		2. Who should do the meta evaluation?	2. Select a meta evaluator	208–209
		3. What criteria or standards should you use to evaluate the evaluation?	3. Select or negotiate standards	210–217
		4. How do you apply a set of meta-evaluation criteria?	4. Rank order standards, determine compliance	218–220
		5. What procedures are used in meta-evaluation?	5. Select procedures for evaluating evaluations	221–222

DESIGN PRODUCTS   Design activities are guided by documents which outline evaluation tasks. Below is a listing of design products that leave a trail for others to study and evaluate the evaluation design. You may have all of these products or only some of them and they may be produced in any order.

DESIGN PRODUCTS *(continued)*

Evaluation Function	Evaluation Products	Content Included
Focusing the Evaluation	Evaluation Overview	description of evaluation object and setting; listing of relevant audiences; evaluation questions and subquestions; evaluation criteria to judge success.
Collecting Information	Information Collection Plan	evaluation questions/sub-questions; variables of interest; information sources; instruments; collection methods; timeline.
Managing Information	Analysis Plan	type of information to be gathered; statistical/valuational criteria; interpretation strategy (who/how); type of analysis specified.
Reporting Information	Report Strategy	audiences to receive reports; number of reports; report content; report format (oral, written); report schedule.
	Follow Through Plans	plans for consultation with key audiences; inservice for staff; dissemination to outside audience.
Managing an Evaluation	Management Plan	tasks to be completed; timeline; personnel reponsible; budget.
	Evaluation Contract	specifies evaluator and evaluator responsibility; summarizes and documents the other evaluation products.
Evaluation of Evaluation	Meta Evaluation Plan	criteria to be used; persons to evaluate.

DESIGN ELEMENTS

Name	Definition	How Design Elements Fit Together in Good Evaluation
Object:	What gets evaluated	*Object* has interest or value to *Audiences*
Purpose:	What the evaluation is to accomplish; why it's being done	*Purpose* is clear, shared and defensible; there is some commitment to use information to be produced relative to *Object*; Some *Audiences* will benefit from *Purpose*
Audiences:	Who the evaluation is for and who will be involved	*Audiences* have an interest in the *Object* and would be willing to help generate and use evaluation information
Evaluation Questions:	Questions about the nature and value of some object which, if answered, could	*Evaluation Questions* are responsive to *Audience* interests or needs and are pertinent to the *Object* and its context

DESIGN ELEMENTS
(continued)

Name	Definition	How Design Elements Fit Together in Good Evaluation
	provide useful information	
Collected Information:	Information about the object or its context that has been aggregated and sorted	*Collected Information* is responsive to *Audiences*; reflects *Object* or context without distortion; and is useful for answering or generating *Evaluation Questions*
Information Collection Methods:	Ways information gets collected (observation, tests, etc.)	*Information Collection Methods* produce good *Collected Information* (as defined above) economically
Instruments:	Forms and records used in information collection	*Instruments* are suitable for *Information Collection Methods*
Analysis Methods:	Ways of understanding collected information	*Analysis Methods* are appropriate to *Collected Information* and will lead to answering or generating useful *Evaluation Questions*
Interpretations and Conclusions:	Values and meaning attached to collected information	*Interpretations and Conclusions* are justified by *Analysis Methods* and are responsive to *Purposes*
Reports:	Communications with audiences about the evaluation or its interpretations and conclusions	*Reports* clearly present *Interpretations and Conclusions* or other relevant information and are useful for *Audiences*
Report Methods:	How communications are made (oral, written, T.V. show, etc.)	*Report Methods* are appropriate for *Audiences* and report content

---

CHECKLIST FOR EVALUATION DESIGN

A. Clarity of Evaluation Focus
   1. Is there an adequate description of what (program, context, functions, products, etc.) is to be evaluated? (Object)
   2. Is the evaluation object relatively stable and mature? Do you know what kind of evaluation it can withstand? (Object, Purposes)
   3. Are the reasons for the evaluation specified and defensible? (Purpose)
   4. Is it clear what planning, implementing, redesign, judging, or other decisions and interests are to be served by the evaluation? (Purpose)
   5. Are all relevant evaluation audiences described? (Audiences)
   6. Are the criteria, values, and expectations that audiences will bring to bear in interpreting information known and described? (Audiences)

7. Have the events in the setting that are likely to influence the evaluation been identified? (Constraints)
8. Is someone available to do the evaluation who has some basic skills in conducting evaluations? (Constraints)
9. Is the setting conducive to or supportive of evaluation (e.g., political support)? (Constraints)
10. Would disruptions caused by the evaluation be tolerable? (Constraints)

B. Evaluation Questions
1. Have key stakeholders' needs and questions been identified?
2. Are questions for the evaluation important and worth answering?
3. Are questions sufficiently comprehensive? If addressed, would they meet the evaluation's purpose?

C. Information Collection
1. Are there procedures available to answer the evaluation questions?
2. Are the **kinds of information** to be collected logically related to the information needs?
3. Are the information collection procedures appropriate for the kinds of information sought?
4. Is the evaluation likely to provide accurate information?
5. Is the evaluation likely to provide timely information?
6. Is the evaluation likely to provide information sufficient to meet its purposes?
7. Is the evaluation likely to provide useful information to each audience?
8. Are the procedures compatible with the purposes of the evaluation?
9. Will information collection be minimally disruptive?

D. Analysis and Interpretation
1. Are information organization, reduction, and storage procedures appropriate for the information to be collected? Safe?
2. Are information analysis procedures specified and appropriate?
3. Are methods and/or criteria for interpreting evaluation information known and defensible?

E. Reporting
1. Are report audiences defined? Are they sufficiently comprehensive?
2. Are report formats, content and schedules appropriate for audience needs?
3. Will the evaluation report balanced information?
4. Will reports be timely and efficient?
5. Is the report plan responsive to rights for knowledge and information with respect to relevant audiences?

F. Management
1. Does the design provide for adequate protection of human privacy and other rights?
2. Are personnel roles specified and related to information collection and management requirements?
3. Is the evaluation likely to be carried out in a professional and responsible manner?
4. Is the evaluation likely to be carried out legally?
5. Has sufficient time been allocated for evaluation activities (instrument development, data collection, analysis, reporting, management)?
6. Are sufficient fiscal, human and material resources provided for?
7. Are personnel qualified to carry out assigned responsibilities?
8. Are intended data sources likely to be available and accessible?
9. Are management responsibilities and roles sufficient to support the evaluation?

CHECKLIST FOR EVALUATION DESIGN
(continued)

10. Is it feasible to complete the evaluation in the allotted time?
11. Can a written agreement (memo or contract) be negotiated to document the considerations about evaluation goals, responsibilities, resources, and criteria?
12. Are there provisions for redesigning or redirecting the evaluation as experience over time may indicate?

G. Evaluating the Evaluation
   1. Is there a commitment to implement sound evaluation?
   2. Is there agreement about criteria to judge the success of the evaluation?
   3. Will the evaluation's credibility be jeopardized by evaluator bias?
   4. Are there procedures planned to assess the quality of the evaluation's design, progress and results?
   5. Are there provisions for disseminating, reporting, interpreting and otherwise utilizing the results and experience of the evaluation?

EXAMPLE OF AN EVALUATION DESIGN (EXCERPTED FROM *DESIGN MANUAL*, APPENDIX B)

INTRODUCTION

This appendix* contains a complete (all 7 Products) evaluation design. The example used is an evaluation design for a 3-day training workshop. To get extra mileage from this example, the 3-day workshop is an evaluation training workshop, in which the hypothetical participants learn about evaluation and produce evaluation designs using the Design Manual (it's a lot like a workshop the authors used to conduct).

So, this example gives you a look at all seven (7) products. It might also give you some ideas how you could use the companion Design Manual to train others.

PRODUCT 1: *Evaluation Preview*

What is to be Evaluated

The object of the evaluation is a workshop developed and delivered by the ETC Project. It is a three-day workshop which gives participants intensive training in evaluation and time to work on their own evaluation designs. Participants are from professional development and teacher preparation programs in colleges and universities and local and state educational agencies. The project received funding from the federal Office of Special Education to develop the materials used in the workshop, but must rely on registration fees to cover some delivery costs. The project is based at a University Evaluation Center which is interested in insuring quality and coordinating the project with its other activities.

HOW THE WORKSHOP WORKS

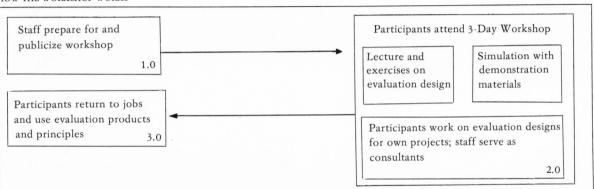

WORKSHOP AGENDA

Day One		Day Two		Day Three	
9:00– 9:30	Introduction	9:00– 9:30	Introduction to the Design Manual	9:00–10:00	Lecture and demonstration: Reporting
9:30–10:30	Evaluation design exercise	9:30–12:00	Participants (each with own Design Manual) complete Products #1 and #2	10:00–11:00	Participants complete Product #5
10:30–12:00	Discussion: Review of Decision Areas from *Sourcebook*	12:00– 1:00	Lunch	11:00–12:00	Panel discussion: Management
12:00– 1:00	Lunch	1:00– 2:30	Exercise and lecture: Measurement Planning	12:00– 1:00	Lunch
1:00– 2:30	Participants read selected case	2:30– 4:30	Participants complete Products #3 and #4	1:00– 3:30	Participants complete Products #6 and #7
2:30– 3:30	Small group exercise: Participants analyze case using Decision Areas			3:30– 4:00	Wrap-up
3:30– 4:30	Summary Review				

Evaluation Purpose

The primary purpose is to produce information which can be used to redesign subsequent versions of the workshop. A secondary purpose is to provide impact and other accountability information to external audiences.

Audiences for the Evaluation

The primary audience is the staff, who want to conduct good, efficient training. Other audiences include: (1) the Federal Office whose primary interest is to see their funds well used to support a quality effort, and (2) the University Evaluation Center and Administration, who hope to promote coordination with other efforts and high quality, visible efforts.

Constraints

The project has a small amount of funds set aside for an internal evaluator (a part-time student). The staff prefer an internal evaluator with whom they can work closely but see the need for credibility of their self-evaluation work. The evaluation must involve participants (federal regulation) and be completed before the end of the funding period.

PRODUCT 2: *Outline of the Evaluation Questions*			
Evaluation Questions	Subquestions	Audiences	Why the Question is Important
Who attended the workshops?	What are their: number? positions? organizational affiliations? evaluation experience?	OSE (funders) University Staff Project Director	The project will change organizations only if key leaders (e.g., deans, chairs) attend
Did participants think it was worthwhile?	Was it: interesting? useful?	OSE (funders) Staff	The "word-of-mouth" network is strong among participants; and, if they don't like it, they won't learn it
Were the learning objectives met?		OSE Staff Project Director	Needed to revise subsequent workshop and to guide any follow-up

PRODUCT 2: *Outline of the Evaluation Questions (continued)*

Evaluation Questions	Subquestions	Audiences	Why the Question is Important
What problems arose?	What problems were related to: preparation? delivery?	Staff Project Director	Staff expect some rough spots; the Director will base staff training on problem areas
How costly was it?	What did it cost? Are there savings possibilities?	University Project Director OSE	The project was funded on a per-participant estimate that cannot be exceeded over the entire workshop series
What uses were made of the training?	What were the: job applications? benefits and effects?	OSE Staff Project Director	This will serve as impact data and will be used as needs data in next year's proposal
Is the workshop content sound?	How sound is it from the point of view of: evaluation methodology? instructional design?	Staff Project Director University OSE	Needed for revision. And, OSE and the University expect to see high quality efforts.
Is the workshop responsive to needs?		OSE University Staff Project Director	The entire workshop proposal is based on identified needs for evaluation improvement

---

PRODUCT 3: *Information Collection: Overall Plan (A)*

Evaluation Questions and Sub-Questions

Information Collection Procedures	1. Who attended? a. number? b. position? c. organization?	2. Did they think it was worthwhile? a. interesting? b. useful?	3. Were learning objectives met?	4. What problems arose? a. preparation? b. delivery?	5. How costly was it? a. costs? b. potential savings?	6. What uses were made? a. actual uses? b. benefits?	7. Is the content sound? a. evaluation methods b. instructional design	8. Is it responsive to needs?
A. Participants (P's) complete registration forms at beginning of workshop	X							
B. P's complete brief questionnaire at end of first day		X						
C. Sample of P's (key respondent) discuss workshop		X	X	X (b)				X

Evaluation Questions and Sub-Questions

Information Collection Procedures	1. Who attended? a. number? b. position? c. organization?	2. Did they think it was worthwhile? a. interesting? b. useful?	3. Were learning objectives met?	4. What problems arose? a. preparation? b. delivery?	5. How costly was it? a. costs? b. potential savings?	6. What uses were made? a. actual uses? b. benefits?	7. Is the content sound? a. evaluation methods b. instructional design	8. Is it responsive to needs?
at end; staff members take notes								
D. Staff keep notes on P's use of materials, questions asked, problems			X	X (b)				X
E. External reviewers rate samples of evaluation designs produced at workshop			X					
F. At post-workshop meetings, staff discuss procedures for developing and producing materials and making arrangements			X (a)	X (b)				
G. Evaluator compiles cost and registration fees					X			
H. Staff members telephone interview sample of P's after training						X		X
I. Selected evaluation and instructional design experts review workshop materials							X	X
J. Evaluation and instructional design experts observe							X	

PRODUCT 3: *Information Collection: How Each Procedure Works (B)*

Procedure	Evaluation Questions Addressed	Schedule for Collection	Respondents	Sample	Instrument(s) Used
A. Participants (P's) complete registration forms at beginning of workshop	1	Beginning of workshop at registration	Workshop participants	All	Registration Questionnaire
B. P's complete brief questionnaire at end of first day	2	End of each of three days during workshop	Workshop participants	All	Reaction Form
C. Sample of P's (key respondent) discuss workshop at end; staff members take notes	2, 3, 4b, 8	Afternoon of last day of workshop	Workshop participants	8–12 selected by staff	Staff notes and Key Respondents Guide Sheet
D. Staff keep notes on P's use of materials, questions asked, problems	3, 4b, 8	Continuous during workshop	Staff	All	Staff Daily Log
E. External reviewers rate sample of evaluation designs during workshop	3	Ratings made two weeks after workshop	Evaluation consultant	3	Reviewer Rating Form
F. At post-workshop meetings, staff discuss procedures for developing and producing materials and making arrangements	4a	Continuous during preparation and delivery of workshop	Staff	All	Staff Daily Logs and other notes
G. Evaluator compiles cost and registration fees	5	1 week after workshop	N.A.	N.A.	None
H. Staff members telephone interview sample of P's after training	6, 8	2 months after workshop	Workshop participants	Approximately 1/3 of participants stratified by type of job setting	Interview Guide
I. Selected evaluation and instructional design experts review workshop materials	7, 8	Materials sent 1 week after workshop; replies completed in 3 weeks	Expert reviews	3 of each type	Reviewer's Guide Questions
J. Evaluation and instructional design experts observe	7	During workshop	Observers	1 of each type	None (observers take own notes)

PRODUCT 4: *Analysis and Interpretation Plan*

Evaluation Questions	Collection Procedure	Analysis Procedure	Evaluation Criteria	Procedures for Making Judgments
1. Who attended the workshop? a. number? b. positions? c. organizational affiliation? d. evaluation expert?	A. Participants (P's) complete registration forms at beginning of workshop.	Analyze questionnaire items regarding the four sub-questions to determine frequencies.	Number of P's needed to cover costs; 90% of participants should match characteristics of intended participants.	Evaluator compares findings to criteria.
2. Did P's think it was worthwhile? a. interesting? b. useful?	B. P's complete brief questionnaire at end of first day. C. Sample of P's (key respondents) discuss workshop at end; staff members take notes.	Analyze relevant questionnaire items to determine ratings of workshop elements. Content analyze staff notes taken during the discussion.	Average ratings of 3-0 or less on 5-pt. scale are considered very low.	Comparison of summarized findings with those from previous workshops.
3. Were the learning objectives met?	C above D. Staff kept notes on P's use of materials, questions asked, problems. E. External reviewers rate sample of evaluation designs during workshop.	Content analyze staff notes to identify evidence that objectives used were not met. Summarize reviewers' rating sheets.	List of learning objectives ranked by importance. All major objectives should be achieved.	Evaluator compares all findings to criteria and presents own summary; reviewers' ratings also presented separately. Project Director makes final determination.
4. What problems arose? a. preparation? delivery? b. delivery?	C above for "b" D above for "b"	Content analyze notes from staff logs and discussion to identify problems, how they developed, and their effects.	Problems such as confusions about materials inadequate facility unproductive diversion from schedule.	Evaluator summarizes information; Project Director and staff review it at staff meeting. Consensus of staff sought.

PRODUCT 4: *Analysis and Interpretation Plan (continued)*

Evaluation Questions	Collection Procedure	Analysis Procedure	Evaluation Criteria	Procedures for Making Judgments
	F. At post-workshop meeting, staff discuss procedures for developing and producing materials and making arrangements. (for "a")			

5. How costly was it?
  a. cost?
  b. savings possibilities?
	G. Evaluator compiles cost and registration fees.	Compare expenditures to budget and to income from fees.	Were there unusual or unjustified expenditures?	Evaluator presents findings to Director who determines savings possibilities based upon comparisons to similar activities.

6. What uses were made of the training?
  a. job applications?
  b. benefits/effects?
	H. Staff members interview sample of P's after training.	Analyze items from interview schedule regarding uses of materials; determine types of uses and apparent effects.	Summary presented. No pre-set criteria established.	Staff discuss, reach consensus about adequacy, as compared to needs data. (Information reported to OSE for any judgments they choose to make.)

7. Is the workshop content sound?
  a. evaluation point of view?
  b. instructional design point of view?
	I. Selected evaluation and instructional design experts review workshop materials.	Compare workshop content to design criteria.
		Compare workshop operation to design criteria.
			Experts selected so that one is familiar with project and at least one is nationally recognized but with no association with project or staff members.	Evaluator summarizes comparison of its content to criteria to identify strengths and weaknesses.

	J. Evaluation and instructional design experts observe workshops and make reports to staff.			
8. Is the workshop responsive to needs?	C above D above H above	Content analysis of staff notes and reports of expert reviews.	All major needs (identified when project began).	Evaluator compares findings to Needs Report.

PRODUCT 5: *Report Plan*

Audience	Content	Format	Date/Frequency	Event
OSE	Description of Project activities and plans; answers to questions 1–3, 5–8	Written report	60 days after funding year	End-of-the-year report
University	Description of Project activities and budget; answers to questions 1, 5, 7, 8	Written report	30 days after funding year	End-of-the-year report
Staff	Evaluation design	Meetings with written summary	2 months before workshop	Staff meeting
	Review of findings and implications; answers to questions 1–4, 6	Presentation by evaluator	2 weeks after workshop	Staff meeting
	Review of findings and implications; answers to questions 7, 8	Presentation by evaluator	2½ months after workshop	Staff meeting
Project Director	Same as for staff	(see above)	(see above)	(see above)
	Progress, problems, and next steps	Informal discussion	Every 2 weeks	Meeting
	Answers to questions 1–8	Written report	2½ months after workshop	Meeting

PRODUCT 6: *Management Plan*

Evaluation Workplan	Person Responsible	Feb	Mar	Apr	May	June	July	Aug
A. Design the evaluation								
· draft the design	Evaluation	X X						
· review	Director and staff		X					
· present to staff	Evaluator		X					
· revise	Evaluator		X X					
· have reviewed by consultant	Director (and consultant)		X X					
B. Develop procedures and instruments								
· draft registration from (Proc. A), questionnaire (Proc. B), and guidelines for expert review (Procs. E and J)	Evaluator		X	X				
· review	Director and staff			X				
· revise	Evaluator			X X				
· produce	Secretary				X			
· train staff for keeping notes on workshop process (Procs. C and D)	Evaluator				X			

PRODUCT 6: *Management Plan (continued)*

Evaluation Workplan	Person Responsible	Feb	Mar	Apr	May	June	July	Aug
develop interview schedule (Proc. A)	Evaluator					X X		
C. Collect information · during workshop Procs. A, B, C, D	Staff and evaluator				X			
· following workshop Proc. E	Evaluator					X		
· send designs to reviewers								
· reviews due						X		
Proc. F · post-workshop meeting						X		
Proc. G · compile budget information						X		
Proc. H · interview a sample of P's							X	
Proc. I · send material to reviewers					X			
· reviews due						X		
D. Analyze information · to answer questions 1–5, 7, 8	Evaluator					X X		
· to answer question 6	Evaluator							X
E. Reports · prepare summaries	Evaluator					X X		
· staff meetings to report findings	Evaluator and Director					X		
meetings with Director	Evaluator and Director	X X	X X	X X	X X	X X	X X	X
· write reports for Director's use in year-end reports	Evaluator							X
· prepare meta-evaluation report	Consultant							X

Budget

Personnel

Evaluator (25% of $4,000 × ½ year)	$ 500
Consultant fees for 2 workshop observations ($100/day × 2 days × 2)	400
Consultant fees for reviews ($100 × 4)	400
subtotal	1,300

PRODUCT 6: *Management Plan (continued)*

Evaluation Workplan	Person Responsible	Feb	Mar	Apr	May	June	July	Aug
Travel and Lodgings								
To Workshop for:								165
Evaluator (carfare = $15, per diem = $50 × 3 = $150)								
Consultant (2) (carfare = 50 × 2, per diem = $60 × 3 × 2 = $360)								460
	subtotal							625
Material and Supplies								
Office supplies								50
Copying								100
Postage								20
	subtotal							170
	TOTAL							$2,095

PRODUCT 7: *Meta-Evaluation Plan*

Evaluation of Evaluation Design

Purpose: To demonstrate a credible and defensible design to funding agent, and to revise evaluation design as necessary.

Method: Send evaluation design to external consultant not affiliated with project; meet with consultant to review design.

Resources: Consultant fees, meeting time and space, checklist.

Criteria: Joint Committee *Standards*.

Evaluation of Progress

Purpose: To revise evaluation as necessary.

Method: Staff will meet with evaluator before, during and after workshop to discuss evaluation instruments and data collection.

Resources: None extra.

Criteria: Utility and accuracy of information.

Evaluation of Completed Evaluation

Purpose: To "certify" evaluation report and determine how to revise future evaluation work.

Methods: 1. Send evaluation report to external consultant who will append a Meta-evaluation Report.
2. Conduct meeting with staff and invited others to review the evaluation report, design and uses; discuss utility and worth.

Resources: Consultant fees; meeting time, promotion and space.

Criteria: Joint Committee *Standards*; utility and economy.

HOW DO YOU GO ABOUT CONSTRUCTING A DESIGN?

There are different ways of constructing an evaluation design. Some ways are better than others in particular situations, and there's probably no one way that's best in all situations. For example, sometimes it pays to act alone and unilaterally, and other times you should proceed in careful concert with others. In any case, you always need to attend to organizational conditions and needs, other people's interests and values, and the purposes that spawned the evaluation.

Designing an evaluation is rarely a linear, one-time-only process. Most often, the design grows iteratively. An architectural design grows much the same way. First, the architect produces a rough sketch (preferably on a tavern napkin). While nowhere near a detailed blueprint, the sketch proposes a complete solution to an architectural problem. It meets the client's needs, is responsive to the site and climate, and makes good use of available resources. Assuming all is "go" (and the project is not abandoned at this point), the architect will work with the client to produce several incremental versions of working drawings. These have more detail than the first napkin sketch and are still complete in that they represent the whole building. Sometimes construction begins now, depending on the skill and style of the builder. Or, one proceeds to make final blueprints which give sufficient detail to guide construction. The initial sketch foreshadowed the final blueprint, and the final blueprints, despite many incremental revisions, carry the vestiges of that first rough sketch.

There are at least four decisions that you should bear in mind as you construct your evaluation design. (Keep in mind the design products, decisions and tasks outlined in the preceding section. They are likely to be the grist of your evaluation design.)

· How much will you plan beforehand? Will you develop a detailed blueprint, or will you "play it by ear," beginning with only a rough sketch (or less) of a design?
· Who will be the evaluator? Who will be involved in the evaluation and who will have primary responsibility for its implementation? What kind of role will those evaluation persons play with staff and key decision makers?
· What will be the scope of your effort? Should you try for a small effort with modest payoff that is most likely to succeed? Or, should you bite off a bigger chunk, taking a greater risk but offering more impact?
· How will you decide when you have a good design? What are the criteria or standards by which all audiences will judge the design? To know if you've successfully arrived at a good evaluation design you must decide in advance what a "good design" looks like.

The first three issues are dealt with in this section. Selecting criteria to judge your evaluation design is a key issue and is highlighted in the section that follows.

DECIDING HOW MUCH YOU SHOULD PLAN BEFOREHAND

Sometimes the amount of evaluation planning is determined by time, expertise, Request-For-Proposal (RFP) guidelines, or the evaluation "model" you have decided to use. In most circumstances, however, you need to determine when to do the bulk of your evaluation planning. Below are some considerations. See also the fixed vs. emergent design discussion on pp. 37–38.

THREE OPTIONS (Different Planning Approaches)

Planning Approaches	Benefits & Drawbacks
Plan in great detail before you begin. Specify carefully each step in the evaluation: what questions you'll address, how, who will get what information, when, and so on. Plan to follow your plan unless you absolutely have to deviate.	*Benefits* - People know what to expect. The plan can be used like a contract, to hold people accountable. Costs and time can be predicted and planned for. *Drawbacks* - Assumes a greater degree of knowledge and control than may exist. Doesn't allow for capitalizing on opportunities. Doesn't allow response to changes. Limits the conclusions to what can be predicted and prescribed.
Wing it. Plan as you go, following the evaluation as it leads you. Begin only with a general purpose, and don't commit yourself to particular questions, methods or interim objectives.	*Benefits* - Can capitalize on opportunity and respond to changing needs and conditions. Is more compatible with how programs and general experience operate. Mimics life. *Drawbacks* - Makes people nervous, which may affect cooperation. Hard to staff and budget. Difficult to get approval from administrators and participants who want more certainty.
Take the "Middle Road" Recognize the Two Planning Errors: 1. It's a mistake not to have a plan. 2. It's a mistake to follow your plan completely Plan as specifically as you can, but recognize, admit and plan for deviations. Be ready to take advantage of changes and respond to emerging needs	*Benefits* - Reduces anxiety among parties to the evaluation because direction and general procedures are known, allows allocation of resources, yet maintains and recognizes legitimacy of deviation, spontaneity. Encourages ongoing contact with audiences. Represents a rational humane approach. *Drawbacks* - Is hardest to do well. Becomes easy to get committed to plans and blind to needs for change. Requires tolerance for ambiguity.

DESIGN ELEMENTS THAT SHOULD BE CONSIDERED BEFOREHAND AND THOSE THAT CAN BE LEFT FOR LATER

Design elements you should almost always plan beforehand are...
· purposes for evaluating
· who will be involved as evaluators, judges and decision-makers
· the kinds of conclusions the evaluation will, and will not, draw
· audiences for the evaluation or process for identifying them

DESIGN ELEMENTS THAT SHOULD BE CONSIDERED BEFOREHAND AND THOSE THAT CAN BE LEFT FOR LATER *(continued)*

· resources available for the evaluation
· legal, organizational and other guidelines that will direct or affect the evaluation
· meta-evaluation procedures and standards
· begin/end dates
· report dates and audiences

Design elements you can define now, but are often OK or preferable to leave for later...
· instrument types and content
· information collection methods
· analysis methods
· verification and aggregation and coding steps
· report content
· report methods
· interpretation methods and criteria

INVOLVING AUDIENCES IN THE EVALUATION DESIGN

There are a number of strategies available to involve key stakeholders in designing evaluation. Regardless of the tactic you choose, it should help assure that the evaluation design is *defensible, clear, internally consistent*, and *mutually agreed upon*.

STRATEGY	BENEFITS AND RISKS
1. Evaluator(s) do evaluation by themselves and informally, "in their head," rather than written or shared with others.	1. Low effort and commonly done. Risks misunderstandings and overlooking something critical.
2. Evaluators do a rough draft of each product. They check it for accuracy, etc., as they interview others. Then they write up the product and get people to sign off on it.	2. Moderate effort. Reduces risks by providing a written agreement up front. Risks overlooking something if people sign without really thinking it through.
3. Evaluators identify key persons from the evaluation audience for the project. They convene them for a planning session in which they (a) brainstorm through the process of doing a product, (b) break into subgroups to write parts of it, and (c) come back together to share, improve, and approve the resulting document.	3. Moderate to large effort. Shares risks, obtains full and early involvement of key persons. Lowers risk of overlooking something. Risks (a) not being able to get them to commit themselves that much or (b) uncovering/encountering serious conflicts early in the process. (That sometimes is a benefit rather than a risk!)
4. Evaluators do a rough draft of each product. They use drafts as input into a session similar to that described for the third tactic. Audiences edit, modify, and sign off on it in the group session.	4. Moderate to large effort. Obtains early involvement but can be perceived as manipulative, if badly handled. Reduces risks of getting embroiled in conflict.

5. Evaluators form an advisory group that represents all audiences and involve them throughout in planning and reviewing.

5. Moderate to large effort. Sustains involvement and promotes acceptance and use. Can be volatile and slow the process. Government requires use of such groups.

KEY PERSONS INVOLVED IN EVALUATION DESIGN

You must decide at the outset who will be responsible for and involved in designing the evaluation. Until primary responsibility is clear, it will be difficult to make any of the important design decisions. See pp. 176–180 in the Management section of the Sourcebook for a lengthier discussion regarding evaluator selection.

Candidates for evaluator role
· internal staff member
· key decision maker
· external consultant
· ad hoc team including line and staff
· external team

Others you might think about involving in a design effort
· clients for the evaluation
· program staff
· program clients
· funding agents
· oversight boards
· consulting experts
· advocacy groups and special interest parties
· parents, community members
· legal experts, attorneys
· union representatives

Ways of involving others
· form advisory groups
· conduct open reviews and panels
· hire them (as consultants)
· interviews and visits
· sign-off lists
· public meetings
· joint working sessions
· task forces, teams

TRAINING AUDIENCES THROUGH THE EVALUATION DESIGN PROCESS

There are a number of *reasons* you may need or wish to train others as a part of their involvement in an evaluation design.

So they can *perform evaluation tasks* adequately. Tasks often requiring training are: generating key evaluation questions, information collection procedures, coding and verification, analysis, and interpretation.

So they can better use *evaluation results*. Such training might be in evaluation approaches and uses, limitations, decision making, problem-solving, ranking and valuing, etc.

So they will *support* evaluation efforts. Topics here might include: general evaluation uses and methods and limitations, or how a particular effort is designed or will proceed.

So they can *do their own* evaluation when you are through. This training might include any of the topics listed above.

DETERMINE THE SCOPE OF THE EVALUATION EFFORT

Decide whether you will start "Big" or "Small." This decision will be affected by a number of variables including resources, time, evaluation expertise, and magnitude of the problem for which the evaluation is to be

DETERMINE THE SCOPE OF THE EVALUATION EFFORT *(continued)*

used. Generally speaking, you are better off beginning modestly (especially if you are relatively inexperienced at formal evaluation) and growing carefully and incrementally. However some evaluations by virtue of what they are evaluating must be grand in scope.

Expenditure Possible	Low		High
Resources available, e.g., money, person hours, equipment, time	Evaluation will be bootlegged; no extra funds available	Budget can support some evaluation activities (person hours, Xeroxing, instrument development)	Substantial and separate support exists for the purpose of evaluation
Expertise Available	Minimal		Maximum
Skills needed, e.g., technical, conceptual, managerial, experiential	Evaluation must be done completely by existing staff who lack evaluation experience	Most of the evaluation will be done by staff; funds exist for training or an outside consultant	Funds and time exist to recruit and hire an experienced evaluator
Impact Anticipated	Small		Large
Magnitude of the impact, e.g., persons affected, dollars/ resource allocation, expected system changes	Evaluation is done primarily to meet a mandate; unlikely that it will have any real impact	At least some of the program components are likely to be affected by the evaluation	The expectation is that the program will be drastically changed or aborted based upon evaluation results

HOW DO YOU RECOGNIZE A GOOD DESIGN?

Keep in mind that there are always a number of alternative designs that are appropriate for an evaluation problem. There isn't a single "right" design, nor is there an infallible design. In order to choose one design over another or to determine when an evolving design has reached maturity, you need to have decided what criteria your design should meet.

This section contains some alternative sets of criteria and standards for judging an evaluation design. Regardless of which set of evaluation criteria is adopted, adapted, or created, there will be tradeoffs when attempting to apply it. Because this is so, it pays to construct an evaluation design a number of different ways—varying design procedures to meet a maximum number of important design criteria.

A useful evaluation design targets on program problems or areas of concern for stakeholders. The design responds to where the program is at the time as well as where it wants to be. To do this, program needs identified by the evaluator as well as important audiences have had to be identified and ranked. The issues uncovered launch a number of evaluation questions that become the starting point for information collection.

After evaluators and stakeholders think through the information needed to address evaluation questions, they must respond to some practical and technical concerns. For instance, what problems might there be in getting information; how accurate will the information likely be; how tough will it be to analyze; how will it be used? Again, it is beneficial to draft several strategies for gathering information, varying the sources, procedures, and analysis. It is preferable to start modestly and grow only in relationship to expanding purposes or questions.

The best evaluation designs are practical; that is, they can be done within the constraints of the environment and your resources. And the most useful evaluations attend to people and how they might be affected by the evaluation. These qualities are more important than which format or method your evaluation design ultimately embraces. Your design, for instance, might take the form of a letter, a grid, a systems chart, or a story. It might include a case study, a series of observations, or a pre/post test. Whatever the format or method, it should consider the issues described in this section.

THE DESIGN CONSIDERS PRACTICALITY ISSUES

The most useful design might not turn out to be practical, or even possible. Look down the following list of issues and consider how they are being dealt with in your design.

Cost$$ **cost has been anticipated**
- dollars, person hours and possible disaffection
- projected benefits (number, type)

**THE DESIGN
CONSIDERS
PRACTICALITY
ISSUES** *(continued)*

· cost of evaluation
· usefulness of evaluation
· audience reaction to cost
· time to complete the evaluation

Politics

you have thought about persons with special interests
· who will be interested in the findings, potential gains or conflicts for particular audiences
· control of final report and its release
· how bias will be limited in report (minority opinions sought)
· what kind of protocol must be anticipated (who must you see first, who must be involved, who is being excluded)
· who will use the information and under what circumstances might they *not* use it
· what groups can stop or change evaluation procedures with their disapproval (unions, professional organizations, clients, administrators)
· whether the contract has established timeline budget, renegotiation strategies and clear responsibility and authority for evaluation tasks

Procedures

the procedures are practical given the purpose
· the criticality of information need has been considered (you're not spending lots of dollars to get more of the same information)
· procedures are commensurate with purpose (finding out how good a 5-hour inservice is does not demand more time than the inservice)
· if the purpose changes, the procedure can change (you've anticipated the unexpected)
· procedures have been okayed by key stakeholders (e.g., teachers know they will hand out tests)

THE DESIGN ANTICIPATES THE QUALITY AND WORTH OF EXPECTED INFORMATION

There is no such thing as a flawless design. Further, there is no such thing as indisputable information. Begin with the assumption that regardless of what the information you turn over looks like, there will be varied interpretations.

Some logical questions to ask yourself:

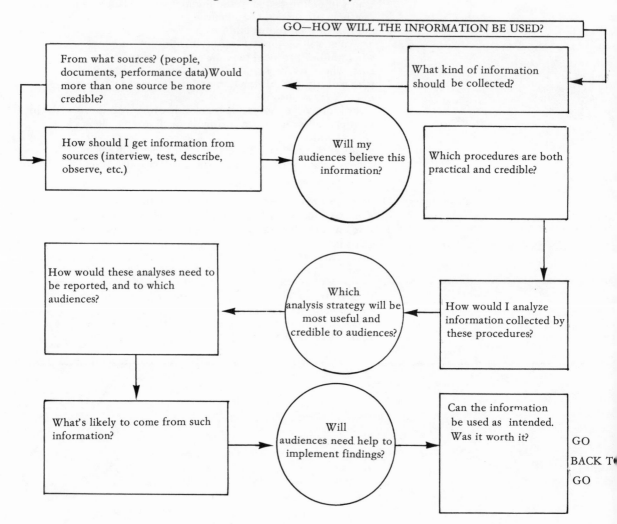

THE DESIGN IS SENSITIVE TO PEOPLE

Evaluations have sometimes been good for organizations and bad for the people in them. This "castor-oil" approach to evaluation has done a good deal of harm. The field of evaluation and professional evaluators do not promote hurtful evaluation; to the contrary, the best evaluations are more useful than harmful to people. Professional evaluation standards highlight

**THE DESIGN IS
SENSITIVE TO
PEOPLE** *(continued)*
the importance of human interactions and ethical considerations. So, being professional in evaluation is being considerate to those affected.

EVALUATION FUNCTION	PITFALLS AFFECTING PEOPLE
Focusing the Evaluation	people affected by evaluation aren't contacted, interviewed, or otherwise considered *result*: key questions not answered results not accepted
Information Collection	procedures involving target audience violate rights of human subjects (self-esteem, civil rights, due process, anonymity, informed consent) *result*: civil suit procedures cost valuable time of personnel and they reap no benefits *result*: disaffection and lack of cooperation procedures are obtrusive and cause people to change their behavior *result*: unrealistic data disruption of the setting
Information Analysis	analysis embarrasses individuals (individual results reported) analysis is too technical for audiences expected to use it analysis doesn't address critical questions of key audiences *result*: information is not valued or used
Reporting	audiences who helped get information aren't given a report audiences aren't given a chance to react to the report before and after its release (consider appending a minority report) the report's release affects people's jobs or plans some people's views are excluded in the report the report embarrasses individuals or units *result*: information is not likely to be used by affected groups
Managing Evaluation	people aren't considered when scheduling evaluation tasks (teachers' units are interrupted, the secretaries are asked to do work) an ill-planned budget forces personnel to work too hard for scant payoffs the person(s) evaluating misuse information being gathered (this includes storing it inappropriately, leaking confidences, or walking around with a smug I-know-something-you-don't expression on their face) *result*: everyone gets really aggravated

THE DESIGN MEETS PRESPECIFIED CRITERIA

An evaluation design is judged from a number of different perspectives; for example, from the perspective of key decision makers, evaluators, program staff, funding agents, and outside observers interested in the evaluation, the program, or both. An evaluation design may not be judged "good" by all of its audiences. This is because as the design is strengthened in one area (e.g., technical adequacy) to meet the needs of some audiences, it makes necessary tradeoffs in other areas (e.g., cost or timeliness) that affect other audiences.

While few designs meet with everyone's approval, it is easier to construct a sound design with the use of criteria that define good evaluation designs. Below are examples of criteria for evaluation designs.

THE JOINT COMMITTEE STANDARDS

Standards for Evaluating Educational Programs, Projects & Materials suggests the following standards as most relevant to designing evaluation (See the section on Meta-Evaluation for more information about the Standards):

· Audience Identification
· Information Scope and Selection
· Valuational Interpretation
· Practical Procedures
· Formal Obligation
· Balanced Reporting
· Object Identification
· Described Purposes and Procedures
· Described Information Sources
· Valid Measurement
· Reliable Measurement
· Analysis of Quantitative Information
· Analysis of Qualitative Information
· Justified Conclusions
· Objective Reporting

SANDERS & NAFZIGER CRITERIA

The following list of criteria is from Sanders & Nafziger, "A Basis for Determining the Adequacy of Evaluation Designs."

I.   Regarding the Adequacy of the Evaluation Conceptualization
    A. *Scope*: Does the range of information to be provided include all the significant aspects of the program or product being evaluated?
        1. Is a description of the program or product presented (e.g., philosophy, content, objectives, procedures, setting)?
        2. Are the intended outcomes of the program or product specified, and does the evaluation address them?
        3. Are any likely unintended effects from the program or product considered?
        4. Is cost information about the program or product included?
    B. *Relevance*: Does the information to be provided adequately serve the evaluation needs of the intended audiences?
        1. Are the audiences for the evaluation identified?

2. Are the objectives of the evaluation explained?
3. Are the objectives of the evaluation congruent with the information needs of the intended audiences?
4. Does the information to be provided allow necessary decisions about the program or product to be made?

C. *Flexibility*: Does the evaluation study allow for new information needs to be met as they arise?
1. Can the design be adapted easily to accommodate new needs?
2. Are known constraints on the evaluation discussed?
3. Can useful information be obtained in the face of unforeseen constraints, e.g., noncooperation of control groups?

D. *Feasibility*: Can the evaluation be carried out as planned?
1. Are the evaluation resources (time, money, and manpower) adequate to carry out the projected activities?
2. Are management plans specified for conducting evaluation?
3. Has adequate planning been done to support the feasibility of particularly difficult activities?

II. Criteria Concerning the Adequacy of the Collection and Processing of Information

A. *Reliability*: Is the information to be collected in a manner such that findings are replicable?
1. Are data collection procedures described well enough to be followed by others?
2. Are scoring or coding procedures objective?
3. Are the evaluation instruments reliable?

B. *Objectivity*: Have attempts been made to control for bias in data collection and processing?
1. Are sources of information clearly specified?
2. Are possible biases on the part of data collectors adequately controlled?

C. *Representativeness*: Do the information collection and processing procedures ensure that the results accurately portray the program or product?
1. Are the data collection instruments valid?
2. Are the data collection instruments appropriate for the purposes of this evaluation?
3. Does the evaluation design adequately address the questions it was intended to answer?

III. Criteria Concerning the Adequacy of the Presentation and Reporting of Information

A. *Timeliness*: Is the information provided timely enough to be of use to the audiences for the evaluation?
1. Does the time schedule for reporting meet the needs of the audiences?
2. Is the reporting schedule shown to be appropriate for the schedule of decisions?

B. *Pervasiveness*: Is information to be provided to all who need it?
1. Is information to be disseminated to all intended audiences?
2. Are attempts being made to make the evaluation information available to relevant audiences beyond those directly affected by the evaluation?

IV. General Criteria

A. *Ethical Considerations*. Does the intended evaluation study strictly follow accepted ethical standards?
1. Do test administration procedures follow professional standards of ethics?
2. Have protection of human subjects guidelines been followed?
3. Has confidentiality of data been guaranteed?

**SANDERS &
NAFZIGER
CRITERIA**
(continued)

B. *Protocol*: Are appropriate protocol steps planned?
   1. Are appropriate persons contacted in the appropriate sequence?
   2. Are department policies and procedures to be followed?

**OFFICE OF SPECIAL
EDUCATION**

The Office of Special Education and Rehabilitation Services, Handicapped Personnel Preparation Program (OSE) suggests the following guidelines for rating the adequacy of program evaluation designs. (U.S. Department of Education, 1981)

EVALUATION: Does the proposal describe an evaluation design which specifies:

a. An appropriate evaluation methodology used to judge the success of each project subcomponent?
b. The kinds of data to be collected for each subcomponent?
c. The criteria to be used to evaluate the result of the project?
d. Procedure for assessing the attainment of competence within the project?
e. A method to assess the contribution of project graduates
   1. toward meeting the needs of children INCLUDING the number of graduates prepared and placed by role;
   2. graduates' length of services; and
   3. graduates' proficiency as judged by employers?
f. A method for assessing the effectiveness and efficiency of project resource usage?
g. A method for assessing the impact of this project on related projects within the institution and the community?
h. At least annual evaluation of progress in achieving objectives?
i. At least annual evaluation of the effectiveness of the project in meeting the purposes of the program?
j. At least annual evaluation of the effect of the project on persons being served by the project, including any persons who are members of groups that have been traditionally underrepresented such as members of racial or ethnic minority groups and handicapped persons, etc.? (p. 35)

**RANK ORDER
DESIGN CRITERIA**

In order to judge an evaluation design: 1) criteria should have been identified (or negotiated) so it is clear how the design is to be judged; 2) stakeholders or independent consultants who will be assessing the design should be identified; and 3) ongoing priorities should be set should tradeoffs in criteria prove necessary down the road.

The Joint Committee *Standards* order the relevant standards for designing evaluation according to these major qualities:

1. usefulness
2. feasibility
3. propriety
4. accuracy

**RANK ORDER
DESIGN CRITERIA**
(continued)

This is one general breakdown of priorities. Each evaluation design should be guided by a set of priorities—they might be usefulness, timeliness, cost, minimal disaffection, maximum information in a prespecified area, technical quality, etc. Remember that it's not enough to have criteria to evaluate the design—you must think about which criteria are the most important in order to make necessary tradeoffs.

REFERENCES

Brethower, K.S. & Rummler, G.A. Evaluating training. *Improving Human Performance Quarterly*, 1977, *5*, 107–120. (IEM)

Brinkerhoff, R.O. Evaluation of inservice programs. *Teacher Education and Special Education*. Vol. III, No. 3, Summer, 1980, pp. 27–38.

Campbell, D.T. & Stanley, J.C. Experimental and quasi-experimental designs for research on teaching. In N.L. Gage (Ed.), *Handbook of research on teaching*. Chicago: Rand McNally, 1963. (Also published as *Experimental and quasi-experimental designs for research*. Chicago: Rand McNally, 1966.)

Carroll, S.J., Jr., & Tosi, H.L., Jr. *Management by objectives: Applications and research*. New York: Macmillan, 1973.

Cook, T.D. & Campbell, D.T. *Quasi-experimentation: Design and analysis issues for field settings*. Chicago: Rand McNally, 1979.

Drucker, P. *The practice of management*. New York: Harper & Bros., 1954. (original MBO piece)

Eisner, E.W. *The perceptive eye: Toward the reform of education evaluation*. Invited Address, Curriculum and Objectives, American Educational Research Association, Washington, D.C. March 31, 1975. (Connoisseurship)

Federal Electric Corporation. *A programmed introduction to PERT*. New York: John Wiley & Sons, 1963.

Guba, E.G. & Lincoln, Y.S. *Effective evaluation: Improving the usefulness of evaluation results through responsive and naturalistic approaches*. San Francisco: Jossey-Bass, 1981.

Hall, G.E. Facilitating institutional change using the individual as the frame of reference. In J.K. Grosenick & M.C. Reynolds (Eds.), *Teacher education: Renegotiating roles for mainstreaming*. Minneapolis: National Support Systems Project, University of Minnesota, Council for Exceptional Children, & Teacher Education Division of CEC, 1978. (CBAM)

Joint Committee on Standards for Educational Evaluation. *Standards for evaluating of educational programs, projects, & materials*. New York: McGraw-Hill, 1981.

Kiresuk, T.J. & Lund, S.H. Goal attainment scaling. In C.C. Attkisson, W.A. Hargreaves, & M.J. Horowitz (Eds.), *Evaluation of human service programs*. New York: Academic Press, 1978.

Levin, H.M. Cost-effectiveness analysis in evaluation research. In M. Guttentag & E.L. Struening (Eds.), *Handbook of evaluation research* (Vol. 2). Beverly Hills: Sage, 1975.

Mager, R.F. *Preparing instructional objectives* (2nd ed.). Belmont, CA: Fearson, 1975.

Patton, M.Q. *Qualitative evaluation methods*. Beverly Hills: Sage, 1980.

Provus, M.M. *Discrepancy evaluation*. Berkeley, CA: McCutchan, 1971.

Provus, Malcolm. Evaluation of ongoing programs in the public schools systems, in *Educational evaluation: Theory into practice*. Edited by Blaine R. Worthen and James R. Sanders. Worthington, Ohio: Charles A. Jones Publishing Co., 1973.

Sanders, James R. & Nafziger, Dean H. A basis for determining the adequacy of evaluation designs, *Occasional Paper Series*, No. 6, Evaluation Center, College of Education, Western Michigan University, Kalamazoo, Michigan 49008, April, 1976.

Scriven, M.S. Pros and cons about goal-free evaluation. *Evaluation Comment*, 1972, *3*.

Scriven, M.S. Goal-free evaluation. In E.R. House (Ed.), *School evaluation: The politics and process*. Berkeley, CA: McCutchen, 1973.

Shumsky, A. *The action research way of learning: An approach to inservice education*. New York: Bureau of Publications, Teachers College, Columbia University, 1958.

Stake, Robert E. The countenance of Educational Evaluation, in *Educational evaluation: Theory into practice*. Edited by Blaine R. Worthen and James R. Sanders. Worthington, Ohio: Charles A. Jones Publishing Co., 1973.

Stake, Robert E. Program evaluation, particularly responsive evaluation. *Occasional Paper Series*, No. 5, Evaluation Center, College of Education, Western Michigan University, Kalamazoo, Michigan 49008, November, 1975.

Stufflebeam, Daniel L. An introduction to the PDK book: Educational evaluation and decision-making, in *Educational evaluation: Theory into practice*. Edited by Blaine R. Worthen and James R. Sanders. Worthington, Ohio: Charles A. Jones Publishing Co., 1973.

Tallmadge, G.K. *Joint Dissemination and Review Panel Ideabook*. Washington, D.C.: U.S. Government Printing Office, 1977.

Thompson, E.K. (Ed.). *Using Student Change Data to Evaluate Inservice Education*. Bloomington, ILL: School of Education, Indiana University, 1981. (NIN "Steps")

Tyler, R.W. Some persistent questions on the defining of objectives. In C.M. Lindvall (Ed.), *Defining Educational Objectives*. Pittsburgh: University of Pittsburgh Press, 1964.

Wolf, Robert L. Trial by jury: A new evaluation method. *Phi Delta Kappan*, 1975, November.

Wolfensberger, W., & Glenn, L. *Program Analysis of Service Systems: A Method for the Quantitative Evaluation of human services*. (3rd Ed.) Vol. I: *Handbook*. Vol. II: *Field manual*. Toronto: National Institute on Mental Retardation, 1975.

Collecting Information

WHAT IT IS

This function involves gathering information to address the evaluation questions. Information sources can include people, documents, performance data, and observations of events. There are a number of methods to gather information including traditional measurement approaches such as tests, ratings, and frequencies, as well as investigative procedures like natural observation, ethnographic description, interviews, case studies, and literature review.

The most important issue related to information collection is *selecting* the most appropriate information or evidence to answer your questions. The information gathered must be relevant to the questions, and there must be enough information to provide convincing answers. Gathering too much information taxes the system and makes the evaluation costly and impractical. The aim is to collect enough information of the right kind at the lowest cost.

To plan information collection, evaluators must think about the questions to be answered and the information sources available. Moreover, they must think ahead to how that information could be analyzed, interpreted, and reported to audiences so it is credible and useful. Sound information collection entails looking ahead through the entire evaluation process to forecast what is likely to happen to the information collected (see Evaluation Questions, pp. 27–32). It also demands practical considerations about how information will be gathered (by whom, when) and how it will be monitored for continuing accuracy.

WHEN DECISIONS GET MADE

Plans for collecting information are usually made after evaluation questions have been posed. (Be wary when decisions about the appropriate information sources or methods precede decisions about what questions are important). After the evaluation is focused and the major questions drafted, a decision usually is made about the general type of information to collect. In most evaluations, information collection is cyclical. That is, some questions are posed which spur information collection. The information then triggers further questions which in turn demand more information collection. This process continues, growing incrementally more specific until sufficient certainty is reached.

WHAT KIND OF INFORMATION SHOULD BE COLLECTED?

The information you collect is the evidence you will have available to answer the evaluation questions. Poor evidence is information which cannot be trusted, is scant, or simply is not relevant to the questions asked. Good evidence, on the other hand, is information that comes from reliable sources by trustworthy methods to address important questions.

The task of selecting the appropriate information sources and methods is initially governed by practical concerns. That is, what's already available, how much money can you spend, what procedures are feasible? The information you finally decide to collect should be determined by what's possible and what best answers important questions. There will be tradeoffs, as you will see in the following sections.

SOME KINDS OF INFORMATION TYPICALLY COLLECTED IN TRAINING PROGRAMS

EVALUATIVE PURPOSES

	To Decide on Goals	To Determine Strategies	To Determine Implementation: is it working?	Recycling: should it be continued?
Descriptive Information	characteristics of job descriptions, proposals, plans, reports current skill, knowledge levels, amount of training rates of use, production, incidences policies, rules patronage patterns kinds of clients served demographic data	characteristics of plans, proposals, user's guides, training manuals data about current services reports from commissions, task groups records of resources available, programs in use people's schedules, positions, jobs, rates demographic data research studies	records of use, attendance records of materials consumed, used, purchased, etc. transactions, behavior reactions nature and frequency of materials produced test scores performance levels pre/post changes	records of use, access rates, consumption effects on pupils, clients costs test scores of pupils, clients patterns of use, nature of use transactions follow-up activities, continued access and involvement case information

SOME KINDS OF
INFORMATION
TYPICALLY
COLLECTED IN
TRAINING
PROGRAMS
(continued)

EVALUATIVE PURPOSES *(continued)*

	To Decide on Goals	To Determine Strategies	To Determine Implementation: is it working?	Recycling: should it be continued?
Judgmental Information	expert opinions consumer preferences, wants beliefs, values criteria, laws, guidelines perceived priorities normative data	expert opinions user/trainee preferences, conve-nience, needs results of feasibility studies, pilot tests, research recommenda-tions from task groups, leaders	opinions of trainees and trainers comparison of test scores to objectives, expectations. qualities of products produced in training expert opinions	opinions of graduates, users opinions of consumers, clients, pupils expert opinions quality of work samples benefits compared to costs

MAJOR SOURCES
OF EVALUATION
INFORMATION

People

how you might
get information
from them

whom you might seek as an information source

conversation
  (face to face
  or telephone)
structured
  interviews
questionnaires
group
  consensus
  strategies,
  e.g., Delphi
  or Nominal
  Group
  Technique

those who originated the idea of the program, project or
  activity
legislators, federal or state agency staff, university
  administrators, department chairpeople committee
those who planned the actual "evaluation object": project
  directors or team, ad hoc committee, instructors
the staff
those who will be held accountable for outcomes: deans,
  chairpeople, instructors, principals, superindendents, etc.
those who will need to make decisions: administrators,
  instructors, students, others
those whose needs are intended to be directly and
  immediately served: students, pupils, teachers, etc.
those who are to benefit intentionally, but not immediately:
  special education pupils, parents, school administrators,
  other teachers
those who may be affected incidentally, positively, or
  negatively: other faculty, non-included students, the public
those whose knowledge or expertise, independent of the
  specific object being evaluated, may provide information or
  insight in addressing the evaluation questions: former
  teachers
trainees, other staff, experts

Performance Data

how to get information about performance	types to consider
"eyeballing" data	test scores
statistical analysis (e.g., inferential, descriptive)	observations of performance
	achievement records
observation	simulations
rating (e.g., using multiple perspectives)	practice teaching
	classroom behavior
interview	social interaction
survey	job success
study of trends	problem solving skills
content analysis	written/oral reports
	work-samples

Documents

how to get information using documents	types to consider
counting numbers of documents (e.g., letters to target audiences)	proposals
	requests for proposals
sorting into types (e.g., materials related to specific objectives)	reports
	schedules
content analysis	minutes
assessing quality of material	memos
considering trends (e.g., watching for general changes in communication patterns)	letters
	course outlines
	work samples (e.g., curricular materials)
gathering factual data (e.g., reading to find out dates, numbers, outcomes, etc.)	student records
	fiscal records
analysis using checklists	expenditure records

Context

how to get information from the context	things to consider
observe	facilities
interview stakeholders	schedules
read reports	organizational patterns
	management styles
	political forces
	economic realities
	attitudes of personnel
	protocols followed
	informal/formal power structures
	distribution of responsibility

SELECTING INFORMATION SOURCES

Once you know what information is available, there are some procedures that help you arrive at the information you should collect. In general, the more of these procedures you have the time and resources to complete, the more sure you'll be of collecting sound and useful information.

1. study what you are evaluating, its context, and related literature to determine what variables appear to be linked to effectiveness (see the previous chapter to review dimensions of an object and setting)
2. interview key stakeholders to determine what questions and variables they think are important
3. rank order the evaluation questions, and search for the variables that most likely would provide evidence to answer the questions
4. determine which sources would give you convincing information about a variable's effect on the program or whatever you are evaluating
5. list and review existing information sources (e.g., past reports, review documents used in program, find out what data is available)
6. select information sources based upon a predetermined set of criteria (see next section) and have this selection reviewed by key stakeholders

---

WHEN EVALUATION QUESTION ASKS ABOUT...

Some Potential Indicators Are . . .

Needs and Goals	characteristics of job descriptions, proposals, plans, reports policies, rules demographic data beliefs, values normative data	current skill, knowledge levels, amount of training patronage patterns expert opinions criteria, laws, guidelines nature and frequency of problems	rates of use, production, incidences kinds of clients served consumer preferences, wants perceived priorities
Training Strategies and Designs	characteristics of plans, proposals, user's guides, instructor's manuals records of resources available, programs in use training literature	data about current services people's schedules, positions, jobs, rates expert opinions results of feasibility studies, pilot tests, research	reports from commissions, task groups demographic data user/trainee preferences, convenience, needs recommendations from task groups, leaders
Implementation of Training	attendance rates and patterns usage of materials, resources perceptions of observers	trainer behavior perceptions of trainees transactions (verbal, other) wear and tear on materials	trainee behaviors perceptions of trainers discard rates and nature

WHEN EVALUATION QUESTION ASKS ABOUT... (continued)			
Immediate Outcomes	materials produced in training trainer ratings observer ratings	knowledge (i.e., test scores) trainee ratings self-report ratings	performance in simulated tasks pre/post changes in test scores
On-Job Usage of Training Outcomes	nature and frequency of usage peer opinions records of use, behavior	trainee perceptions observed behavior performance ratings	supervisor opinions quality of work samples test scores transactions of trainees with others
Impacts (Worth) of Training	changes in policies, rules, organization perceptions of clients patterns of use rates cost/benefit analyses	performance ratings performance of clients (e.g., test scores) opinions of experts, visitors, observers	promotion records perceptions of clients, peers, relatives consumer opinions quality of work samples treatment, sales records

---

DETERMINE IN ADVANCE THE CRITERIA INFORMATION SHOULD MEET

There are a number of considerations when selecting information; and, often, accommodating one consideration such as "cost effectiveness" forces you to trade off another such as "technical accuracy." It's up to evaluators and their audiences to prioritize criteria *their* information must meet. To help make those decisions, some criteria for evaluation information are listed below along with descriptions of information that meets such criteria, rationale for why criteria are significant, and some tips on what might be done to meet the criteria.

Criterion	Information that meets criterion	Significance of meeting criterion	Procedures for meeting criterion
Credibility	Information that is believable to audiences because it is accurate (see below), was produced by competent, trustworthy persons and interpreted in light of defensible criteria	Only information that can be trusted by audiences will be used	Selecting a competent evaluator who is considered skilled by important audiences. Interpreting the information from several value bases, or including minority reports
Practicality	Information produced by reasonable efforts that are not too costly or disruptive	Complex information sources and analyses can be costly and have little practical significance	Prioritize audience questions, adhere to fiscal and practical constraints

Criterion	Information that meets criterion	Significance of meeting criterion	Procedures for meeting criterion
Timeliness	Information produced in time to meet audience needs	Late information is useless to key stakeholders	Plan backwards; target the completion date and then determine lead time necessary to produce
Accuracy	Information that is relevant and trustworthy, and not flawed with errors due to collecting methods, processing or analysis	Inaccurate or flawed information not only misinforms but can mislead audiences	Monitor information, specify how and why it will be analyzed, bring in outside consultants to reanalyze complex or large data bases
Ease of analysis	Information that personnel have the capability (competence and support system) to analyze	You have to be equipped to analyze the information you collect	Anticipate the type of information and analysis you'll have; make sure you have access to someone who has experience in dealing with such analyses
Objectivity	Open and direct information which has not been unduly distorted by the personal or professional invest-ments of evaluators or certain audiences	Information biased by a particular perspective is dismissed; even objective sections of reports perceived to be nonindependent are ignored	Multiple perspectives; multiple value bases reported; meta evaluations at certain stages; independent observers; reviews of reports; appended minority reports
Clarity	Unambiguous and understandable information	Highly technical reports, or sloppy reports, cannot be read or understood by audiences who need to use them	Give drafts to non-technical readers for review; keep rewriting for clarity; use summary sheets and graphs
Scope	Information that is broad enough to provide a credible answer to a question, but not so broad as to be diffuse or unmanageable	Excess information is costly and cumbersome; scant information leaves too many questions unanswered	Balance comprehensive information against information overload by rank ordering questions, feeding back information to see when you have

Criterion	Information that meets criterion	Significance of meeting criterion	Procedures for meeting criterion
			enough, producing quality not quantity
Availability	Existing data or data that are cheap and easy to get, e.g., records, reports, files, test scores, survey results, demographic data	Available data are usually free, and less likely to be contaminated or biased by being collected for the evaluation purpose	Check existing information files and reports for several "generations" back; check data bases across horizontal and vertical layers of the organization (e.g., other departments and higher adminis-trative levels)
Usefulness	Information which is timely and relevant to important audience questions	Evaluation information that cannot be used, or is not ready in time to be used, is not worth collecting	Make sure key stakeholders have been identified and their questions listed. Return to them for reactions to the information you plan to collect. Seek commitments from stakeholders to use information
Balance	Information that does not inordinately represent one point of view, value, perspective, etc. (e.g., collecting only *strengths* of a workshop)	Audiences realize that all aspects of the program were studied; program strengths aren't sabotaged when planning to meet identified needs	Make sure both advocates and critics are approached; use multiple and objective observers when possible
Cost effectiveness	Information that is worth the resources (dollars, people, time) spent to get it	Even useful information can cost too much to be fiscally or ethically defensible	Draft costs in terms of people, dollars, time. Forecast "costs" for prioritized evaluation questions and have these costs reviewed by important stakeholders

WHAT PROCEDURES SHOULD BE USED TO COLLECT INFORMATION?

Most often a number of procedures are useful for collecting information to answer a question. For instance, information to answer "How are students achieving?" might be collected by tests, observations of students, interviews with supervisors, or analyses of written assignments. There are multiple ways to collect information for most any question. And usually, the more measures you use, the more sure you can be of your results. This is especially true when whatever you are measuring (e.g., program, inservices, or trainees) is complex and made up of a number of variables, as one measure rarely captures the richness and variety of such evaluation "objects."

Selection of procedures is dependent upon resources. Information collection procedures must be practical; should you choose to use multiple procedures to collect information, considering time, cost, and interruptions to staff becomes even more important. Collection procedures, like information sources, must be selected with analysis and reporting in mind. That is, "Will this procedure produce information in a form that we have the capability to analyze and in a form our audiences will find credible?"

SOME QUANTITATIVE COLLECTION PROCEDURES AND INSTRUMENTS

Using these procedures results in numerical data. We call such data "convergent" in that phenomena (opinions, performance, behaviors) are "reduced" and put into categories that can be assigned a number. Then, these numbers can be summarized and otherwise manipulated.

Quantitative data collection procedures -

Procedure	What it Measures or Records	Example
Behavior Observation Checklist	Particular physical and verbal behaviors and actions	Record how frequently teachers use a new questioning technique
Interaction Analysis	Verbal behaviors and interactions	Observers code faculty classroom interactions.
Inventory Checklist	Tangible objects are checked or counted	School bulletin boards are checked for inservice related materials
Judgmental Ratings	Respondent's ratings of quality, effort, etc.	Experts rate the adequacy of the college's curriculum
Knowledge Tests	Knowledge and cognitive skills	Faculty are tested on knowledge of special education laws.

Opinion Survey	Opinions and attitudes	Superintendents are asked to rate their attitudes toward PL 94-142
Performance Tests and Analysis	Job-related and specific task behaviors	Principals are observed and rated on how they conduct an interview
Q-Sorts, Delphi	Perceived priorities	Parents prioritize teacher inservice needs
Self-Ratings	Respondents rate their own knowledge or abilities	Students rate how well they can administer different diagnostic devices
Survey Questionnaire	Demographic characteristics, self-reported variables	Teachers report how frequently they use certain resource center materials
Time Series Analysis	Data on selected variables are compared at several time points	Frequencies of key practicum behaviors of students are charted over the course of a new semester-long seminar

SOME QUALITATIVE COLLECTION PROCEDURES

These procedures produce narrative information. (While narrative information can be converted into numerical categories, that would usually serve an antiethical purpose.) Qualitative procedures tend to capture broader and more open-ended perspectives about complex phenomena. These data are often harder to analyze and summarize.

Procedure	What it Measures, Records	Example
Wear and Tear Analysis	Apparent wear or accumulation on physical objects	Learning center materials are inventoried before and after a workshop to determine usage or removal.
Physical Evidence Analysis	Residues or other physical by-products are observed	Waste-basket contents are inventoried after workshop to see what material was thrown away
Case Studies	The experiences and characteristics of selected persons in a project	A few graduates from each degree program are visited at their jobs, and interviews conducted with their colleagues

SOME QUALITATIVE COLLECTION PROCEDURES (continued)	Procedure	What it Measures, Records	Example
	Interviews, Group or Individual	Person's responses and views.	Department chair interviews students about course adequacy
	Panels, Hearings	Opinions, ideas	A panel of teachers reviews the needs assessing survey data to give interpretations
	Records Analysis	Records, files, receipts	Resource Center receipts are analyzed to detect trends before and after inservice
	Logs	Own behavior and reactions are recorded narratively	Practicum students maintain a log of activities
	Simulations, "In Baskets"	Persons' behaviors in simulated settings	Students are video-taped introducing a simulated inservice session
	Sociograms	Preferences for friends, work and social relationships	An IEP committee pictures their interdependence for conducting meetings
	Systems Analysis	Components and subcomponents and their functional interdependencies are defined	An evaluator interviews staff about program, depicts these perceptions in a systems analysis scheme
	Advisory, Advocate Teams	The ideas and viewpoints of selected persons	Teams are convened to judge the merit of two competing inservice plans
	Judicial Review	Evidence about activities is weighed and assessed	A "jury" reviews the data collected on a new practicum to decide if it should be repeated

SOME CONCERNS TO BEAR IN MIND WHEN DESIGNING INFORMATION COLLECTION PROCEDURES	Concern	For Instance . . .
	Availability	Make a list of data already available (records, reports, etc.) and see if you can use it to address evaluation questions. For example, a pre/post look at performance appraisal reports on trainees could indicate whether training is making an on-the-job difference.
	Need for Training Information Collectors	Trained information collectors usually collect better (more reliable) information. Interviewers, product raters, observers, etc. will do a better job if they know what to look for and how to tell if it's there.
	Pilot Testing	This is a fancy term for trying something out before you use it. Interviewers might try out a telephone interview with a few role-played participants to see whether and how well the interviewee notices and describes different training outcomes. Or, test a questionnaire on two groups of role-played trainees—one who loved the session, and another who hated it. The questionnaire group scores should be different.
	Interruption Potential	The more a procedure disrupts the daily flow of training life, the more likely it is to be unreliable—or even sabotaged. Try to be unobtrusive: An analysis of trash can contents can tell you something about whether trainees valued your materials—and is less disruptive than a questionnaire asking them to tell you if they valued them.
	Protocol Needs	Sometimes you can't collect (or shouldn't collect) information without first getting necessary permissions and clearances. Following traditional protocol is always a good idea: A letter from the employee's boss telling when and why you want to interview him or her gets you permission and makes cooperation a lot more likely. If you're not likely to be able to get needed clearance or permission, look for alternative information sources.
	Reactivity	You don't want *how* you measure something to change too drastically what you're after. A typical "laundry-list" questionnaire to survey training preferences can, for example, shape and re-prioritize a respondent's reaction; a simple interview question: "Tell me what you'd like" might get a very different response. Or, an observer's presence can suppress—or elicit—certain behaviors.
	Bias	Self-selected samples are often biased in ways that will contaminate conclusions. A follow-up questionnaire to trainees might elicit returns from extreme groups only. Or, a post-test administered only to those trainees who stayed until the very end of training may yield biased scores, since this sample of trainees may be more diligent, motivated, etc. Make sure the sample of what you'll measure is most likely to represent what you're after.
	Reliability	Consider how to get the most accurate information. When, for example, multiple observers, interviewers, or raters are used, *train* them to promote and check for consistency. Be sure that *when* or *where* you collect data isn't adversely affecting your data. Take time to make instruments readable, clear and error free.

SOME CONCERNS TO BEAR IN MIND WHEN DESIGNING INFORMATION COLLECTION PROCEDURES *(continued)*	Concern	For Instance . . .
	Validity	Will the collection procedure produce information that measures what you say you are measuring? Be able to support that the information you collect is, in fact, relevant to the evaluation questions you intend it for. Be sure that what you collect is a real indicator of the claims you make. "Graduates" of training might, for example, have knolwedge from your training; and/or they might *claim* to use it. Does that mean they *do* use it? Be sure, too, that your information collection procedure records what you want it to. A performance appraisal might, for example, record more about personality than behavior (what it supposedly measures).

CONSIDER INTERACTION EFFECTS

Remember that no collection procedure automatically meets, or violates, quality criteria. Reliability, cost effectiveness, validity, or ethics all depend upon the appropriate relationship of

the information source
with the
information collection procedure
considering the
evaluation question
given the
particular setting

This means that an excellent instrument with a reliability coefficient of .86 is still worthless if it is not investigating a relevant concern or if it is administered to an inappropriate group. In every evaluation situation, there will be tradeoffs in meeting criteria for sound information collection. That is why the important criteria should be determined at the beginning and reviewed throughout the evaluation.

HOW MUCH INFORMATION SHOULD YOU COLLECT?

Sampling is selecting a portion of a whole group taken to represent the whole group. The portion is known as the *sample*; the whole group is called the population. When you sample, you do so to learn something about a population without having to measure (interview, observe, etc.) all of the population.

Sampling is like a shortcut. It allows you to save time and money by selecting only a portion of all potential members of a population to provide information. Like any shortcut, sampling risks basing decisions on inadequate information. If you needed to choose a hotel for a convention, a tour of fifty guest rooms would provide a more complete rating than would a tour of five rooms. But, the five-room tour is quicker and easier, and you can make an estimate of the whole population (all the rooms) within a known degree of certainty.

Whenever you evaluate anything or any person you inevitably sample. That is, you don't collect information on *all* aspects of that thing or person. For instance, in evaluating whether a trainee should be certified, you would assess only a sample of competencies for each individual.

Often, it is wise to sample events, evaluees and respondents because you can generalize from your sample to the larger population, such as a course, a workshop, or a group. But you don't always want to sample among evaluees or respondents. If your purpose is to make diagnostic decisions about trainees, you have to evaluate a sampling of competencies from *each* trainee.

THE OPTIONS: DIFFERENT KINDS OF SAMPLING METHODS

There are two general kinds of sampling methods: random and purposive (called also objective and subjective). Random methods are used to produce samples that are, to a given level of probable certainty, free of biasing forces. They allow use of inferential statistics to generalize findings with calculable degrees of certainty. Purposive methods are used to produce samples that will represent particular points of view or particular groups in the judgment of those selecting the sample.

Here's a chart of some commonly employed sampling methods. Each is named and described, and a brief example of its use provided.

Some Sampling Techniques

Method	How it Works	Example
Random straight random sampling	One selects, via random method (such as a random numbers table), a predetermined portion of a population. The proportion of the population sampled determines the level of precision of the generalization to the larger population. The larger the sample, the more precise the generalization.	To determine the level of preparation of the average teacher, the SEA surveys a random sample of teachers accredited in the state.
quota sampling	The samples are drawn within certain population categories and can be made in proportion to the relative size of the category. A sample of parents, for example, could be drawn randomly from predetermined lists of upper income pupils, lower income pupils, Caucasians, blacks, Hispanic parents, or whatever other subpopulation categories were of interest. The quota sample ensures that the sample will include access to low-incidence subpopulations who would likely not be drawn in a straight random sample.	The university sends surveys to 5% of the graduates in each of several income and social categories to determine the perceived utility of the curriculum and its responsiveness to cultural differences.
Stratified samples	Samples are drawn for each of several "strata," such as freshmen, sophomores, juniors or seniors; or, teachers, administrators, and directors. Stratified samples are useful when you have more, or a different, interest in one particular stratum than another. You identify strata of greater interest, then take larger samples from them. Each stratum is considered a population.	The school district sends an inservice attitude survey to all of 15 principals, 50% of 40 administrators, and 10% of 1500 teachers.
matrix samples	This method samples both respondents from a defined population *and* items from an instrument. The notion here is that, when the respondent pool is sufficiently large and there are many instrument items, it is more efficient to have each respondent respond to only a certain subset of the items. If these item subsets are randomly generated, and respondents randomly drawn, generalization is possible to the entire population and the entire instrument. This method is particularly useful in broad-scale surveys or testing programs—but only, of course, where an individual's scores are not needed.	To determine whether a district-wide workshop impacted on knowledge of new state laws, 10% of all attendees were given tests. To keep tests brief, each person answered only 10 questions from the 50 items on the entire test.
Purposive key informants	This method of sampling individuals is employed to access those persons with the	Workshop staff conduct a de-brief

Some Sampling Techniques *(continued)*

Method	How it Works	Example
	most information about particular conditions or situations. Union representatives or de-facto leaders among teachers could be a prime source of teacher attitudes and opinions; community leaders, respected individuals, etc., could yield rich information on community issues and so forth.	with 6 participants to get their feedback. These 6 were selected because they emerged as small group leaders.
expert judges	This method involves sampling those persons with exceptional expertise about certain conditions or factors of interest. When information about best practices or recent advances is sought, an hour interview with an expert in the area can short-cut many hours of literature review and reading.	The university conducted case studies of employment of graduates who were deemed the most successful in the program to see if *their* preparation was sufficient, and to get their ideas for revision.
extreme groups	This intentionally seeks out conflicting or extreme viewpoints. Whereas the random methods aim to account for bias and converge on the average or typical case, the extreme group sample purposely ignores the middle ground or common viewpoint to learn about the atypical, extreme view. The known detractors of a program, be they small in number and inordinately biased, can offer rich clues as to a program's potential flaws—and even strengths.	Follow-up interviews are conducted with students who drop out of the program.
grapevine sampling	This entails a growing sample, where each successive sample member is determined by clues or explicit directions from the prior members. One might ask a principal, for instance, to be directed to the most voluble (or negative, or positive, or reticent, etc.) teacher in the school. That person would be interviewed then asked to recommend another person to the interviewer, and so forth, until the interviewer is satisfied that a sufficient sample has been obtained. Direction to the next case can be asked for explicitly or derived from each case's notes. The same method can be used in a survey questionnaire, much the same as a chain-letter operates.	In evaluating a technical assistance system, the evaluator interviewed first the teachers who got service. Then, went to the person who advised the teacher to use the service and also to the person who gave the service, using these contacts to get more contacts until repeats were encountered.

IMPORTANT
QUESTIONS TO
ADDRESS BEFORE
DETERMINING
WHETHER AND
HOW TO SAMPLE

Q: Should you use a sample?

A: Your most accurate alternative is always to get information from an entire population. But, this is also costly. Each additional sample member entails added costs of instrumentation, administration, analysis, and handling and storage.

Sampling can help with some typical sorts of problems. For example: an inservice coordinator received three telephone calls from irate teachers who just attended an inservice workshop, complaining of a poor instructor and disorganized session. The coordinator, before taking action (e.g., to change instructors) needs to decide whether these three teachers represent all who attended or whether they are a vociferous minority. A quick telephone call to a small, random sample of attendees could help determine this. Or, a few calls to some especially trusted attendees (a purposive sample) could also be used. In any case, the coordinator should also delve into the particular complaints from the vociferous three, for they are a "sample-of-opportunity" from which something of value can be learned; perhaps, for instance, they represent a small portion who are opposed to any inservice and thus their concerns need to be heard.

Q: What kind of sampling is most appropriate?

A: It happens often in training and personnel preparation that random samples are drawn when other—more purposive—sampling would be more useful. The best key to correct sampling is to reconsider why you are collecting information in the first place. What is it that you want to learn about, change, or report about?

For example, consider the typical case of sending a follow-up survey to graduates of a program or participants in an inservice. Usually, a random sample of attendees is drawn to receive the survey. But, this method assumes that you wish to make an inference (an estimate) about *all* attendees. Very often, however, the purpose is to make some judgments about the program (curriculum, workshop, etc.) itself, not about the typical or average attendee. Thus, it might make more sense to draw a sample of those whose judgments and opinion could mean the most or be most useful. This might be high-scoring graduates (or poor ones), or specially qualified attendees, persons with a lot of experience, etc.

The point is to choose a sampling method that will work best for your purpose. This means you have to be quite clear about your purpose. And, of course, you want to use a sampling method that suits your resources.

Q: What sampling unit should you use?

A: Sampling units are the basis on which you'll sample. Examples are:

People (e.g., teachers, trainers, parents, pupils)
Organizational units (e.g., schools, classes, districts, buildings)
Special groups (e.g., persons who received different sorts of experiences or treatments, users of different resources)

The sampling unit is very much related to the kinds of samples you intend to draw. It's thus dependent on your purposes for collecting information.

Q: How large a sample do you need?

A: The size of the sample you will draw will depend on four factors: (1) the amount of certainty you need, (2) the nature of the population, (3) how much money you have to spend, and (4) the nature of the information collection procedure.

▶ Certainty

Larger samples will give you greater certainty. For example:

A larger survey return on test population (e.g., 150 vs. 20) will increase the

IMPORTANT
QUESTIONS TO
ADDRESS BEFORE
DETERMINING
WHETHER AND
HOW TO SAMPLE
(continued)

certainty of estimates of population characteristics within fixed degrees of precision (e.g., ± 5%).

Most standard statistical texts (see references) contain tables that show you how large a sample is needed to achieve given levels of certainty.

A longer observation period or more periods, will enable you to record more, and more varied, behaviors.

A test or survey containing 100 items vs. 10 items will produce a more reliable estimate of the trait it measures.

The amount of certainty you need can be determined partially by projecting the consequences of a "wrong" (inaccurate, untrue) decision. If you're basing a major decision on data you're collecting—say whether to graduate a trainee, or refund a workshop—then you will want a lot of precision and certainty. If, on the other hand, you can live with a rough estimate, a smaller sample may do.

▶ How much variability is there in the population or trait about which you might make an estimate?

When variability is high, you need a larger sample. Some examples of variability are:

How many kinds of graduates complete a program?
How large a range of reactions to a training session might there have been?
How many different kinds of records might be in the files?
How many different behaviors constitute good (vs. bad) performance?

▶ Resources available

A larger sample will cost you more time and money. Along with greater certainty come greater costs. In all endeavors, there's a point of diminishing returns. You should consider whether the increase in certainty is worth the extra costs. And, consider, too, that a larger sample takes more time to access and handle data from: can you afford delay?

▶ Effectiveness of the information collection procedure

Not all procedures produce a 100% yield. If you expect: low return rates; inaccurate or partially complete records; partial completion of interviews, tests, observation; variably successful site visits; poorly attended meetings and hearings, etc; then you should think about increasing your sample size. The idea is to not just *try* for an adequate sample, but in fact *get* an adequate sample.

Q: Is your sample likely to be biased?
A: Yes. You will have some bias in any sample. The point is to anticipate and control it if possible; to consider and report it if not. Bias causes inaccuracy in estimates to a population. You might have a large enough sample to have good certainty, for example, but a bad (biased) sample can mean you draw an inaccurate decision despite high certainty. Some causes of bias in training programs are:

▶ Low response rates: Whenever you get less than 100% of your intended sample back, you run risks of response bias, more bias with lower returns. Those who actually respond might be significantly different from the population. To avoid low response:

Use smaller samples and spend your effort and money in more vigorous pursuit of the respondents.
Use a briefer instrument.
Pursue non-respondees.
Include a "reward" for response (money, a gift, a summary report, etc.). A teabag has been known to work: "Complete our survey, then have a cup of tea!"
Make return as easy as possible (stamped envelopes, self-mailers, etc.).

▶ Out-of-date population lists.

IMPORTANT
QUESTIONS TO
ADDRESS BEFORE
DETERMINING
WHETHER AND
HOW TO SAMPLE
(continued)

▶ Lack of complete data for some subgroups, such as poorly maintained records for handicapped and students.
▶ Use of the wrong sampling unit for the population you're interested in.
▶ Biased population listing, such as using the PTA roll for *all* parents.

**CRITERIA TO AIM
FOR WHEN
SAMPLING**

FREEDOM FROM UNWANTED BIAS

You need to be sure that some unplanned or unknown factor has not unduly biased the sample(s) you obtain. Some instances and examples of bias are:

lists and pools of names that are used to generate samples can be, themselves, biased. The classic example of this sampling error resulted in the famous 1932 headline, "Landon Beats Roosevelt." The pollsters took names from the phone book, which biased (1932) the sample to upper socio-economic strata.

the presence of an observer affects the samples of behavior that can be observed

some behaviors occur infrequently (e.g., managing violent pupil behavior) and wouldn't likely occur in a random sample

the timing of an information collection procedure is related to samples. Lesson plans sampled in September may be more conscientiously completed than those in March, for example. Or, behaviors in the morning may be different from the afternoon.

a directive from an authority to submit samples of lesson plans might influence respondents to submit their "best" work

a questionnaire mailed to parents in one school and carried home by pupils in another might reach different sorts of parents

EFFICIENCY

Samples should be no larger than what's necessary to obtain the desired level of certainty. Too much data is not only costing extra resources but places unnecessary demands on respondents and participants.

CHARACTERISTIC

Your sample should consider known incidence rates, distributions, and proportions in the population. When samples are drawn from larger populations to make inferences about certain characteristics or traits, you need to be sure that your sampling procedure accounts for what's known to be related to that trait. This often requires stratification. If, for example, you wished to sample district opinion on school programs, you would want to sample across socioeconomic levels, for these factors are known to be related to expectations and values about schooling. Or, your sampling procedure (purposive) would seek input from a spectrum of existing special interest groups.

REPLICABILITY

You should document the procedures by which you sample so that potential bias might be identified or so that others could repeat your procedures.

HOW WILL YOU SELECT OR DEVELOP INSTRUMENTS?

Instruments are the tangible forms which both elicit and record information you collect. There are many kinds of instruments: interview protocols, questionnaires, tests, checklists, observation records, etc.

Instruments have to be carefully chosen or designed. Sloppy or improper instrumentation can spoil an otherwise well planned information collection effort.

The tasks involved in instrumentation are deciding what you need, choosing to select or develop them, and developing if you have to.

COMMONLY USED INSTRUMENTS IN TYPICAL COLLECTION PROCEDURES

Surveys
Open-ended instruments
Forced-choice instruments

Interviews
Closed formats where questions and responses are read to respondent
Semi-open formats where questions are fixed, and interviewer transcribes interpretations of responses onto form
Open formats, where general guidelines are provided to interviewer; responses are transcribed in notes or on audio-tape

Observations
Open formats, where observer makes notes or general reactions, behaviors, etc. of subjects
Logs, where observer records own reactions and behaviors
Sign systems where specific behaviors are counted each time they occur to provide a record of certain behaviors that occur in a given time interval
Category systems, where behavior observed is classified in certain categories to produce a record of the kinds of behavior that have transpired in a given time interval

Tests
Multiple choice tests
Other forced-response formats; true-false, matching, etc.
Short answer, fill-in-the-blank
Essay tests

Inventories
Open-ended, where respondents make notes about certain objects; items as they find them
Checklist formats, where respondents check off—or count and enter numbers—next to listed items

Site visits, expert reviews, panel hearings
In these procedures, you can think of people *themselves* as "instruments." Kinds of "instruments" in these procedures might be:
Experts
Consumer representatives
Staff members
Public
Parents, etc.

GENERAL
SPECIFICATIONS
FOR AN
EVALUATION
INSTRUMENT

1. What **content** is needed?
   This relates directly to the variables you've decided on. The content of an instrument should be limited to and inclusive of these variables.

2. What **language** requirements exist?
   This can relate to the reading level of respondents, the kinds of examples and references to be used, avoidance of jargon or inclusion of definitions, foreign language translations, etc.

3. What **analysis** procedures will be used?
   If machine scoring or automatic coding is needed, the instrument must provide for these options. If sub-group analyses are projected, then demographic data must be included.

4. What **other special considerations** apply?
   This might include special versions for handicapped respondents, need for special directions, etc.
   In reviewing specifications, it's a good idea to construct a "blueprint" or list for each instrument you'll need. Also, you may want to get some special consultant help from your friendly local psychometrician at this point.

5. Determine how much **precision** is called for.
   Sometimes you plan to use data for relatively fine discrimination, such as ranking proposals for levels of funding or deciding how much remediation to provide different course participants. In other cases, less discriminating precision is needed, as in deciding whether a record meets completeness criteria or if participants are in favor of an evening or daytime workshop session. Don't be overly precise.
   Some variables distribute across a broad range of increments, such as clock-time spent in a learning module or the number of graduate courses completed. Others do not, and to measure them in precise increments lends an artificial degree of precision; examples of this are "participants rated satisfaction at 3.237 on a 10-point scale," or "3.7 participants completed the exercise."

6. Capacities of **intended** respondents.
   There is little to be gained, and reliability to be lost, when respondents and participants in information collection are asked to make discriminations beyond their abilities. Asking teachers in a questionnaire, for example, to list their undergraduate training courses would be less desirable than having someone analyze a sample of personnel files to get the same information.

7. **Suitability** for planned analysis
   Knowing what you'll do with data once they're collected helps decide how much precision to go for. If you think, for example, you'll want to see if amount of training is related to success on the job, you'll need relatively discriminating measures on each variable.
   Precision can be increased in a procedure by providing more detail and definition in instrument items and response guidelines and categories. Interviewers, for example, could read from a list of clearly defined uses of inservice outcomes, rather than ask for respondents' own interpretation.

GENERAL SPECIFICATIONS FOR AN EVALUATION INSTRUMENT
(continued)

Or, proposal judges could rate each of 20 defined variables instead of making a global judgment.

Asking respondents (raters, observers, reviewers, etc.) for more objective vs. subjective responses can increase precision—but may limit richness and interpretation. Observers could, instead of rating teachers' "warmth and receptivity" count the instances of certain behaviors (e.g., verbal reinforcement, patting a child's head, smiling).

CHECKING TO SEE WHAT INSTRUMENTS ARE AVAILABLE

Before developing a new instrument, invest time in checking to see whether one already exists—even if it would need to be refined or adapted.

- friends and colleagues—ask them
- publishers of tests and materials
- catalogs (see references at end of chapter); especially helpful for training programs are the *ETC Instrument Catalog* and *Mirrors of Behavior*
- other projects and programs like yours
- libraries, resource centers, etc.

ASSESSING THE ADEQUACY OF INSTRUMENTS FOR YOUR PURPOSE

content: Do they contain what you need? Are variables appropriate? Is there irrelevant or missing content?

precision: Will they be precise enough, or *too* precise, for your needs?

availability: Can you get them? In time? Will copyright laws let you use them?

norms: When norms are used or provided, are the referent groups similar to those you'll use?

price: Can you afford them? Are they worth it?

technical accuracy: We'd recommend that you see the "Checklist" in the Appendix.

DEVELOPING YOUR OWN INSTRUMENT

1. List specifications for the instrument.

   content: what variables should it address?

   precision: how precisely and surely must it measure? What kinds of decisions will depend on the data produced?

   language requirements: will the instrument be read by 4th graders or Ph.D. candidates? handicapped persons? bilingual persons?

   analysis planned: machine scoring? special coding? analysis along with other instruments?

   demographic data needs: how much will the instrument need to record information about respondents themselves or the administration setting?

2. Clarify the *conceptual design/basis* for the instrument.

   An instrument shouldn't be a haphazard collection of items and directions. It needs a conceptual design—the "glue" that hangs it together. Some examples are:

   "Respondents will be asked to recollect their initial ability levels before the workshop, then rate their growth on each of the several workshop objectives"

   "The six typical behavior problems will be presented, and respondents will outline a proposed treatment strategy. Responses will be scored according to how well respondents incorporate Schwartzian theory"

   "The hidden observer will watch for, and list, behavior indicative of Schwartz's Syndrome"

"The questionnaire will list many resources, some of which the agency has disseminated. Then, it will ask people to check those they use most often"

3. *Block out* ("blueprint") the instrument
   Outline the major sections, where you'll want directions, how many items you want for each objective, etc.
4. Produce a *draft* of the instrument
5. Get the draft *reviewed*. Have it checked for:
   ease of reading and clarity
   content
   technical flaws (e.g., dual stems, overlapping response categories).
6. *Revise* the draft (Note: the more often you do this and Step 5, the better it will get)
7. *Try out* the instrument (see next sub-section) to be sure it has sufficient reliability and validity for your needs.
8. Revise again, and try-out again until:

ASSESS THE
INSTRUMENT

Validity: The instrument provides truthful, useful and authentic information about what it measures or records

Reliability: The instrument measures and records accurately. (You want a minimum amount of error in the scores and information they produce.)

Non-reactivity: Instrument does not adversely change or otherwise affect what is measures and records. (Sometimes, some items on a test will give clues to correct answers on other items; questionnaire items may "key" a response; interview questions and phrasing may suppress certain information, etc.)

Appropriateness for responders and users: Language levels, examples, formats and item structures are suitable for the intended users.

Sufficient precision for intended analysis and usage; The instrument produces data in categories (e.g., scores, ratings) at least as fine as the finest discrimination you intend to make. (If, for instance, you wanted to sort users of resource services into four categories, you would need an item [or group of items] with at least four levels of response categories.)

Economy: The instrument is not too costly to select, develop, try-out, revise, aggregate, analyze and interpret. Nor is it too demanding of respondent's and user's time, patience and attention.

CHECKLIST FOR
INSTRUMENTS

Introduction

☐ there is a clear statement of the instrument's purpose

☐ the respondent is told how information resulting from the instrument will be used

☐ those who will see the data are identified

☐ the respondent is told why s/he was selected to complete the instrument

CHECKLIST FOR INSTRUMENTS
(continued)

Introduction

- [ ] the privacy of confidential information is insured
- [ ] the anonymity of the respondent is guaranteed (if appropriate)
- [ ] motivators for responding are supplied
- [ ] directions for returning the instrument are adequate (when, where, and how)

Item Stems

- [ ] the stem is relevant to the stated purpose of the instrument
- [ ] the stem focuses on one center (has one key verb)
- [ ] the wording of the stem is appropriate to the reading level of the respondents
- [ ] the possible response is not biased by the wording of the stem (giveaway hint for plural)
- [ ] "supply" items identify the appropriate unit of response
- [ ] each stem is independent of other stems
- [ ] the level of analysis necessary to respond to the stem is appropriate to the capabilities of the respondents

Directions

- [ ] directions are given when necessary for each section
- [ ] the language used is appropriate to the level of the respondents
- [ ] the directions are clear and complete
- [ ] an example item is provided (if necessary)

Directions

- [ ] directions are provided for responding to items which "do not apply"
- [ ] the respondent is told if other materials are needed to complete the instrument

Format

- [ ] individual items are appropriately spaced
- [ ] items are grouped in a logical order (by content, type, etc.)
- [ ] sufficient space exists for the desired response
- [ ] instrument is easy to read
- [ ] instrument is not too long
- [ ] instrument is "pleasing to the eye"

Responses

- [ ] response categories are unidimensional
- [ ] response categories are non-overlapping
- [ ] response categories are exhaustive
- [ ] response categories are relevant to the stems
- [ ] "not applicable," "I don't know," "no opinion" options are provided where appropriate
- [ ] a sufficient amount of space is left for supply responses
- [ ] space is provided for comments where appropriate
- [ ] a sufficient amount of space is left for supply responses
- [ ] space is provided for comments where appropriate
- [ ] guidelines are provided for comments

HOW DO YOU ESTABLISH THE VALIDITY AND RELIABILITY OF INSTRUMENTATION?

Validity and reliability are characteristics that must be present in your data collection efforts or you risk collecting information too inaccurate to be usable.

Validity refers to how truthful, genuine and authentic data are in representing what they purport to. To be valid is to make truthful claims; instruments must measure what they intend and claim to measure. Data produced by instruments must authentically represent the traits and phenomena you use them to represent.

Reliability relates to the accuracy of measures. The more error in a measure, the more unreliable it is. Reliability often means different things in different kinds of measures, but in general it represents the trustworthiness of data produced. We might know that a bath scale, for instance, is capable of producing valid indications of weight: the number of pounds is a valid measure of weight. But if the bath scales' indicator slips and is loose and its viewing glass is scratched and dirty, it is highly likely that any one weighing will produce an erroneous result. The scale is unreliable.

Reliability and validity are achieved through the careful design, try-out and revision of instruments and information collection procedures.

In thinking about how you can approach increasing the reliability and validity of your collection efforts, you should recognize and keep two facts "up front":

Neither reliability nor validity is a "one-time" phenomenon. You must be continually aware of them, working to increase them and deal with problems that arise throughout the life of an evaluation.

There is not on *a priori* level of minimum reliability or validity that can be set for your measures. The more you increase these characteristics, the more sure you can be of your results, and you can use them with more confidence.

In this section, we briefly characterize kinds of validity and reliability and present some general steps and considerations you can take to increase reliability and validity. Then, for each of five (5) commonly used quantitative instrument types, we present some techniques you can use to determine and increase reliability and validity.

KINDS OF VALIDITY AND RELIABILITY

Validity

Content Validity: does an instrument contain the right stuff? Are test items consistent with course content? Are behaviors listed related to diagnostic ability? Do rating items represent a meaningful range of criteria?

Concurrent Validity: does a measure produce results consistent with some other independent measure? e.g., do self-ratings of knowledge correlate with scores in a knowledge test?

KINDS OF
VALIDITY AND
RELIABILITY
(continued)

Predictive Validity: this is the ability of a measure to faithfully predict some other future trait or measure; e.g., does score on the interview for admission predict success in the graduate program?

Construct Validity: this relates to the truthfulness of the theoretical construct underlying a measure and requires considerable research to establish and investigate. An example of construct validity inquiry would be research to determine if persons who achieve good scores on workshop objectives do, in fact, achieve good pupil learning results. Or, whether"ability to give positive reinforcement" is related to pupil learning.

Reliability

Stability, repeatability: a test or measure that provides consistent scores from instance to instance is reliable: stable over time. A content rating of a product, for instance, should not produce different scores depending on when and where the analysis takes place.

Inter-judge or rater agreement: a rating should reflect the characteristics of the object being rated, not vagaries and differences among users of the instrument (the judges). This kind of reliability is vastly improved by training of raters and judges.

Equivalency: this relates to the degree of consistency between two alternate forms of the "same" test or measure. If tests are equivalent (produce the same scores) then differences over time (e.g., after a workshop) can be inferred to be the result of instruction, not the result of having taken the test before.

Internal Consistency: this relates to how well a group of items or a measure "hangs together." It tells you how unidimensional the measure is—whether items are measuring one trait. Estimates of this kind of reliability can be made by checking the degree of correlation between split-halves of the test, or by other measures requiring only one administration of the test (see references).

GENERAL
QUESTIONS AND
CONSIDERATIONS
ABOUT VALIDITY
AND RELIABILITY

Q: How do you get valid data?

A: Validity is not so much a characteristic intrinsic to some data. It's more related to how you *use* data. Self-ratings of knowledge are known, for example, to be quite an accurate estimation of actual knowledge. To use self-ratings in a certification program as a basis for grading, however, would likely be an invalid use. Use of self-ratings in a workshop, however, as a means for participants to select paths of study, would be far more valid.

Consider, then, how you'll use information. Will it provide a genuine and authentic measure of what you want to use it for? Might it be easily contaminated by another factor (as in the case of self-rating for certification)?

Q: How do you maximize the content validity on an instrument?

A: When constructing a test, rating scale, questionnaire, checklist or behavioral observation, you want to be sure that what you're measuring (the items on the form) are the right stuff. This is largely a judgment issue. Seek advice from colleagues, experts, literature and research. Ask:

GENERAL
QUESTIONS AND
CONSIDERATIONS
ABOUT VALIDITY
AND RELIABILITY
(continued)

does content reflect what's important in this workshop, course, program, etc.?

is there agreement that these variables are important?

does the literature, other programs, or research support these variables as being correct?

is there a logical connection between what you're measuring and what you need to know?

Q: How do you maintain validity?

A: Because validity is related to how data get *used*, you need to monitor and reflect on the uses of data you collect to avoid invalid applications. A department chair should not, for example, use grades assigned to students to compare faculty—or whose students are learning the most. Nor should an inservice coordinator base decisions of who in the district needs what training on preferences expressed from a volunteer survey.

An intended use could be quite valid; an actual use could be quite invalid. Monitoring usage of data, facilitating interpretation (See the "Reporting" chapter), and exploring meaning in data empirically and reflectively will increase validity and the utility of your evaluation.

Q: How do you design an instrument for reliability?

A: Reliability is related to error in measuring. An instrument that contains a number of errors (that is, it's unclear, vague, confusing and difficult to use) is bound to be unreliable. You can achieve needed levels of reliability very often by trying out an instrument and revising it based on feedback.

make sure directions are clear

be sure there's only one way to respond to and interpret an item

eliminate items with dual stems (e.g., "How useful and interesting was the workshop?"

Adherence to the criteria on the Instrument Checklist (pp. 98–99) will help you improve or assess reliability.

Q: Do you need to monitor data collection?

A: Yes. Instruments used differently in different situations will produce non-parallel, unreliable data. You need to be sure that data collection gets carried out the way it's intended and is consistent from instance to instance.

Q: Who should administer the instrument?

A: Train experts, judges and raters when you use rating instruments. Without training and adequate direction, raters are likely to apply varying criteria and to "see" different things. If you want to treat their data equivalently, then you need to train them. If you will use their judgments independently, then you'll need to know what rules they used, criteria they applied, their perspectives, etc. to reliably interpret their opinions.

Q: How can you increase the reliability of ratings?

A: Use more and more specific rating variables. For example, global judgments ("How did you like the workshop?") can easily be unreliable. To get more precision into your data, break the global concept into several subconcepts.

WAYS OF
ESTABLISHING
RELIABILITY
AND VALIDITY
FOR DIFFERENT
KINDS OF
INSTRUMENTS

HOLISTIC RATING SCALES

Holistic rating scales: where ratings on several items are added together to compute a total score.

Example
Student Diagnostic Test Administration Ability

		4	3	2	1	
☐ gives directions properly	excellent	( )	( )	( )	( )	poor

☐ checks comfort level
☐ repeats questions when necessary
☐ etc.

Total score = _____

Uses: The *total score* on the instrument (e.g., "Student's Diagnostic Ability") is used to rank student, grade performance, etc.

1. Reliability Concerns
   a. *Can different raters use it accurately?* Or, do results depend on who does the rating? To check this kind of reliability, have different raters rate the *same* behavior sample (e.g., a videotape), then compare scores. Train raters, then revise the instrument until scores are within acceptable limits. Make sure directions are clear and that rating scale "anchors" are clearly defined for each item.
   b. *Are the items reliable?* If all items are meant to rate the same general skill, they should be internally consistent, each correlating with the total score. Cronbach's "coefficient alpha" or one of the Kuder Richardson formulas should be used. If the instrument rates a varied set of skills, then you don't necessarily want high internal consistency. In this case, look for consistency over time, as in a repeated measure of the same subject.
2. Validity Concerns
   a. *Is the content meaningful?* Does it measure the "right" variables? This is a judgment call. Have a draft version of the instrument reviewed by experts in the area which you're rating.
   b. *Does the score represent the variables it's meant to measure?* You can test this empirically in several ways. One might be to have raters use the instrument on some videotape samples, some of which are known to show "good" behavior and some "bad." A valid rating should tell a good one from a bad one. Or, for example with a workshop rating scale, you might give the rating to two simulated "extreme" groups. Tell one group it was a great workshop and the other it was awful; scores should correlate with group membership.

SINGULAR ITEM RATING SCALES

Singular-Item Rating Scales: where an instrument contains several rating items (as on a workshop reaction survey), but each item is scored independently and you don't calculate a total score for each instrument.

Example
* Uses Schwartz question methods:
☐ always   ☐ frequently   ☐ seldom   ☐ never
* Can use a ratchet wrench:
With amazing grace ( )   ( )   ( )   ( ) Wretchedly

WAYS OF
ESTABLISHING
RELIABILITY
AND VALIDITY
FOR DIFFERENT
KINDS OF
INSTRUMENTS
(continued)

Uses: The total score is *never* computed. Rather, item scores are reported for diagnostic purposes, reporting progress, impact, etc.

1. Reliability Concerns
   a. *Do raters affect scores?* (see preceding instrument discussion of this question)
   b. *Is "halo effect" a factor?* Because the items are meant to rate different (independent) variables, you want to be sure that a person's score on some items doesn't influence their score on others. Your raters have to be able to see the differences among the items being rated. You can check for this by having raters rate a sample (e.g., a videotape) of someone *known* to vary on the different items. Correct halo effects by repositioning items, by careful writing of items and scales, and by training raters.
   c. *Is it consistent over time?* Check this by administering the rating to the same subject more than once when you *know* the variables rated haven't really changed. The item scores from different administrations should correlate highly.
2. Validity Concerns
   a. *Is the content valid?* Does the instrument assess the right set of variables? Again, this requires some expert judgment to be sure that what you've included on your instrument is defensible and fits your program.
   b. *Do items really measure the variables?* This requires some empirical testing, which could be extensive. Use of videotaped or other known good/bad samples can be used to see if items discriminate as intended.

BEHAVORIAL OBSERVATIONS

Behavioral Observation: where behaviors are observed then counted or categorized on a checklist type of instrument.

Example

* The teacher hyperventilated

☐ 3 or more times ☐ 1–3 times ☐ never during the lesson

Uses: These instruments categorize particular verbal or other behaviors to be used diagnostically, record progress and growth, or assess changes as a result of training.

1. Reliability Concerns
   a. The main concern is to see whether observers can indeed see and accurately record the intended behaviors. Often, considerable training and instrument revision is needed to achieve tolerable limits of error. Careful definition and redefinition of items helps assure consistent usage.
   b. Another reliability concern is sampling. You need to be sure that the behaviors actually observed are representative of what you wish to make inferences about. If you wish to be able to draw conclusions about typical behaviors, then you must be sure what you observed was typical. Often multiple observations of the same subject are necessary.
2. Validity Concerns
   a. *Is the content valid?* There should be a rationale, based on research, expert judgment or other value bases, that the behaviors you will count are meaningful.
   b. *Can the instrument discriminate instances from non-instances of the behavior?* A useful procedure here is the extreme groups method, where you record behavior of two extremely different samples (e.g., a good diagnostician at work and a bad one). Your items, and your total score, should discriminate the two.

WAYS OF ESTABLISHING RELIABILITY AND VALIDITY FOR DIFFERENT KINDS OF INSTRUMENTS *(continued)*

SURVEY INSTRUMENTS

Survey Questionnaire: where respondents are asked to classify and categorize their reactions, characteristics, etc.

Example

* Did you see the film *The Great Prune Robbery*? ☐ Yes ☐ No
* Rate your feeling about prunes. Love them ☐   ☐   ☐   ☐ Hate them

Uses: These forms collect data on a broad range of variables, some of which are related to one another, and some not. Item scores are generally used to characterize traits of groups and sub-groups.

1. Reliability Concerns
   The major reliability concern is whether the instrument is stable over time. Is someone's response affected by when they completed the form? Would they respond the same way again? To check for stability, readminister the form to some respondents, then compare their responses. If item responses change—and what they're rating/responding to *hasn't* changed—you've got a reliability problem.
   Often, you can increase reliability by writing more items and/or by making items more specific. But be careful about length increases. A longer questionnaire will have a lower return/completion rate, and you'll trade greater reliability for bias.
2. Validity Concerns
   a. Expert judgment, prior research, etc. will help you determine whether you've included the right variables.
   b. Whether the form and items are valid for a particular use/group of respondents is a developmental issue. You should review draft versions with potential respondents and make appropriate changes.
   c. Whether the items measure what they intend to can be checked by comparing scores to some other, concurrent measure. Again, extreme groups—either real or simulated—can be used. Or, you can compare survey scores to some other kind of data known to be valid for the respondents.

KNOWLEDGE TESTS

Knowledge Test: where forced response items are grouped in an instrument to assess a particular knowledge (skill, competency, etc.) domain.

Example

* Check the behavior(s) below that is/are typical of a Schwartz Syndrome adult

☐ insults small mammals without provocation
☐ drinks from wrong side of glass
☐ believes septic tank can back up into refrigerator
☐ eats no vegetables except ketchup
☐ all of the above
☐ none of the above

WAYS OF
ESTABLISHING
RELIABILITY
AND VALIDITY
FOR DIFFERENT
KINDS OF
INSTRUMENTS
(continued)

Uses: Usually, total scores or scores on subtests are used diagnostically or to assess learning.

1. Reliability Concerns

   The most usual reliability concern is internal consistency: how well the items "hang together," and are they related to the other items. A split half or one of the other consistency measures listed in the references at the end of this chapter can be used. Adding more items and rewriting items (e.g., getting rid of ambiguous distractors, etc.) will enhance reliability. In general, reliability accrues to the carefully constructed test that is revised, revised again, then again.

2. Validity Concerns

   a. Is the content right? To determine this, you need expert judgment about the *scope* of the instrument; is it adequate for the domain you are testing? You also need a judgment about the *relevance* of the items to the tested domain. Again, expert judgment, prior research, and analysis of curriculum can be used. Revise the instrument drafts until you receive satisfactory judgments about scope and relevance.

   b. Does it measure validly?
      - try out your tests on known extreme groups. Test scores should correlate with group membership.
      - compare test scores against another, independent, criterion measure, such as expert judgments, other tests, ratings, etc.
      - correlate *item* scores with *total* scores. Items that don't discriminate (i.e., aren't related to total score) may be invalid.

CHECKLISTS AND INVENTORIES

Checklist: where tangible items or characteristics are observed, then counted, coded or classified (e.g., a content analysis checklist, an inventory of tangible goods).

Example

* How many times did teachers check out the film "Cattle Prods in the Classroom?" _____ times

* Does the *diagnostic* section make a specific reference to Schwartz Syndrome? _____yes _____no

Uses: These instruments are a lot like behavioral tallies, except they count and record characteristics of tangible items (e.g., the content of a report, or what's on a bulletin board).

1. Reliability Concerns

   a. Here (as in observation) you need to be sure that scores represent what got measured versus who did the measuring. Check this by comparing scores from different observers who observed the same thing. You can increase this reliability by training your checkers/observers and by carefully specifying items.

   b. When total scores are used (versus item-by-item reporting) you need to be sure that a score of "15," say, was arrived at in the same way by different observers. You need to have good internal consistency. Inter-item correlations should be high. When items are scored and reported independently, inter-item correlation is not an issue.

WAYS OF ESTABLISHING RELIABILITY AND VALIDITY FOR DIFFERENT KINDS OF INSTRUMENTS
(continued)

2. Validity Concerns

   a. Is the scope of items (characteristics) sufficient to represent the trait being assessed? This calls for expert judgments of drafts of the instrument.

   b. Are items relevant to the trait? Again, expert judgment can be used, research and theory could be referenced.

   c. Can observers in fact "see" the characteristics they're being asked to observe and check for? This requires careful item construction and specific phrasing and should be checked empirically.

   d. Does the checklist measure validly? Do scores represent the intended traits? An extreme groups method can be used, wherein checklist scores should discriminate instances from non-instances. A checklist to assess a report's adequacy, for example, could be tried out on a known complete report and a known incomplete report. Or, you could correlate the checklist score against some other independent measure of the object.

HOW CAN YOU PLAN THE INFORMATION COLLECTION EFFORT TO GET THE BEST INFORMATION AT THE LOWEST COST?

The information collection phase of evaluation is often its most costly activity. It is also the activity that produces the "meat" in the evaluation effort: information. The whole information collection effort should be carefully choreographed so that it will get you the most information at the lowest cost. You will want to make maximum use of each data collection instance, to save repeated demands on your resources and respondents.

From the economy standpoint, the ideal information collection plan would tap just one source. This hypothetical source would be so rich and accurate that it would adequately address all the questions of the evaluation. Unfortunately, this ideal source (an oracle, perhaps) does not exist, and one must consider many varied sources and procedures. But, the trick is to get the maximum mileage out of the sources you are going to access. For example, if you're going to be analyzing students' work for one purpose, are there other purposes the same analysis might serve?

The more sources of information (more perspectives) you get for one question, the more sure and whole your conclusions will be. Evaluation needs the richer understanding multiple sources can bring. The error or bias inherent in any single measure can be counterbalanced by using multiple perspectives and information collection procedures.

Information collectors should pay due respect to Mr. Murphy and his laws: what can go wrong, will. To get the data you've planned on, you need to watch what gets done. And, you must protect the vested public interest and trust by maintaining adequate ethical and moral safeguards. Collecting information is a complex process, and it relies on many steps being carried out adequately and often by different persons. Breakdowns in logistics can seriously harm the quality of data collected, or even render it unusable.

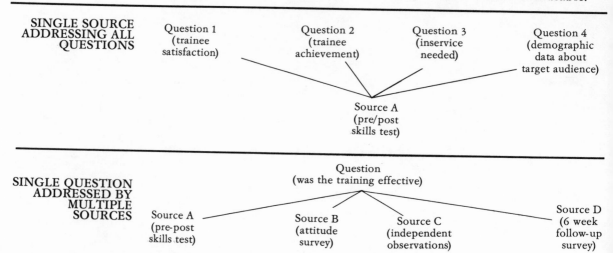

MULTIPLE MEASURES FOR MULTIPLE QUESTIONS

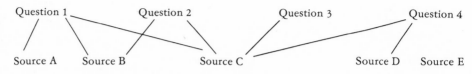

MULTIPLE MEASURES ANSWERING MULTIPLE QUESTIONS

EXAMPLE: A TRAINING WORKSHOP

Here some sources serve more than one question (like "Source C"). Also, each evaluation question is addressed by more than one source.

Here's the same multiple measures for multiple questions relationship pictured in a "matrix." *

Evaluation Questions

Information Collection Procedures	Knowledge Test	Behavioral Observation	Workshop Evaluation	Follow-Up Survey Questionnaire
Did they learn it	X			
Did they like it		X	X	X
Did they use what they learned		X		X
Did using what they learned make a difference		X	X	X
Was the training successful	X	X	X	X

* Frank Courts and Richard Quantz developed this very useful matrix format while working for the ETC project at the University of Virginia.

EXAMPLE: INFORMATION COLLECTION PLAN FOR A SCHOOL DISTRICT NEEDS
ASSESSMENT

QUESTIONS

INFORMATION COLLECTION PROCEDURES	1. What are pupils attitudes toward handicapped classmates	2. What are the achievement deficits of handicapped pupils?	3. What problems do teachers face in mainstream classrooms	4. What current services do handicapped children receive	5. What problems do handicapped children encounter in mainstreamed classrooms?
A. Administer questionnaire to sample of pupils	X				X
B. Interview parents of handicapped pupils	X	X	X	X	X
C. Visit and observe a sample of mainstream classrooms	X		X		X
D. Analyze test scores from sample of handicapped pupils		X			
E. Interview sample of teachers	X	X	X	X	X
F. Analyze records of pupil personnel services office				X	

NOTICE

▶ Some data collection procedures (like B) do double duty (quintuple duty really).

▶ Multiple sources are provided for each question.

▶ Keep adding rows (more procedures) and moving "X's" around until you're satisfied you've optimally blended economy and multiple perspectives (see the Design Manual for more specific steps).

CONSTRUCT THE LOGISTICAL PLAN

Who will conduct the called for observations, ratings, etc. How likely are they to respond to various formats and procedures (e.g., interviews, questionnaires, self-report/observations measures)? Is their educational and experiential background such that special terminology is required to avoid ambiguity and elicit complete and accurate information? Is a special incentive required to insure full participation? Will they be willing to provide the information required? What biases or particular problems of the group should be considered in designing the procedure? Can they handle the job?

Just *when* are observations to be made, instruments delivered and picked up, etc.? The setting and timing of an information collection procedure must be carefully considered. Would teachers' perceptions of problems be characteristically different in the beginning of the year as opposed to the end of the year? Various legal, contract, or policy constraints must also be considered. Would the teachers' union cooperate with a survey or observations, and if so, under what conditions? Will you hand out instruments after a break? Before lunch?

Where will observations be made, interviews conducted, instruments administered? Special characteristics of the setting can influence data collected. An interview in *her* office might net different reactions, or be less controlled, than one in *yours*. A particular room or setting may contain clues and uses that will bias results.

What *timing, schedules,* are respondents and collectors to follow? The sequence or frequency of some information collection procedures can affect results. Essays graded first may be graded more harshly, final interviews in a busy schedule may be cursory, etc.

How are instruments, records, etc. to be returned? To whom? By when? A mailed survey, even though completed, may never get returned if it's a hassle to do so; participants in a rush to leave a workshop may not find someone to turn their rating forms to, etc.

It is a good idea to put your plan into writing, so it can be more easily checked over, monitored and adhered to. Gantt charts are especially useful, for they can show busy periods, overloads, slack times, etc.

See the following page for another example of a logistic planning form, called a "work plan." It shows when and how procedures will get carried out.

EVALUATION WORKPLAN

Instrument	Instrument Status	Evaluation Questions Addressed	Administration Schedule	Administrators	Respondents	Sample	Data Analysis Procedure	Report Available
1. Practicum Preference Form	Completed	B1	before practicum placement	self administered	Student	All students	Frequency, compare to site profile	4 weeks after practicum placement
2. Student Practicum Log Analysis Form	Completed	B1, B2, B3, E1	monthly	self administered	Evaluator	Logs from each student	Frequency of activities, mean time per activity area	End of semester
3. Student Self-Rating Form	Completed	C1, C2, C3, C4	weekly	self administered	Student	All students	Frequency trend over time	Monthly
4. Supervisor Rating Form	Completed	C1, C2, C3, C4	bi-weekly	self administered	Supervisor	All supervisors	Frequency trend over time	End of semester
5. Two step Graduate Questionnaire:	Completed	D1, D2, D3	annually	self administered	Graduates	All graduates	Frequency analysis, central tendency trend by years	End of year
6. Graduate Follow-up Questionnaire: Employers	Completed	D3	annually	self administered	Graduate employers	All; contingent on graduates'	Frequency analysis, central tendency trend	End of year
7. Site Profile Analysis Form	Completed	B1	end of semester	evaluator	Evaluator	One per site	Content analysis; compare to Student	End of semester

Service Review Sheet						Sample of Records		
							central tendency	year
9. Contact Record Analysis Form	Ready for field test	A1, A2, A3	end of semester	evaluator	Evaluator	Record for all students	Content analysis frequency, mean time	End of semester
10. Resource Center Usage Form	Completed	A5	end of semester	evaluator	Evaluator	New Materials	Frequency by materials categories	End of semester
11. Drop Out Record Checklist	Completed	C4	annual	evaluator	Evaluator	All drop-out records	Content analysis	End of year
12. Module Feedback Form	Blueprint completed	A2, A3, A5	upon module completion	self administered	Students	All Students	Mean ratings	End of semester
13. Module Test Form	To be developed	A4, B1	upon module completion	self administered	Students	All Students	Mean ratings	End of semester
14. Diagnosis Analysis Checklist	Completed	C1, C2	end of practicum	evaluator	Evaluator	One per student	Content analysis frequency and rating scores	End of semester
15. Diagnosis Observation Sheet	To be developed	C1, C4	end of practicum	faculty	Faculty	One per student	Frequency by client type	End of semester
16. Lesson plan Analysis Sheet	Completed	C2, C3	end of practicum	evaluator	Evaluator	Random: 3 per student	Content analysis frequency, rating scores	End of semester
17. Classroom Observation Record	Blueprint Completed	C2, C3, C4	end of semester	faculty	Faculty	One per student	Frequency by client type	End of semester

Follow appropriate protocols, procedures and customs, and simple good manners.

Any information collection procedure makes demands on the time and attention of others. At best, failure to follow polite customs and protocols will earn you a bad reputation and cast the evaluation in a bad light; at worst, you may get bad, or no, data.

Get needed releases, permissions and clearances

In many cases, some information and data will simply not be available at all, unless certain permissions and releases are obtained. Some files and records, even persons, are not routinely accessible without prior arrangements. Or, you may obtain data but not be able to use or reference it because you don't have a needed release.

Monitor for consistency and good measurement practice

The more complex your procedures are, and the more they rely on others (e.g., a cadre of interviewers or document analysts), the more sure you need to be that everyone is playing by the same rules.

All aspects of the distribution, administration and return of instruments should be consistently carried out in all instances. If pupils in one school, for instance, did not receive test instructions while others did, their scores might likely be adversely affected. An interviewer who clarifies, repeats and rephrases questions will gather different responses than the interviewer who does not. In these cases, anomalies and differences in the data collection procedure can influence their results. Procedures must be designed so as to inhibit such anomalies, and monitored and reviewed to detect confounding anomalies when they occur.

Depart from your plan when you need to

There may be opportunities to gather unplanned for information. Don't let slavish adherence to a plan shut you off from other information. Likewise, don't stick to your plan if a need arises to vary. If, for instance, an interviewer has traveled 50 miles to meet with a superintendent but finds that some circumstance prohibits the superintendent's participation, it would probably be unwise to reject the offer to interview the assistant superintendent. The best laid plans are bound to need revision in the face of current events. Such revisions ought to be made when needed, but take care to document them when they occur and consider their potential consequences to the data collected.

Use appropriate coding, aggregation and reduction techniques (See next chapter: "Analyzing Information")

In many instances, data resulting from evaluation efforts will require reduction and aggregation just to be handled efficiently. In general, the larger the scope of information collection—the greater the number of completed instruments or forms—the more complex the aggregation and reduction scheme will have to be. On the other hand, it is critical to bear in mind that aggregation and reduction of *any* sort, while it can aid communication and interpretation, can remove meaning. For this reason, the less reduction, the better; the closer data are to their original, raw form, the richer they will be.

For example, a large-scale questionnaire survey requires careful planning to ensure that each form is returned, and pertinent data gleaned from it and prepared for analysis. Coding forms to record and portray each instrument's data need to be designed. The task of transferring data from completed instruments to a coding form is a simple clerical task, but one which if ill-planned or carried out lackadaisically can ruin the entire data collection effort. The aggregation and recording system must be accurate, so that the data are not changed by the aggregation process. The system must also be comprehensive, ensuring that all instrument items are recorded; in addition, extra information, such as date of receipt or other pertinent variables, may be included on the coding form. Finally, the aggregation system must be simple. Unnecessary complexity is likely to introduce error and contaminate the data needlessly.

Safeguard information with appropriate handling and filing procedures

Care must be taken to ensure that data and all reports based on it are responsibly handled, distributed and stored. Irresponsible or otherwise inadequate handling can do great harm to persons and their rights. Short of legal or ethical infringements, irresponsibility in the handling of data could do grave harm to future data collection efforts. We all live in a world of decreasing privacy and should do all we can to be attentive to persons' rights and feelings.

For all data collected, a record should be maintained and stored so that it might be retrieved, to verify or re-analyze it as may be necessary. Thus, an original set of survey forms should not be destroyed as soon as a frequency analysis is complete, for it may be useful at a later date to return to these raw data for verification or a new analysis.

HOW GOOD IS YOUR INFORMATION COLLECTION PLAN?

If you *had* the information you plan to collect for a given purpose/question, are you willing to defend the "answer?" If no, you need to plan to get more data.

Are there additional existing sources of information you haven't included?

Are there procedures planned whose payoff is so minimal they aren't worth the cost?

Is the additional perspective or added certainty you get from an additional source worth the cost?

Do you need, and can you use, the information you are planning to collect?

Are logistic arrangements sufficient to carry out all steps of each procedure?

Have safeguards and quality control checks been planned?

Are responsibilities and assignments clearly defined?

Are quality control checks being made to assure you that your plan is working?

Are sufficient records being maintained to document activities occurring?

Are human rights, customs and protocols being honored?

Are data being protected from breaches of ethics and promises?

Are data being organized, filed, and stored to maintain accessibility?

REFERENCES

Babbie, E.R. *Survey Research Methods*. Belmont, CA: Wadsworth, 1973.

Bruyn, S.T. *The Human Perspective in Sociology: The Methodology of Participant Observation*. Englewood Cliffs, N.J.: Prentice Hall, 1966.

Dalkey, N.C. *The Delphi Method: An Experimental Study of Group Opinion*. Santa Monica, CA: Rand Corporation, 1969.

Demaline, R.E. & Quinn, D.W. *Hints for Planning and Conducting a Survey and Bibliography of Survey Methods*. Kalamazoo, MI: Evaluation Center, Western Michigan University, 1979.

Ebel, R.L. *Measuring Educational Achievement*. Englewood Cliffs, N.J.: Prentice Hall, 1965.

Furst, N.J. *Systematic Classroom Observation*. In L. Deighten (Ed.), *Encyclopedia of Education*. New York: MacMillan, 1971.

Gronlund, N.E. *Constructing Achievement Tests*. Englewood Cliffs, N.J. Prentice Hall, 1968.

Guba, E.G. & Lincoln, Y.S. *Effective Evaluation: Improving the Usefulness of Evaluation Results Through Responsive and Naturalistic Approaches*. San Francisco: Jossey-Bass, 1981.

Patton, M.Q. *Qualitative Evaluation Methods*. Beverly Hills, CA: Sage, 1980.

Payne, S.L. *The Art of Asking Questions*. Princeton, N.J.: Princeton University Press, 1951.

Pennsylvania State Department of Education. *Suggested Methods for the Identification of Critical Goals*. Harrisburg, PA: Author, 1975.

Richardson, S., Dohrenwend, H.S., & Klein, D. *Interviewing: Its Forms and Functions*. New York: Basic Books, 1965.

Shaw, M.E. & Wright, J.M. *Scales for the Measurement of Attitudes*. New York: McGraw-Hill, 1967.

Sudman, S. *Applied Sampling*. New York: Academic Press, 1976.

Webb, E.J., Campbell, D.T., Schwartz, R.D. & Sechrest, L. *Unobtrusive Measures: Nonreactive Research in the Social Sciences*. Chicago: Rand McNally, 1966.

Analyzing and Interpreting Evaluation Information

WHAT IS IT

Analysis is the process of finding out what the information collected by the evaluation means. Analysis involves working with the data that have been collected to determine what conclusions these data support and how much support they provide for, or against, any conclusion. The purpose of analysis is to summarize from the data the messages it contains in order to bring this information to bear on tentative conclusions or decisions.

In most cases, analysis is done in stages. That is, the information is coded or organized so that some sense can be made of it (e.g., you put it in a frequency distribution, a percentage breakdown, or a set of lists). Once you "eyeball" your data using experience and common sense, you decide whether more analysis would be helpful and, if so, what kind. A more detailed analysis, while still preliminary, might entail using description (e.g., the average score, the high points on a response sheet, content analysis of how many times a topic was mentioned in an interview). Again, some interesting questions might emerge (e.g., "Persons in Friday's training session did better than those in Thursday's. Why?" or "Experienced teachers seem to be doing better in training than student teachers. Is the difference significant?") At this point, a secondary analysis using more sophisticated methods might be in order. For example, an inferential or correlational analysis might be done, external observers might be brought in to interview and observe, or a new data collection effort might be planned.

WHEN ANALYSIS DECISIONS ARE MADE

Early in the planning of an evaluation, some major analysis issues get decided. These early decisions are related to the purposes for the evaluation. For example, an evaluation to decide whether one training approach works better than another likely will find itself involved in some kind of comparative analysis, where the effects of training Strategy A are compared to information about the effects of Strategy B. On the other hand, an evaluation that will describe an innovative practicum might be more involved with qualitative analysis.

Later in the evaluation process when you decide on the kind of information to gather (test data, interviews, observations, etc.), the kinds of analysis to be performed are further narrowed and decided. And, you decide how to organize and store it when it is collected. Then, when information is finally collected—an interview round completed, a questionnaire returned, an observation report finished—analysis decisions are confronted again. Is it worth analyzing? What does it mean?

Analysis proceeds when data "come in" from information collection. First, data are organized and coded, then checked to see if they are complete and sound enough to warrant your time for analysis. Then, analysis for meaning begins and often cycles back through more information collection.

HOW WILL YOU HANDLE RETURNED DATA?

Data must be properly handled and stored in order to prepare it for analysis. This includes coding data (when called for), aggregating and organizing it, and storing it for safekeeping and ready access. The main idea is to organize data in ways that facilitate its use, and keep it from getting lost or forgotten.

Results of questionnaires, objective tests, checklists, observation records, and other quantitative methods used in training programs are readily and easily used if organized and coded. A coding system enables you to record the results of returned instruments on a single record. This code sheet can be scanned to get a "feel" for the data, and then data can be easily prepared for computer analysis.

There are two basic kinds of coding approaches you can use for quantitative data:

-numerical codes, where you break the narrative data down into smaller "pieces," for example, phrases, paragraphs, words, or sections, then assign numerals to each according to the rules of your coding scheme.

-literal codes, where narrative data are broken down and assigned to different literal categories, again according to the coding rules you establish.

EXAMPLE OF INTERVIEW DATA CODED NUMERICALLY

		Content Categories				
Nature of Problem		Assistance Provided		Results of Assistance		Perceived Value
Code #	Category	Code #	Category	Code #	Category	Code #	Category
10.	Instructional	20.	Demonstration	30.	Problem solved	40.	Very positive
11.	Scheduling	21.	Materials	31.	Problem persists	41.	Appreciative but qualified
12.	Diagnostic	22.	Instructions	32.	Problem improved	42.	Ambivalent
13.	Behavioral	23.	Referral to resource center	33.	Problem deferred	43.	Negative
14.	Administrative	24.	Referral to other teacher	34.	Other	44.	Other
15.	Other	25.	Other				

Normally, these categories could be drawn up only *after* narrative data were scrutinized. If categories were known and limited prior to inquiry, a questionnaire method would have been more efficient than interview.

When you code numerically, you are doing quantitative analysis of what used to be qualitative data. This might be useful, but it might also drastically sap your rich qualitative data of much of its meaning.

The codes above are strictly nominal (the numbers have no "value," they can't be added, subtracted, etc.)

EXAMPLE CODING
SYSTEM FOR
INTERVIEWS WITH
TRAINING
DIRECTORS

Categories

A. Context of problem requiring assistance
B. Kind of assistance provided
C. Results of assistance provided
D. Attitude of recipient about assistance received

How the categories would be used to code:

1. The interview summary could be cut up into pieces (or certain phrases, sentences, etc., transcribed) then sorted into categories labeled A, B, C, or D.
   OR
2. The coder could read the interview notes, circling phrases, sentences, etc., and marking them with the appropriate A-D code.

Nominal codes can be used simply as organizers. That is, you categorize and file the qualitative information (or interview in this case) using a nominal code. But when you analyze the data for meaning, you return to the qualitative information using the labels only to retrieve the data you want.

EXAMPLE CODING
SCHEME FOR
PORTION OF
A SURVEY
QUESTIONNAIRE

1. Your department   _____
2. Your faculty rank _____
3. How long have you been at Upstate U.?
   ☐ 0–3 years
   ☐ 4–10 years
   ☐ more than 10 years
4. Rate your agreement with the following comments:

Strongly Agree	Agree	Neutral/ Undecided	Disagree	Strongly Disagree
☐	☐	☐	☐	☐

Coding Scheme

Item 1 Column 1-2	Item 2 Column 3	Item 3 Column 4	Item 4 Column 5
00 = Blank	0 = Blank	0 = Blank	0 = Blank
01 = Accounting	1 = Instructor	1 = 0–3 years	1 = Strongly Agree
02 = Anthropology	2 = Assistant Professor	2 = 4–10 years	2 = Agree

EXAMPLE CODING SCHEME FOR PORTION OF A SURVEY QUESTIONNAIRE *(continued)*	Item 1 Column 1-2	Item 2 Column 3	Item 3 Column 4	Item 4 Column 5
	03 = Art	3 = Associate Professor	3 = more than 10 years	3 = Neutral/Undecided
	—			
	—	4 = Professor		4 = Disagree
	—	5 = Other		5 = Strongly Disagree
	39 = Sociology			
	40 = Special Ed.			
	41 = Speech & language pathology			
	42 = Other			

GUIDELINES FOR CODING & ORGANIZING DATA

1. *Use coding sparingly*
   Any coding you do transforms the data you have and potentially reduces the meaning. On the other hand, when you have a lot of data, coding is sometimes necessary for further analysis. In general, the larger the scope of the data collection effort, the more likely it is such procedures are necessary.

2. *Use the simplest coding scheme you can*
   Coding is like a second layer of data collection, and as such it can fall prey to reliability problems. If a coding scheme is complex and difficult, error is likely to be introduced. As a result, data will be made less reliable and useful.

3. *Carefully choose coding variables*
   You can code more than just the responses recorded on an instrument. Additional data may be useful for analysis. Some examples of additional coding variables are:

   When instrument was returned (e.g., early, late, serial, order)
   Who returned instrument (e.g., any demographic variables of interest)
   How instrument was returned (e.g., by mail, in person, by a friend, telephone response)
   Condition of instrument or other physical indicators (e.g., written on, dog-eared, crisp and clean, done in crayon)
   Whether respondent wrote *additional comments*, showed other signs of interest, care, etc.

4. *Train coders to accurately complete coding tasks*
   Normally, coding data is a simple clerical task. But, some training is probably in order. You don't want a bad job of coding to ruin an entire information collection effort.

5. *Design for coding*
   Incorporate coding into the instruments were possible. Design the instrument you use for the easiest possible coding.

GUIDELINES FOR CODING & ORGANIZING DATA *(continued)*

6. *Keep records*

Maintain a record of each coding and processing step so that these steps can be retraced if necessary.

7. *Maintain ethics*

Safeguard your data from breaches of ethics, human rights, laws, privileges and commitments (anonymity, confidentiality) made or implied by the evaluation.

OPTIONAL CATEGORIES FOR ORGANIZING AND FILING DATA

Organized by:

information collection procedure: all the teacher interviews are filed together, all work samples, analyses, etc.
evaluation question
chronological sequence (first month's data, second round together)
source (all teacher data together, all trainer data together)
program element (all course data, all practicum data)

Stored within:

discs and magnetic tapes to be accessed by computer
folder systems in file cabinets
a rolodex system, using numerical or narrative filing
a cross-referencing card (or rolodex) file that references data by some of the categories listed above, such as program element, source, evaluation question, when collected, etc.

Example:

Assume that data are filed in folders, one for each information collection method (or some other basis). Each document, for example, an interview summary, could be assigned a code, say:

05-B-12-02-6

05 - in file folder #5
B - an interview
12 - Schwartz Elementary School
02 - prepared in Spring 81
6 - workshop participant

A code like this lets you locate data when it's needed, regroup it for different analyses, and get it back to the right folder.

ARE YOUR DATA WORTH ANALYZING?

Sometimes problems with data collection "spoil" some or even all of the data you've collected so that you might not want to take the trouble to analyze it. You should "clean" the data removing those bits (e.g., partially completed instruments) that you don't want to analyze. Inspection of the data you have on hand may indicate that more collection of information is needed. Or, it may indicate that you need to restructure your analysis procedures.

With quantitative data collection instruments (e.g., a test, a survey questionnaire), verification takes place when all the data are returned and coded. In qualitative inquiry methods, such as case studies or site visits, data collectors often analyze and check their notes and findings as they proceed, in order to optimize information collection opportunities.

PROBLEMS TO LOOK FOR WHEN VERIFYING DATA	Problem	Example
	1. incomplete response, or interrupted collection process	An interview with a superintendent gets cancelled part-way through; or, so many interruptions occur that the response is fragmented and inconsistent.
	2. coding errors; inconsistent coding	Two coders produce different results on the same instrument; code numbers are entered in wrong column on a form.
	3. respondents aren't a representative sample of the population	Only those who stayed until the end of a workshop completed the final rating form.
	4. low return rate of instruments, and/or a low response rate on items	Many of the surveys from the sample aren't returned and/or of the ones that were returned, many are incomplete.
	5. returned data which aren't from a representative sample of the population	Only parents who have handicapped children returned the questionnaire, even though they were sent to all parents in the district.
	6. administration and monitoring procedures which are not implemented as they were planned	Observations of some teachers occur one month after the workshop instead of three months as intended; some interviewers didn't explain questions.
	7. unusual responses; responses outside of the possible range	A classroom teacher who indicates that he/she serves 100 handicapped students per day.
	8. unlike responses on similar items by a respondent or like responses on opposite items	Respondent indicates a "high" rating on interest level of workshop and a "high" rating on how boring the workshop was.

PROBLEMS TO LOOK FOR WHEN VERIFYING DATA
(continued)

9. a series of like responses which seem to indicate that the respondent was not attending to individual items

The "middle" response (3) is circled for many items in a series of five-point rating scales, showing a particular pattern, on unrelated topics.

10. persons rating or observing the same thing classify it differently

In a behavioral observation, raters do not have uniform results because they are focusing on different aspects of the activity.

SOME VERIFICATION AND "CLEANING" PROCEDURES

"Eyeball" methods
scanning the code sheets can identify odd-ball responses, blank spaces, incorrect entries, etc.
incomplete interviews will be short
pages missing from forms
questions left blank

Spot-checks
arbitrarily select code sheets and compare against questionnaires
choose completed forms (e.g., tests) at random and check for accuracy and completeness

Audit
information collection procedures are retraced to ensure no breaches of good measurement practice invalidated data (e.g., a survey sent by mail in one district but carried home by pupils in another may not represent comparable samples. Or, failure to follow appropriate protocol or obtain needed releases may render data unusable.)

Group meetings of analyzers, interviewers
data collectors meet and discuss the procedures used
comparisons are made
problems that may have invalidated data emerge

Follow-up, repeated measures
persons interviewed are recontacted to elicit reactions to interview process
adherence to protocol is verified
unreliable information is identified

Ratings of accuracy, reliability
instruments (or interviewers) themselves ask respondents to rate the soundness of their own responses
respondents judge how thoroughly or reliably they could make responses. Example: "How accurate are your estimates of client load?"
☐ Extremely: based on good records
☐ Quite: based on memory
☐ Poor: I'm not very sure

GENERAL GUIDELINES FOR VERIFYING DATA

1. *The more complex the instrumentation and coding scheme* (e.g., a 12-page questionnaire), *the more likely there will be errors.*
2. *The larger the data collection effort, the more likely you'll obtain odd-ball information.* The tradeoff is that when there's a lot of data, a few bad items or messed up instruments will have less overall consequence.
3. *When precision demands are high—important decisions will ride on the data collected—you should do careful screening and cleaning of data.* Project proposals have not been funded because clerks mistotaled rater's point awards!
4. *If planned analysis procedures are extensive and expensive, then it becomes more important to spend time being sure you have data worth analyzing.*
5. *Set—and use—verification rules.* The verification step sometimes results in some data being discarded or analyzed separately; the purpose, after all, is to weed out bad data. You need "rules" to go by here. A survey analysis scheme may determine, for instance, that any instrument with less than 75% completion will be rejected from the sample. Or you may decide not to analyze further any interview data resulting from a session that lasted less than 10 minutes. Such rules are necessarily arbitrary and probably cannot be made until one has a notion of how the data actually look.
6. *Consider the possible biasing effects of verification rules.* As you decide not to use certain data, you run the risk of bias. Partially complete tests may represent slow readers; partially completed questionnaires may derive from a unique (e.g., negative, turned-off) sub-population; incomplete interviews may represent the busiest, most influential interviewees.
7. *Consider sub-analyses for weeded-out data.* Rather than discard potentially erroneous data, you may learn something useful from a separate analysis of it.
8. *Consider and deal with sampling effects.* You need to know if the samples you have are what you've planned on. Has some quirk in the information procedure given you a bad sample?

   a. Review the actual conduct of the data collection procedure looking for consistency and aberrations.
      - were instructions followed uniformly?
      - did collection occur under similar circumstances?
      - are returns especially low or unbalanced?
      - did raters or interviewers follow parallel procedures and rules?
   b. *Adjust analysis procedures where you suspect sampling problems.* You may be able to account for sampling errors if you determine the nature of differences in the samples you have.
      - compare the characteristics of your obtained sample to know what's known about the population.
      - determine the characteristics of the sample you in fact have. For example, in a low-return circumstance, see if those who did return survey forms represent a particular subgroup (e.g., recent graduates).
      - check a few non-respondents to determine how they differ from respondents.
   c. Collect more information; re-conduct the information procedure to procure a better sample.

SOME CRITERIA FOR VERIFICATION

1. All data collected should be verified, if only by a quick spot check.
2. Verification should not destroy or discard data that could represent a special opportunity (e.g., following up a low-return sample, determining why refusers refused).
3. Use consistent verification rules within each data set. Varying rules for same set of data (e.g., a set of questionnaires) could inordinately bias your analysis.
4. Document verification procedures, especially when data are rejected from analysis.
5. Increase verification attention as major decisions ride on results of analysis.

HOW WILL YOU ANALYZE THE INFORMATION?

The process of analysis is cyclical, and it works in a "Sherlock Holmes" fashion. Your initial data are beginning clues. You formulate hunches and tentative conclusions based on these clues, then work with your data (or collect more) to determine how well your hunches are substantiated or hold up. This leads you to more clues, then to more analysis and/or collection. As you move through these cycles, you learn and become more certain.

This section present procedures for guiding analysis and provides you with several examples of different kinds of analysis and considerations for assessing the sufficiency of the data and analyses you have completed.

GUIDELINES AND PROCEDURES FOR ANALYSIS

There are four (4) steps that you should consider in conducting analyses:
review the questions (or purposes) to be addressed by the evaluation
prepare descriptive analyses and frequency distributions (in quantitative data) for each set of data and display the results
prepare a summary of basic issues, trends, relationships and questions evident in the data
assess the available evidence in light of the issues and questions to be pursued.

1. *Review the questions to be addressed.*
   The evaluation questions that guided information collection were, of course, already identified before you got to this point. But now, they should be reviewed to help guide the analysis.

   a. Are the questions still appropriate in light of what's happened in the program and evaluation up to this point?
   b. Are there new questions that should be addressed?
   c. Are the questions sufficiently clear to guide analysis? Do you know what they mean?

   It is important that the evaluation clients and audiences be collaborated with and considered in this review.

2. *Prepare descriptive analyses.*
Descriptive analyses are meant to reduce the data into a briefer form so that its key features become more evident. The kind of analysis done depends on the kind of data you have gathered. In general, there are two kinds of descriptive analyses available:

a. Quantitative methods—included here are:
   1. descriptions of central tendencies, such as means, modes, medians
   2. descriptions of dispersion in the data, like range, standard deviations, variance
   3. frequency distributions, that show frequencies of response, numbers who chose certain options, etc.
   4. comparison of individual scores to group scores (percentile ranks, etc.)
b. Qualitative methods
   These methods are used to organize narrative information (like interview records, student essays, sample reports) into briefer narrative summaries that highlight key features of interest.* Again, what you use depends largely on the data you have. Some commonly used options are:
   1. checklist analysis, in which "yes-no" decisions are made as to whether a report contains certain information, a document has a key component, etc.
   2. content analysis, in which a document's characteristics and content are classified in different categories
   3. précis, summary analysis, in which narrative data are collapsed into briefer summaries

3. *Note basic issues, trends, relationships and questions.*
The point of this step is to decide what you have and what you want to do with it next. You review your preliminary analyses and determine what the data appear to be telling you.

Your options for completing this step range from a quick eyeball to more elaborate methods.

a. informal notation of hypotheses, questions, issues, etc. The least any evaluation should do is scan the preliminary analyses and make notes about what seems to be evident.
b. formal listing of hypotheses, issues, questions, etc. These listings, along with the preliminary analysis summaries, can be provided to several persons for their review and revision.
c. group reviews which can generate issues and questions or review and comment on those already listed.
d. formal hearing and panel reviews by key persons/experts.
e. preparation of working papers based on some major topics (e.g., the context, program description, effects). These papers would provide in-depth consideration of the preliminary analyses in light of the assigned topic.

---

* Often, you may decide not to reduce qualitative data in a descriptive summary, but to analyze it just like it is.

4. *Assess the available evidence.*

This is a "go-no-go" decision point. Considering the questions that the preliminary analysis stimulated, do you have what you need to perform more analysis? Do you need to recycle and collect more data?

Some decisions to make here are:

a. Are there issues, questions, hunches, etc. worth pursuing via further analyses? Are such questions sufficiently explicit that they can be used to guide further analyses?

b. Is there sufficient data to carry out the analyses needed to pursue the questions
- are samples of sufficient size?
- will missing data endanger conclusions?

c. Do the data you have available meet the requisite assumptions (e.g., homogeneity of variance, linearity) for the further analyses that are projected?

IMPORTANT PRINCIPLES AND CRITERIA TO GUIDE ANALYSIS

Don't oversimplify.

Evaluation questions almost always relate to complex dynamic phenomena. The analytic procedure must be sensitive to such complexities and not reduce them for analytic convenience to an oversimplistic notion.

Account for differential effects and conditions.

You should avoid overall measures and analyses that assume an unrealistic uniformity. Program functions differ from location to location; participant needs, interactions and outcomes will differ by participant characteristics. Analyses should be conducted for different sub-groups or should account for sub-group differences.

Use multiple techniques.

Different analytic techniques employ different assumptions about the data. Where possible, multiple analyses based on different assumptions should be used.

Make sure assumptions of techniques to be used are met by the data you have.

A common violation in evaluation studies is to treat ordinal data (ratings, etc.) as if they were interval (data which can be added and averaged). Often, parametric statistics (t-tests, F-tests) are applied when their assumptions (e.g., that the group represents a "normal curve" or is homogenous) cannot be met. Sometimes this is acceptable, for the violation doesn't make much difference (that is, the analysis technique is robust and can compensate for the faulty assumption). There are methods for estimating statistically the extent to which assumption-violations weaken results.

The rule is: be aware of the assumptions, and account for violations. *Just because an analysis operation is mathematically possible, doesn't mean it should be done.* Check with someone who has expertise in statistics for guidance when applying a statistic.

Use methods appropriate for audiences and purposes.

Analytic techniques should be chosen not to dazzle but to inform. Very often, the best, most communicative and convincing method will not be the most sophisticated. Choose one that will get the informing job done in the simplest, most direct way possible.

Use methods that are practical and affordable.

Do not plan collection efforts that require computers if you do not have ready computer access. Consider costs for expert judges, consultants, etc. Use resources available, such as graduate students, local expertise, libraries and computer centers.

Keep it simple.

Save the sophisticated and fancy techniques for journal articles and professional conferences. Most evaluation consumers are plain folks who need more to be informed than dazzled with analytic virtuosity.

Don't be overly rigorous.

The use of rigorous analytic methods intended for interval and ratio data allows the use of powerful statistic tools. When assumptions for such methods as covariant analysis or factor analysis can be met and the methods will yield needed information, use them. But, in transforming data to allow use of these powerful techniques, you should be careful that you haven't transformed the meaning of the data you have.

ANALYTIC
PROCEDURES
COMMONLY USED
IN TRAINING
PROGRAM
EVALUATION

There are two basic types of analytic procedures used in evaluation of training programs:

1. quantitative procedures for analyzing data consisting of numbers; and
2. qualitative procedures for analyzing primarily narrative data. Descriptions and examples of these procedures follow.

QUANTITATIVE PROCEDURES AND EXAMPLES

Here's a chart that lists three major kinds of quantitative analyses: *descriptive statistics, correlational analysis*, and *hypothesis testing*. The chart lists procedures

ANALYTIC
PROCEDURES
COMMONLY USED
IN TRAINING
PROGRAM
EVALUATION
(continued)

for each kind, showing the major sorts of questions they address and for which level of measurement data each is appropriate.

Following the chart is a description of each type and some example analyses.

Commonly Followed Analysis Methods for Some Kinds of
Quantitative Data Typically Collected in Personnel Preparation Programs
(behavior observations, objective tests, rating scales, questionnaires)

Analysis Questions to be Addressed	Level of Measurement* (see notes below)		
	Nominal	Ordinal	Interval/Ratio
1. What do the scores "look like"? e.g., the distribution of answers to each of six multiple choice questions, the number of times participant questions were asked for each workshop unit	frequency distribution bar graph (histogram) line graph (frequency polygon)	frequency distribution bar graph (histogram) line graph (frequency polygon)	frequency distribution bar graph (histogram) line graph (frequency polygon)
2. What is the typical score; what represents the middle of the group? e.g., the topic most people want on the inservice agenda, the average number of years teachers have worked for the school	mode	mode median	mode median mean
3. How much do the scores "spread out"? e.g., the percentage of graduates getting jobs within six months, the high and low scores on the knowledge test	proportions percentages	range semi-interquartile range	range semi-interquartile range Standard Deviation
4. How does an individual score compare to the rest of the group? e.g., the rank of each state for number of federal projects awarded, the rank of each trainee on the supervisor rating		percentile rank	percentile rank standard scores
5. How do sets of scores change together? e.g., the relationship between amount of training received and number of supervisor citations	correlation (see correlation chart, p. 137)	correlation (see correlation chart, p. 137)	correlation see correlation chart, p. 137)

ANALYTIC
PROCEDURES
COMMONLY USED
IN TRAINING
PROGRAM
EVALUATION
(continued)

Commonly Followed Analysis Methods *(continued)*

Analysis Questions to be Addressed	Level of Measurement* (see notes below)		
	Nominal	Ordinal	Interval/Ratio
6. Are the sets of scores from different groups "really" different? e.g., the average performance rating of employees receiving training compared to those who were not trained	non-parametric tests, e.g., Chi-square	non-parametric tests e.g., median test para-metric tests e.g., when ratings thought of as interval data	parametric tests e.g., difference between mean (t-test), analysis of variance

*Measurement Scales
Nominal: categories, names
   Discrete: no underlying order; e.g., names of school buildings
   Continuous: underlying order; e.g., low, medium, high for parents' income levels
Ordinal: numerical categories with some underlying order, ranked according to that order; e.g., scoring
   1 to 5 for top five training priorities
Interval: numerical categories scaled according to the amount of the characteristic they possess, intervals
   are of equal value and zero is just another point on the scale; e.g., scores on PL 94-142
   knowledge test.
Ratio: same as Interval except that zero represents a complete absence of the characteristic being
   measured; e.g., this year's training budget.

Descriptive statistics

Frequency distribution

A frequency distribution is a collection of scores (usually raw scores) that have been arranged together in order from low to high values with the number of people (or other unit of interest) having each value presented. A frequency distribution is usually presented in a table listing the numbers of individuals with scores in each category or as a bar graph (histogram) or line graph (frequency polygon).

Mean, Median, and Mode

The mean, median, and mode are three different ways to describe the "central tendency" of a group of scores. The mean is obtained by adding together all of the values in a group of scores and dividing that sum by the total number of scores. The median is the score in a group of scores above which exactly half the score values are found and below which half are found. The mode is the value that occurs most often in a given group of scores. Much of the time, all of these ways to pick out a "typical" score will give you pretty close to the same answer. This is the case when the frequency distribution is nearly "normal" or forms a "bell-shaped curve."

But in skewed score distributions, these statistics can be quite different. For example, because a few people earn a lot of money in a city, the *mean* personal income might be high ($44,000); yet, half the people in the city might earn less than $20,000, the *median* income level.

Range and Standard Deviation

The range and standard deviation are two ways to describe the "dispersion" or spread of a group of scores. The range is the difference between the highest and lowest values in a group of scores. The standard deviation is the square root of the average of the squared deviations from the mean of the group. It is also the unit of measurement used to express "standard scores." A standard score is used to indicate the number of standard deviations a corresponding actual or "raw score" is above or below the mean. Scores that spread out a lot will have a high standard deviation and a broad range. Scores that cluster together (are much alike) will have a narrow range and a lower standard deviation.

Percentile rank and standard scores

Percentile rank and standard scores are two ways to describe how an individual score compares with the rest of the group. The rank is the percentage of cases which fall below a given individual score. A standard score is expressed in terms of standard deviation units above or below the mean of the group. The standard score scale depends on the numerical value assigned to the mean and to the standard deviation. For example, if the scale is set with the group mean (whatever it is) equal to 50, and the standard deviation (whatever it is) equal to 10, then an individual score (whatever it is) that falls half a standard deviation above the mean would receive a value of 55.

EXAMPLE #1   EXAMPLES OF DESCRIPTIVE STATISTICS

A large city school district was in the process of developing a one-day training workshop for its special education staff related to new requirements for planning and delivering services to students in special education. Since they planned to do the training in two groups anyway, they decided to randomly assign staff to the first or second session and then give a knowledge test to both groups after the first session to help decide if the training made a difference.

They administered a 75 point test to thirty people in each group, tabulated the results, summarized each group's performance, and compared the two. Here is a summary of what they found:

EXAMPLE #1
(continued)

Total Scores for Each Staff Person on Public Law (PL) 94-142 Test

	Without Training	With Training		Without Training	With Training		Without Training	With Training
1	15	29	11	22	20	21	14	33
2	19	49	12	24	34	22	20	45
3	21	48	13	49	28	23	30	35
4	27	35	14	46	35	24	32	39
5	35	53	15	52	42	25	34	36
6	47	39	16	44	43	26	42	48
7	46	23	17	64	46	27	40	63
8	38	74	18	61	47	28	38	57
9	33	72	19	55	40	29	54	56
10	67	50	20	54	54	30	56	65

SUMMARY OF DESCRIPTIVE STATISTICS ON KNOWLEDGE TEST

	Mean	Standard Deviation	Variance	Number
Without training	39.30	14.98	224.29	30
With training	44.60	13.36	178.39	30

	Median	Mode	Maximum	Minimum
Without training	39	38	67	14
With training	44	35	74	20

LINE GRAPH (FREQUENCY POLYGON) FOR KNOWLEDGE TEST

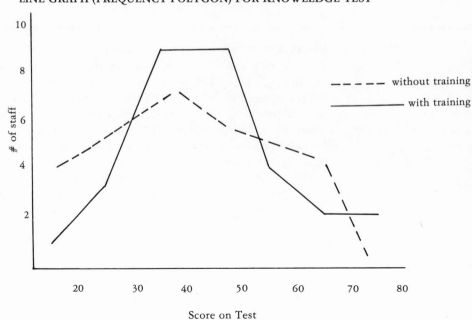

EXAMPLE #2   Here's another way of displaying similar information. In this case, the numbers (means, etc.) have been replaced by verbal statements representing a specific score category (like 0–2 = "low," 3–5 = "high"). The data shown are from a school survey.

	Respondents		
Variable	Regular Teachers	Special Education Teachers	Administrators
1. Self-rating knowledge on:			Note: response rate low
a. handicapping conditions	low	high	low
b. individualized instruction based on IEP	medium	high	low
c. resources/referrals	high	high	medium
2. Rating of knowledge by others:			
a. handicapping conditions	low	high	low
b. individualized instruction	low	high	low
c. resources/referrals	low	low	low
3. Problem ranking (highest 2)	inadequate planning time	inappropriate requests	too much paperwork
	getting enough help	too much paperwork	parent relations
(lowest 2)	knowledge of methods	knowledge of methods	knowledge of methods
	parent relations	access to resources	getting enough help
4. Knowledge test of District procedures for 94-142	low	high	medium/low
5. Training preferences	want release time	think classroom teachers need more theory	want release time dollars
	prefer in building	don't think selves need training	want involvement in training design
	less theory, more "skills"		

EXAMPLE #3   Here's another example of descriptive statistics used to portray the results of a checklist analysis of records maintained in a resource center.

Materials Re:	Total in % Available	Frequency of Use Sept.–Nov.	% of Total Usage	Increase/Decrease Over Last Year Same Quarter
Federal Regulations	15%	6	9%	1% increase
filmstrips		2		
articles		0		
handbooks for implementing		2		
etc.		0		
etc.		2		
Classroom & Behavior Management	40%	4	6%	2% decrease
texts		2		
problem diagnosis kits		0		
films		0		
intervention strategy pamphlets		1		
articles		0		
special technique handbooks		1		
etc.		0		
etc.		0		
Testing & Assessment	30%	27	41%	2% increase
reading		13		
mathematics		7		
career education		1		
values clarification		0		
etc.		6		
Classroom Methodology Packets	15%	29	44%	no change
Houzon-Furst Questioning		0		
SCI Sets		2		
Learning Center Packages		2		
etc.		15		
etc.		10		
	100%		100%	

Total Frequency = 67

Correlational analysis

Correlational analysis gives you an estimate of the size and direction of the linear relationship between two variables. It can usually be a number between -1 and $+1$. It *does not* provide an estimate of how likely it is that one variable *causes* changes in another. It is often used to a) describe relationships between variables more clearly, b) explore possible cause and effect relationships to be pursued later on, or c) supplement other evidence about how events seem to influence each other when a randomized experiment is not a reasonable alternative. Recommended types of correlation coefficients to use with different combinations of measurement scales are presented in the chart below.

Chart Showing Correlation Coefficient
Appropriate to Scales of Measurement for Variable X and Variable Y*

Scale of Measurement for Variable Y*	Scale of Measurement for Variable X			
	Discrete-Nominal	Continuous-Nominal	Ordinal	Interval/Ratio
Discrete-Nominal	1. a. *Phi (ϕ) b. Contingency Coefficient (C)	(5)	(8)	(10)
Continuous-Nominal	5. ** ↑	2. a. Tetrachoric b. multicell	(6)	(9)
Ordinal	8. Rank Biserial (r_{rb})	6. ** ←	3. a. *Spearman Rho (ρ) b. Kendall's Tau (τ)	(7)
Interval/Ratio	10. *Point Biserial (r_{pb})	9. Biserial (r_b)	7. ** ↑	4. Pearson (r)

* a special case of the Pearson r
** an undefined correlation coefficient, the preferred alternative is in the adjacent box indicated by the arrow

Chart adapted from G.V. Glass & J.C. Stanley, *Statistical Methods in Education and Psychology* (Englewood Cliffs, NJ: Prentice Hall, 1970), p. 158; and from D.E. Hinkle, W. Wiersma, & S.G. Jurs, *Applied Statistics for the Behavioral Sciences* (Chicago: Rand McNally, 1979), p. 96.

EXAMPLE OF CORRELATIONAL ANALYSIS

An agency has begun providing training to all its clerical employees to help them follow new legal client record requirements. In some agencies, nearly everyone has been trained, while in others, very few have been. In order to determine possible training impact, the agency analyzed data (already on hand) of errors in records and violations of record regulations leading to state reprimands (serious violations). Based on the correlation data shown below, they argued that the training didn't seem to affect overall error rates but was related to reducing serious violations.

Relationship Between Proportion of
Clerks Trained and Branch Office Error Rates

Proportion of Clerks Receiving Training	Average No. of All Errors*	Average No. of Serious Errors*
0– 20%	16	6
20– 40%	12	6
40– 60%	18	4
60– 80%	13	3
80–100%	15	1
Correlation Coef. =	−.07	−.97

* Monthly per-clerk rates

HYPOTHESIS TESTING

When you have information on two or more groups of people, like those who attended a workshop and those who did not, you can use that information to estimate whether those groups are "really" different. Hypothesis testing is a way of deciding whether differences found between groups are likely to be "true" differences or ones that could simply have come about by chance fluctuation in the data. Some characteristics of the groups that you would be most likely to compare include means, proportions, correlations, and variances (the standard deviation squared). The particular analysis you would use depends on a number of things, like the estimates you would like to test, the levels of measurement you have (e.g., names, ranks, intervals, ratios), and how you selected the groups you have information on (e.g., is information from one group independent of others).

EXAMPLE

After the large city school district (see Example #1 for Descriptive Statistics) put together their descriptive summaries, they performed a *t-test* to decide if the two groups (special education staff who attended a training workshop and those who did not) differed on the knowledge test. They also decided that they wanted to be 95% confident that any differences between the mean scores of the two groups were not due to chance. They computed the following "t" value and probability based on the information for the two groups.

	Number	Mean	Standard Deviation
Without training	30	39.30	14.98
With training	30	44.60	13.36

difference = 5.30   t = 1.45   probability = 0.15

They concluded that the 5.3 point difference between mean scores of the special education staff who did and did not attend the training workshop could have happened by chance alone. This finding, along with feedback from the first group of workshop participants, prompted the trainers to revise the workshop for the second group.

QUALITATIVE ANALYSIS METHODS

These are methods used to derive meaning from rich descriptive materials such as interview summaries, case studies, site visit reports, sets of records, and so forth. Such materials are usually primarily narrative (versus numerical).

As with quantitative analysis, there are many procedures and approaches available. And, there is a rich literature on the topic; see the chapter bibliography for some useful references. We have included here only a very brief and superficial sampling of the options, trying to relate these especially to the kinds of qualitative data that might be collected in a training program evaluation.

Qualitative analysis procedures differ from quantitative approaches in that they are not so mechanistic and prescriptive. The steps in computing an "F"-test are fixed and unvarying; there are no equally specific and pre-determined steps for conducting a qualitative analysis. Rather, there are conceptual frameworks, cues and guidelines that an analyst may find helpful. But you will not find a cookbook.

The social phenomenon approach*

This approach provides six (6) units for inquiry and interpretation based on a continuum of levels of social phenomena, from the smallest level (an act) to the largest level (a complete setting). The next table describes these six levels and shows two kinds of analysis—static and phase—that can be used to guide inquiry into each level.

---

* This is borrowed loosely from John Lofland, *Analyzing Social Settings* (Wadsworth Publishing), Belmont, California, 1971.

Different Questions to Guide Inquiry
Defined by Levels of Social Phenomena and Kinds of Analysis

	Static Depiction of Phenomena	Depiction of Phases, Stages and Sequences
1. Acts: specific, brief action	What are acts comprised of? What categories do they represent? What labels can be assigned? What acts recur?	What led up to an act? What sequences occurred within a single act? What stages of acts recur?
2. Activities: action of a longer or continuing duration, especially by groups	What patterns and categories of activities exist? Are there characteristic types of activities, actors, and results?	Are there stages and phases that can be identified for all, or different kinds of, participants?
3. Meanings: the verbal signs of people involved that define and direct their action	What basic ideas do actors hold? What are norms and expectations? What explanations are given by participants?	What transformations in meaning occur? What changes in viewpoints, norms, expectations, etc. happen? Are there patterns or stages of change?
4. Participation: how people behave, react, etc. in a given setting	What kinds of persons (or personalities) are involved? What labels characterize participants? What levels and patterns of involvement exist?	Are there cycles or stages of participation?
5. Relationships: among several persons in a given time, in a given setting	What kinds of interactions and interrelationships are there? What hierarchies exist?	Do relationships move through stages and patterns of change?
6. Setting: the entire setting under study conceived of as a whole unit	What label or type characterizes a setting? What general types of settings can be discerned?	What stages or phases has the setting passed through? At what stage or phase is the setting now?

Example

A state department of education provided grants to several schools to conduct inservice training. As part of an evaluation effort to determine what kinds of benefits, changes, and impacts those grants had helped stimulate, they commissioned several case-studies to be conducted—one per site—by a graduate class from the local university. The case-study reports were then provided to readers (a few readers per case). The readers were asked to study the cases, guiding their analysis using the Activities, Participation, Relationship and Setting Categories from the preceding table. Then, they were asked to report their conclusions, citing the categories, as to what evidence supported or refuted the hypothesis that teachers and pupils had benefitted from the inservice.

Content analysis

Content analysis is a way of objectively and systematically identifying particular characteristics of documents, records, or any other kind of retrievable communication. Four major characteristics of content analysis include:

the process is carried out using specific rules and procedures;
it is systematic;
it aims toward generalizable conclusions;
analysis is of what is actually present, not an "interpretation."

Good classification categories should have the following characteristics:

they reflect the purposes of the study;
they should be exhaustive—cover all of the possibilities;
they should be mutually exclusive—have no or little overlap;
they should be independent—classification of one piece of information should not determine the classification of another;
they should reflect a single classification principle—e.g., classify only what is "in print."

Example

As part of an overall staff development program, a school district had established a technical assistance system to facilitate mainstreaming activities in the elementary schools. The Technical Assistance staff had the general impression that things were not going as smoothly as they could be, but they did not feel that they had a good handle on what was going on. As an initial step, they decided to interview a group of teachers in one building to get an idea of how the system was being used and what the teachers' attitudes were about it.

Following a semi-structured interview, key categories for summarizing comments were selected (some qualitative, some quantitative) and the relevant responses from each teacher were recorded. A section of this interview summary is in the next table. This analysis provided a manageable level of information for the technical assistance staff to use to start focusing on a variety of strengths and weaknesses of the system.

Example of Content Analysis (*continued*)

Interview Summaries

Interview	Background	Context of Problem	Categories		Summary: Attitudes toward T.A. System
			Assistance Requested/Provided	Results of Assistance	
7	Music tchr	Problems in providing music training for deaf student	Request help (materials, suggestions); Spec. Ed. tchr met w/music tchr and suggested materials emphasizing rhythm exercises	All of the children responded to the rhythm materials	Good system to have available.
8	4th grade tchr 23 students 2 handicapped children	Has child who is confined to a wheelchair—is always left out of activities during recess	Request training in recreational activities which don't require the use of the legs; P.E. tchr met w/classroom tchr leaving lots of ideas for recreational activities for small or large groups of children	Handicapped child suddenly seen as "special" by classmates because he knew games they didn't—they all wanted to learn	Tchr found that many of these activities could be done right in the classroom—and made good use of them on rainy days during recess time; has since shared many of the ideas w/other tchrs. Tchr had to buy own materials.

Tchr felt that no help was offered.

wasn't doing such a bad job of record-keeping after all

Request forms to simplify record-keeping; Building Team member discussed problems of recordkeeping w/tchr

Recordkeeping seems inadequate

4th grade tchr 22 students 3 handicapped children

Summary (in frequencies)

Tchrs	Problem Type	Requests Made	Results of Assistance	Summary of Attitudes
(9 interviews)				
(2) 1st grade	(1) reading	(4) materials	Negative = 4	(2) system is poor action taken, no help offered
(3) 3rd grade	(3) behavior	(4) consultation	Positive = 7	
(2) 4th grade	(1) motivation	(2) training		(3) materials difficult to access
(1) 5th grade	(1) handwriting	(1) referral		
(1) Spec. area	(1) music			(5) system is helpful
	(1) physical	Requests Provided		
	(2) recordkeeping	(5) materials		
		(2) direct contact w/child		
		(2) training		
		(4) consultation		

Records analysis

Qualitative analysis of records is distinguished from a quantitative analysis. A quantitative analysis might employ a checklist or aggregation form for gathering and summarizing, quantitatively, the numerical information from existing records. A qualitative approach would use a variety of techniques (e.g., content analysis, searching for clues and patterns, etc.) to pursue one or more questions, hunches, or tentative hypotheses. A useful approach for records analysis is called "tracking." Here, the evaluator forms one or more tentative hypotheses (e.g., "the teachers are using what they learned in the inservice"). The assumption is that when things happen, "tracks" are left. So, one searches for tangible evidence in a variety of records, looking for tracks that confirm, or disconfirm, the hypothesis.

Example

A district had been operating its resource center and teacher awareness program for several months. It wished to determine whether teachers had in fact made use of the center's resources in their school duties. Their working hypothesis was, " . . . Yes, there has been use!" Then, they projected what kinds of records and other tangible indicators would reflect such use, had there in fact been any.

They selected a small sample of teachers who had made several resource center visits and checked out materials. Then, from those teachers, they collected lesson plans, reports, faculty meeting minutes, principal's evaluation and classroom visit reports, and reports to parents. These materials were then intensively scrutinized, and evidence indicating usage of resource center materials was noted.

HOW WILL YOU INTERPRET THE RESULTS OF ANALYSES?

Interpretation is bringing meaning to the results of analysis; deciding on the significance and implications of what the data show. Interpretation involves making claims, such as: "The student can prepare an adequate lesson plan," or "Pat Jones is unable to interpret diagnostic data," or "The workshop helped teachers individualize instruction."

Interpretation of data also involves valuing and necessitates comparison of what the data show against some value, standard, expectation or other referent. Here are some sample results; *descriptive only* . . .

"Three site visitors felt that the workshop was a failure . . . "
Participants rated 'interest' at $\bar{X} = 3.2$ on a 1–5 scale"
"The teacher engaged in Schwartzian questioning techniques twice during the lesson"
"Participants achieved perfect (100%) scores on the post-test"
"No record contained a parent signature"

In the absence of referents, none of these data expositions has meaning beyond its descriptive function.

Now here are some possible *referents* . . .

the expertise (knowledge, experience, etc.) of site visitors
research on the expected and acceptable interest ratings of workshop participants
beliefs and values about proper teaching behaviors
previously established standards for performance (e.g., on tests)
laws and regulations

Comparing data against these referents allows interpretations (valuing). To continue, here are some example interpretations . . .

The workshop did not function as well as expected
Participants' interest was low and could explain poor performance
The teacher uses proper questioning technique
Participants met workshop knowledge objectives
Records are out of compliance with regard to parent signatures

POSSIBLE REFERENTS TO BE USED IN EVALUATING TRAINING

Expert judgments, opinions, viewpoints
Staff expectations, arbitrary standards
Public (democratic) viewpoints, e.g., as determined from a consensus or voting procedure
Special interest viewpoints (e.g., a handicapped parents group)
Research studies and reports (e.g., linking interest to learning)
Institutional standards, guidelines
Commonly accepted practice (e.g., adult learning theory)
Regulations, laws (e.g., federal guidelines)
Accreditation or licensing standards (e.g., AMA, NCATE, CEC, ASHA)
Probabilities, rates of occurrence, predictable likelihoods
Norms, expected scores, cutting scores

PROCEDURES FOR JUDGING FINDINGS

Statistical tests of significance
Consensus methods (Delphi, nominal group technique, Q-Sort, etc.)
Voting, democratic procedures
Discussions, meetings, reviews
Hearings, panel reviews
Debates
Jury trials
Individual opinions
Expert judgments

GUIDELINES FOR INTERPRETING

1. *Deal with multiple and conflicting evidence*
   In evaluation, not everything and usually hardly anything lends itself to a summation process of interpretation where you can "add up" the scores from several data sources and arrive at a convenient single conclusion. One cannot, for example, rely on a formula such as "$(2 \times$ participant reaction$) + (.07$ trainer's perception$) + (3 \times$ work accomplished$) =$ success of workshop."

   Our knowledge of many variables and the interrelationships among them is limited and prevents us from such manipulations. More often, we must rely on a holistic approach, wherein we react and judge based on a reaction to the whole of something as we consider data about its element parts. Or, we must interpret each element or part alone and report these, leaving holistic judgments to evaluation consumers. You cannot expect to provide consensus or resolution if there is none.

2. *Don't assume that statistical significance is the same as practical significance* or that lack of statistical significance has no practical significance.

3. *Beware of regression effect*
   Remember that a group selected for measured low performance on some variable will show improved measured performance as an artifact of measurement error. That is, error not showing up the first time in an extreme sample is likely to be caught the second time around.

4. *Look for confirmation and consistency with other sources of information*
   Often, single data sources will not, despite more analysis, yield more information that you can use. If, for example, workshop participants rated satisfaction high, check other bits of data before interpreting that they were satisfied. Did they stay for the whole session? What do instructors say? How did they behave while there?

   When you find obvious inconsistencies—e.g., participants said they liked the session, but no one came back after lunch—look for a third source, or yet more information.

5. *Know when to stop*
   Remember that you'll never be certain; any and all data are to some extent inconclusive. Some guidelines to know when to stop are:

   with quantitative data, you arrive at a level of certainty you're willing to defend
   with qualitative data, you encounter redundancy, or regularity
   remember: You never conclude analysis. You stop doing it.

6. *Consider and cite limitations of the analysis methods you use*
There are limitations inherent in the analysis techniques you use and the assumptions necessary for their use.

For example, a correlation coefficient does not account for all variance, and it does not merit causal inferences.

7. *Consider and cite limitations based on external phenomena and other data you have*
No findings exist in a vacuum, and all must be interpreted against other data. For example, an interpretation might note that "Participants rated satisfaction low, yet all of them attended the optional sessions."

Or, "Supervisors were satisfied with student performance, but student performance test scores were below criterion."

Or, "Participants did not show a gain in knowledge, but they had just received notice of staff cutbacks and the interest in training was minimal."

8. *Audiences may, and often should, be involved in interpretation*
This process sheds more light on what data mean and helps analyses be more responsive. In this way, interpretation overlaps with reporting. (See especially cases S-4 and L-1 for examples where audiences were asked to help interpret findings.) Should strong disagreements emerge regarding what data mean, consider appending a minority report.

CRITERIA FOR INTERPRETATION	

CRITERIA FOR INTERPRETATION

1. Ensure that norms and referents are appropriate for the population or characteristic you are judging
2. Cite and provide rationale for particular referents used in interpretation
3. Formulate and explain interpretations in light of contextual and confirming, limiting, or disconfirming information
4. Use summations and holistic interpretation techniques appropriately
5. Cite limitations and clearly explain degrees of certainty warranted
6. Provide alternative explanations and interpretations where appropriate
7. Seek out and include "minority" opinions on opposing interpretations when appropriate

Reporting in Evaluation

The general purpose of reporting is to communicate information to interested audiences and to help them make use of information from the evaluation. Reporting is *not* a static, one-time event nor is it necessarily a product, such as a written report. Rather, reporting is an ongoing process that might include oral, visual, or written communication that commences before an evaluation begins and likely continues beyond its conclusion.

The content of reporting is not constrained to communicating the findings of evaluation. It includes communicating information about purposes, context, activities, results, and implications of programs and evaluations. It includes, too, communication among evaluation staff when more than one person is involved in an evaluation.

Reports are the only way some audiences have access to the evaluation. Sometimes the report can serve as the sole information base from which decision makers will work. This is especially true as time or distance elapses between the evaluation and the planned use for evaluation information. Reports, then, are extremely important. It is important that they are timely, open and frank, and as balanced as possible in their descriptions of strengths and weaknesses of what is being evaluated.

WHEN ARE REPORTING DECISIONS MADE?
The initial decisions for reporting are made as part of the overall evaluation plan. But you must expect to reconsider these decisions during the course of an evaluation effort. Special problems requiring reporting will crop up; opportunities and needs for special reporting will occur. Expect to vary from the original plan and to replan reporting as you go along.

WHO SHOULD GET AN EVALUATION REPORT?

Reports are written for people. The content of a report is determined by who will be using the information and why. The report format (whether it should be a written report, oral report, formal presentation or news release) is also determined by the audience—who needs to understand this information and how can you best present it for their understanding.

Your report audiences are the persons, groups, and agencies whose information needs and interests guided the evaluation or whose actions support the evaluation. They must be kept apprised of an evaluation's operation and results.

Audiences differ in the kinds of interests they have in an evaluation. Some will be decision makers; some will be reactors and providers of further information; some will be informees only. In all cases, audiences are defined by the "stake" they hold in an evaluation, or by what is being evaluated. In this respect, evaluation audiences and evaluation purposes are closely related.

GUIDELINES FOR IDENTIFYING REPORT AUDIENCES

Be comprehensive. You should take care not to ignore a particular audience. Return to the original purposes and audiences for the evaluation, and be sure your report plan accounts for each of the evaluation's audiences.

Differentiate audiences by purposes. Remember that when you report to someone you're doing it for a reason. It's good communication practice and certainly more efficient to make communications as specific and to-the-point as possible. Audiences should not "automatically" be everyone who has anything to do with a training preparation effort. Many times an evaluation will produce only one report (mistake #1) and then give it to anyone and everyone who has anything to do with the program (mistake #2). Deluging people with unwanted information can hurt the credibility and utility of the evaluation, and it is probably as bad as not giving an audience some information they should have received. Nearly as bad as leaving someone out is "junk-mailing" an audience. Choosing an audience carefully according to just what they need, then reporting to them in a timely, direct and appropriate manner, respects their needs, not to mention their time.

Attend to human rights, ethics, laws and guidelines. Review each intended report audience to ensure that, in providing information to that audience, you don't infringe on or violate the rights of another. Consider both the timing and editing of your report in advance. Who will be the last audience to review and edit? Who will decide when and how the report will be released? Evaluation reports usually become publicly accessible under freedom of information laws. Anonymity assurances, protocol, and other ethical considerations can be potentially violated and ought to be considered prior to reporting.

GUIDELINES FOR
IDENTIFYING
REPORT
AUDIENCES
(continued)

Reconsider audiences throughout the evaluation. Audiences for reports need to be reconsidered during and after an evaluation. Usually, an evaluation's original design is modified as evaluation work progresses and may require new audience considerations. Finally, when an evaluation has collected and interpreted information, you need to consider what audiences need to be involved in its further interpretation and who should receive what kinds of reports.

TYPES OF REPORT
AUDIENCES

- funders and supporters
- oversight agencies, advisory boards, licensing groups
- staff and consultants
- clients (students, trainees)
- administrators
- professional groups and organizations
- libraries, resource centers and clearing houses
- projects and programs similar to what you've evaluated
- the public
- others with a stake in the evaluation

ALTERNATIVE
PURPOSES FOR
EVALUATION
REPORTS

to demonstrate accountability: to show that objectives have been met, activities undertaken, resources expanded, and persons involved.

to convince: an advocacy argument providing evidence that activities have been effective in meeting objectives, or that worthwhile benefits have been achieved, or that a position or decision is justified.

to educate: enlightening audiences about how programs work, who they involve, why they are needed, what problems they face, what resolutions might be possible.

to explore and investigate: providing information that can help solve problems, shed light on successes and failures, and identify new directions.

to document: recording what has taken place for future use such as research and development.

to involve: attempting to draw uninvolved (or underinvolved) people and resources into activities.

to gain support: arguing for the worth and importance of activities, resources, outcomes, etc.

to promote understanding: providing information that can be used to interpret activities, problems, or outcomes in light of audiences' beliefs, knowledge, or values.

to promote public relations: demonstrating particular intentions, activities, and problems to enhance positive feelings.

decision making: providing information that can be used to design or revise programs and standards, direct staff development, redirect evaluation activities, rank order needs, or select alternatives.

Don't limit the purpose for reporting to decision making.
Recent research (Alkin, Daillak and White, 1979; Patton, 1978; Braskamp, Brown and Newman, 1980) reinforces the notion that evaluation can and does have impact beyond being "used" in decisions. It can reduce decision makers' uncertainty, make people more aware, reinforce policy, and create support, to name a few additional purposes. Further, this research shows that evaluation data can rarely be linked

directly to a decision. To limit reporting purposes to decision making is to drastically limit the potential ability of evaluation in personnel preparation.

CONSIDERING AUDIENCE NEEDS IN EVALUATIONS OF PERSONNEL OF TRAINING

Students (Trainees)

Report about progress and mastery for continued learning; through reporting, students also should be kept informed about program changes and the uses for their feedback.

Trainers, faculty, consultants, leaders

Report to these persons about their effectiveness, style, and results to improve their effectiveness, or report to them as a group or program unit for general staff development.

Staff

Program training staff need regular feedback on the program's progress and development and their own effectiveness. Internal evaluation reports can clarify issues and value conflicts, identify problems, and stimulate motivation and progress.

Public

Report about funding, program intentions, progress and results to enhance support, involvement, and awareness.

Funders

Most agencies or organizations require annual or other regular reports. These should concentrate on accountability, major impacts, and goal achievement.

Colleagues, other professionals, other organizations

Report in journals, newsletters and professional meetings to share your experience, successes and failures.

Disseminators

Report to agencies (your SEA, the National Diffusion Network (NDN), the Joint Dissemination and Review Panel (JDRP) and the National Inservice Network (NIN) at Indiana University, for example) and to journals to disseminate promising practices. Reports to them should concentrate on replicability information and proofs of accomplishments.

WHAT CONTENT SHOULD BE INCLUDED IN A REPORT?

Report content is simply what a report is about. Reports can be comprehensive, covering the setting, history, growth and achievements of a project. Or a report can be quite specific; for example, a report on why a problem emerged, how well a group of trainees performed a task, or what transpired at a meeting.

No matter what the purpose is for a report or who the report is for (or even how informal it is), it should be balanced, clear, and grammatically and technically sound. Each report, even if it is a memo, serves as a sample of the evaluation; biased, sloppy, or late reports have irrevocable and negative effects on key audiences.

TYPICAL KINDS OF REPORTS

Announcements and releases

These are brief, usually single-topic reports that highlight key decisions or aspects relating to a project or evaluation. Included would be information about evaluation designs, decisions to evaluate, purposes, staff, resources, schedules, etc.

Progress reports

These are reports on milestone accomplishments, major events, or significant achievements and activities that occur.

Interim and preliminary reports

These focus on predetermined time intervals (e.g., each quarter, semester) in the evaluation and report on the events and conclusions of that interval. They may include preliminary findings, modifications to plans, or progress toward goals. Some typical topics for interim reports are:

situation appraisals: How did the first workshop go; is the revised practicum installed; are we on schedule?
analyses of problems; Why was attendance low? Why are trainees unable to use new procedures?
assessments of quality: How good are the new workshop materials?
research conclusions: Did the new materials produce better impact? Has the revised workshop schedule raised attendance?
justifications: This is why the workshop has been revised to include consultation. These are the reasons for shortening the workshop.
updates: Schedule for interviews and training of field persons: the new plan for trainee follow-up.

Concluding reports

These are reports that occur at the end of an evaluation or program or at the end of a major period, such as the first year. Some usual kinds of concluding reports are:

main report: containing comprehensive information about evaluation purposes, objects, activities, findings and conclusions
executive summary: a précis of the main report, highlighting conclusions
popular report: a summary version, in simple language, of the main report
technical report: detailed information about information collection strategies, sampling, analysis procedures, data collection, etc.

TYPICAL KINDS OF REPORTS
(continued)

follow-up reports: (usually meetings, conferences, panels, or hearings) presentations containing interpretations, consequences, implications, and next steps concerning the results and conclusions of the evaluation

Internal reports

These are reports intended for internal use of the evaluation; they are "consumed" by the evaluation and enable it to move ahead. Questionnaire data, for instance, might be aggregated and displayed, then given to (reported to) a group for analysis and interpretation.

Internal reports might be produced any time by the evaluation and can be planned or spontaneous. Most often, the audience for internal reports is evaluation staff or helpers. Sometimes, reports are written only for the file. Some examples of internal evaluation reports can be found in the following examples.

PRELIMINARY PRESS OR ORGANIZATIONAL RELEASE TO ANNOUNCE AN EVALUATION

a. the reasons for, and purposes of, the coming study
b. the goals and objectives of the study
c. the groups and others involved
d. some of the crucial issues involved (e.g., the desegregation order, socio-economic variation among the schools)
e. the organization of the study (e.g., subgroups, task forces)
f. the variables to be investigated and the general information methods to be used
g. a time-line for the study, listing its major planned events and report schedule

---

MEMORANDUM REPORT TO KEY STAFF SENT PRIOR TO PRESS RELEASE

a. copy of drafted press release
b. a delineation of roles to be played by personnel
c. the duties and responsibilities of staff in supporting the study
d. the kinds of changes that might result—and would not result—from the study
e. request for reactions to press release

SUMMARY INTERIM REPORT

Introduction reviewing the major purposes, scope and goals of the study and delineating the audiences and content for the report
the general design
progress to date, noting what data were collected, what persons were involved, what reports had been made, and what problems (if any) had been encountered
next steps: this would outline the work that remained and show a plan for its accomplishment. Here, for example, a task force's filing system would be explained, their plans for preliminary analysis reviewed, and their sub-group organization and meeting schedule explained.

INTERIM DATA SUMMARIES

This report would be technical in nature and intended for use by groups in their preliminary analysis. The data summary would be organized by the major information collection procedures (e.g., tests, interviews, questionnaires, cumulative folder data) and would display the aggregated information in a form (reduced, if necessary, as with questionnaire data) amenable to analysis. This allows key audiences to anticipate findings.

MAIN CONCLUDING REPORT DISSEMINATED TO KEY AUDIENCES

I. Introduction
   A. Intent of document
   B. Audience(s) addressed
   C. Basic definitions (e.g., need, model training program, XYZ training approach)
   D. Limitations and caveats
   E. Overview of document
II. Basic information
   A. Background
   B. Group(s) involved
   C. Focus of the study (which schools, audiences, objects, etc.) - see *Focusing the Evaluation*
   D. Information collected
   E. Uses made of the information
III. Design of the study
   A. Objectives (evaluation questions)
   B. Logical structure and rationale
   C. Procedures
   D. Reports made (with brief summaries)
   E. Schedule - calendar of events
IV. Results
   A. Summary tables and displays of the data collected
V. Conclusions
   A. Interpretations and recommendations
VI. Evaluation of the study
   A. Summary assessment of its strengths and weaknesses, limitations
VII. Next steps
   A. What will happen next; programs to follow; further evaluation
VIII. Appendices

CONCLUDING TECHNICAL REPORT AVAILABLE UPON REQUEST

I. Introduction
   A. Primary intent
   B. Audience
   C. Basic definitions
   D. Limitations and caveats
II. Questions and information collected
   A. Enumeration (e.g., listing of the 4 major questions, the 10 variables, the information sources in each of the 6 sites)
   B. Comparison to objectives (a matrix showing how information collected was used to relate to the objectives of the study)
III. Sampling plan
   A. Definition of population (e.g., the 6 sites, levels assessed, contextual factors re: each site)
   B. Sampling specifications (numbers and types of samples drawn, numbers within each sample, such as how are variables assessed at each of the levels, the stratified random samples, etc.)
   C. Procedures (how each sample was drawn, by whom, when)
IV. Information collection plan
   A. Instruments and procedures (descriptions of tests administered, Delphi group constitution, site visit plans, etc.)
   B. Comparison to information needs (a matrix showing how instruments and procedures relate to particular needs assessment questions, *see Information Collection*)

**CONCLUDING
TECHNICAL
REPORT
AVAILABLE UPON
REQUEST**
(continued)

V. Information processing
  A. Screening and cleaning procedures (for each procedure, tell how data were verified and screened, noting recollection where it occurred)
  B. Aggregation and filing (description of how the data were reduced, filed and made ready for analysis)
VI. Preliminary analysis
  A. Preliminary analysis procedures (description of the subcommittees formed, concerns looked for, questions addressed, comparisons made among sites on attendance data, etc.)
  B. Preliminary analysis results (a description of each conclusion reached, e.g., the trends identified, issues defined)
VII. Needs analysis
  A. The questions addressed
  B. Procedures used (a description, for each information set, of how analysis was performed, e.g., a Delphi ranking of 10 variables, computation of school-scores for each variable. This would *include* new information collected.)
  C. Analysis results (displays - e.g., bar graphs, charts, and accompanying discussion of each major analytic procedure's results)
VIII. Appendices
  These would contain raw data summaries, the internal data reports, and other documents and reports that support the technical report and would be needed to replicate the analysis.

**CONCLUDING
PRESS RELEASE**

Study Team Recommends Staff Development
brief history of study and purposes
who was involved
what information was collected
results and conclusions
next steps
announcement of public report hearings

**REPORT
MEETING(S) WITH
KEY GROUPS
(EXAMPLE
AGENDA)**

I. Introduction by the superintendent: (a) purposes, scope and general design for the needs assessment; (b) major parties involved; and (c) overview of the agenda (15 min.)
II. Review of the assessment (30 min.) by the chair of the task force team (with overhead projector)
  A. The objectives of the study
  B. The procedures used (transparency: matrix of objectives and procedures)
  C. Results of analysis (transparencies of cumulative bar graphs, school comparisons, etc.)
  D. Conclusions of the study (overview of advocacy team procedures and convergence team conclusions
  E. Evaluation summary of limitations and caveats re: needs assessment
III. Questions for clarification: led by superintendent, task force team chair and evaluator; in which questions pertaining to clarification are raised by audience and answered by appropriate respondent (15 min.)

BREAK for Coffee and Rolls - (20 min.)

REPORT
MEETING(S) WITH
KEY GROUPS
(continued)

IV. Panel discussion (evaluator, task force chair, principals) (60 min.)
V. Evaluation: participants react to meeting, rate report, and note further questions and interests (5 min.)
VI. Closing (by superintendent) (5 min.)

HOW WILL REPORTS BE DELIVERED?

There are many more ways to skin the reporting cat than the traditional written report. The main message of this section is to consider alternative means and to choose them wisely. Also included in this section is one example of some effective visual display techniques.

OPTIONAL STRATEGIES FOR REPORTING

written documents: technical reports, interim progress reports, conference proceedings
media releases: press, TV, radio
meetings and small group discussions, presentations, luncheons
hearing, panel reviews, presentations to groups (e.g., PTA)
direct mail leaflets, pamphlets, newsletters
staged interviews of key participants with dissemination provision (e.g., "live" coverage, transcripts)
memoranda, letters
professional journals, publications
slide-tape, video, multi-media presentations, films
mock jury "trials," socio-dramas, theater
training sessions, workshops, conferences

GUIDELINES FOR CHOOSING ALTERNATIVE REPORTING STRATEGIES

Make use of multiple sensory channels (in written reports, use graphics: charts, tables, figures, displays)
Include provision for interaction and checking for comprehension (in written reports: use review questions, discussion summaries, etc.)
Be as simple as possible
Encourage audience participation (in written reports, this can be a tear-off response form)
Make optimal use of audio-visual display techniques
Incorporate varied displays
Gain the attention of the intended audience

USE CHARTS, GRAPHS, AND TABLES IN YOUR REPORT

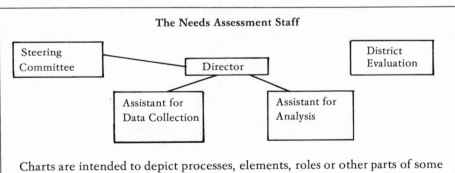

The Needs Assessment Staff

Steering Committee — Director — District Evaluation
Assistant for Data Collection — Assistant for Analysis

Charts are intended to depict processes, elements, roles or other parts of some larger entity and their organization or interdependencies.

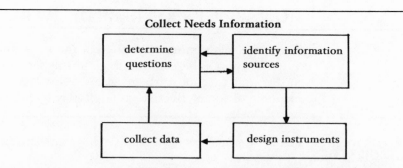

Collect Needs Information

The functions network is often used for program planning and analysis. It is used to show relationships of functions within a system. Arrows leading into a box indicate inputs to that function, and arrows leading out from a box indicate outputs of that function.

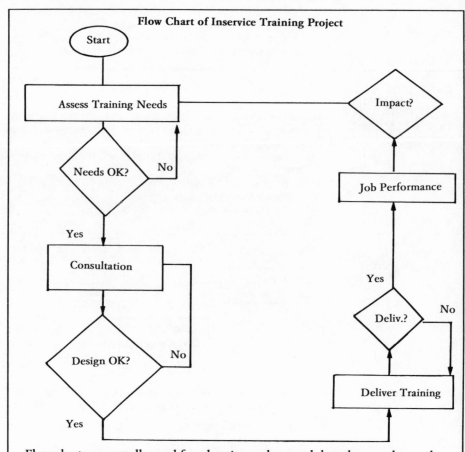

Flow Chart of Inservice Training Project

Flow charts are usually used for planning and control, but they can be used to report how a process works. Most flow charts make use of five symbols. An oval represents a starting and finishing place. Inputs and outputs are represented by parallelograms. An action is represented by a rectangle, and decisions are represented by diamond shapes. Arrows indicate direction of flow.

GRAPHS

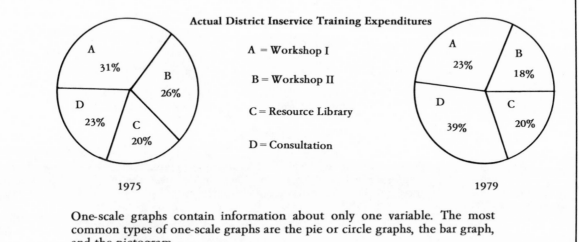

Actual District Inservice Training Expenditures

A = Workshop I

B = Workshop II

C = Resource Library

D = Consultation

1975   1979

One-scale graphs contain information about only one variable. The most common types of one-scale graphs are the pie or circle graphs, the bar graph, and the pictogram.

Pie or circle graph is the simplest of the one-scale graphs. It can show only parts of the whole (all parts must total 100% or 360°). Two or more circle graphs can be used to provide a comparison.

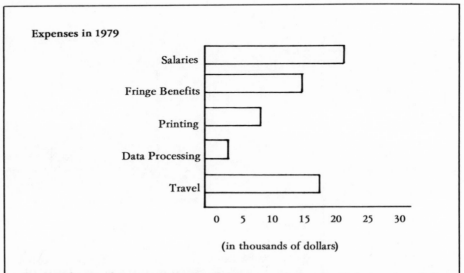

Expenses in 1979

(in thousands of dollars)

Bar graphs are the most versatile of the one-scale graphs. Relative size of the various categories of the single variable is indicated by the length of line or bar. Greater precision is possible with this than with the circle or area charts, and there is less chance for misinterpretation.

Expenditures in 1980

Salaries	$ $ $ $ $ $ $
Fringe Benefits	$ $
Printing	$ $
Data Processing	$
Travel	$ $ $ $

$ = $1,000

The pictogram is a modification of the bar graph. Rather than using a line to represent quantity, figures are used. This is often the most visually attractive graph, although it often sacrifices precision.

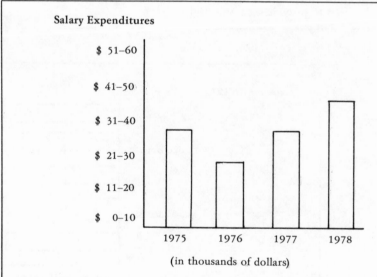

Salary Expenditures

$ 51–60
$ 41–50
$ 31–40
$ 21–30
$ 11–20
$ 0–10

1975   1976   1977   1978

(in thousands of dollars)

Two-scale graphs

The column graph contains two scales while the bar graph contains only one. Either graph can be horizontal or vertical, but usually the one-scale is better horizontal and the two-scale graph is better vertical.

GRAPHS
(continued)

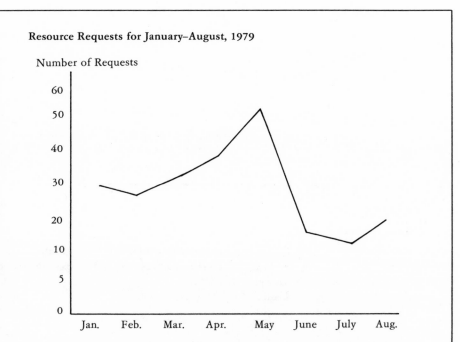

Resource Requests for January–August, 1979

Number of Requests

More lines may be plotted on the line graph to provide information for additional comparisons. Be careful not to provide too much information; four or five lines are usually the maximum.

The line graph can be used to convey the same types of information as the column graph, but the line graph is better when there are several points which must be plotted or where there are small changes between the points.

TABLES   Tables present information, numerical or verbal, in rows or columns arranged so that relationships and trends can be readily identified. They may be quite simple, showing single variables, or quite complex, showing multiple variables and depicting several interrelationships.

Percentage of Workshop Participants
Who Achieved Objectives at 80% or Higher Level

	Objective 1 Diagnosis	Objective 2 Interpretation	Objective 3 Prescription	Objective 4 Evaluation
Workshop A	78%	93%	97%	100%
Workshop B	90%	94%	88%	73%
Workshop C	82%	80%	78%	75%
Workshop D	64%	53%	47%	68%

TABLES
(continued)

INCIDENCES of Crime in Schools (annual average)

		Minor	Major	Total
Socio-Economic Status of Schools	High	n = 73	n = 4	77
	Low	n = 81	n = 36	117
Total		154	40	194

The relationship apparent in the table above is that minor crime rates are about the same in "high" and "low" socio-economic schools, but major crime rates are dramatically higher in the "low" status schools.

CRITERIA AND GUIDELINES TO ASSESS REPORT FORMAT

Determine whether the chosen format(s) will meet the following criteria:

1. Comprehensible and engaging to audiences
2. Suitable for content (e.g., don't press release the results of a complex analysis of variance)
3. Useful for the purpose(s)

WHAT IS THE APPROPRIATE STYLE AND STRUCTURE FOR THE REPORT?

The medium is part of your message. That is, how a report is styled and structured can have a major impact on how it's received.

This section contains a listing of suggestions, research findings and guidelines that relate to incorporating appropriate styles and structures into reports, be they written, oral or some other format. This section also provides some examples of report structures (organization).

EXAMPLE ORGANIZATION FOR AN EVALUATION REPORT

I. **Précis, or abstract (written report only)**: this enables a "nutshell" view of a report's content and lets a reader know if further reading is warranted.

II. **Table of contents (written report only) or other guide to organization**: this should clearly label portions of the report and indicate where they are and how to access them. In an oral report (meeting, etc.) an agenda can serve this function.

III. **Introduction**: this should relate the purpose of the report, its intended audience, its scope and coverage, including limitations, and how it is organized. Where selection among report parts is intended, the structure of such parts and decision rules for selection should be clearly provided. A preface, acknowledgments, or disclaimer section may also be called for in the introductory content. In an oral presentation, support this portion with a handout or audio-visual graphic.

IV. **Body of report**: this should contain whatever is "promised" in the introduction and be clearly organized around functional aspects related to the report's purpose. A report intending to explain the methods of a needs assessment might well be organized in a method-by-method presentation. Some other common organizing principles for report content are:

A. *Chronological*: arranging information by when it happened, series of events, stages, etc.

B. *Functional or conceptual stages*: arranging content by major functional steps, such as design stage, implementation, analysis, interpretation, etc.

C. *Purposes, goals or objectives*: organizing content by the particular goals, questions, or objectives of the study.

D. *Methods*: presenting content by each of the major procedures in the needs assessment, such as survey, research analysis, interviews, testing, etc.

E. *Conclusions, findings, results*: content can be organized according to each particular conclusion or result of the needs assessment.

F. *Organizational, administrative units*: content might be arranged by the unit, persons or groups who completed different parts of the study.

V. **Summary**: this section should briefly review and highlight the major aspects of the report, its conclusions, significance, etc. This content may also contain, where appropriate, devices for readers and audiences to check their understanding and interpretation of the report. A "Question and Answer" or discussion session can be added after this in an oral presentation.

VI. **Closing**: this should indicate implications for further related work or reporting and contain any content necessary for audiences to place the report in a proper context and perspective, relative both to what has gone before and what may, or should, next occur. This aspect of a report may also be used to provide or reiterate guidance to the audience as to how they might further understand, use, or benefit from the report.

KEY
CONSIDERATIONS
ABOUT CONTENT
WHEN PUTTING
THE REPORT
TOGETHER

Selection of Content

Content should be limited to what's needed to get the reporting job done or to meet the evaluation purpose(s). The ill consequences of including irrelevant content are far greater in a "live" reporting format than they are in a written report. An oral presentation, for example, allows little provision for the listener to pick and choose from a "table of contents" those bits of the report most suitable to his/her needs. Audiences exposed to irrelevant content are likely to tune out the entire report, often with more damaging consequences than if *no* report has been attempted.

Balanced Content

There are two or more sides to every story (probably more). Evaluation findings are rarely conclusive. Alternative explanations and interpretations are offered, along with the available evidence to support or refute them. Sometimes minority perspectives are appended. Evaluation should neither report only positive results if there are also negative results nor vice versa. This is not only ethical practice. The continuing power of evaluation as a force for change rests in its credibility and acceptance by involved persons. Biased, unbalanced reporting will destroy that power base.

Multiple Perspectives

Determine content from the audience's point of view. A report must be comprehensible and have meaning to the recipient audience. Content should be compatible with their point of view, experience and knowledge. Examples, for instance, must be within—and preferably in the forefront—of the audience's experience.

Direct and Simple Language

Keep it simple. Reports should not be overly complex, don't use references and language not readily understandable to intended audiences. Education, as most professions, has a regrettable tendency to use jargon and to use complex language and presentation in transmitting ideas. Evaluation should take extra care to use simple language, brief examples, and ordinary expressions and terminology.

Clarity

Be clear. Reports should be prepared and delivered so as not to introduce unnecessary ambiguity. Evaluation results often have multiple interpretations and are seldom precise and definite. Make sure your report does not add further ambiguity. Findings should be clearly and simply presented and, where appropriate, alternative interpretations clearly listed and explained. Opinions and other subjective expressions should be clearly defined as such.

Focus

Be direct. Reports should directly address the purposes for which they are intended. This means they should not ramble, or "beat around the bush,"

KEY
CONSIDERATIONS
ABOUT CONTENT
WHEN PUTTING
THE REPORT
TOGETHER
(continued)

but should in the sparest and briefest manner address their points. An audience's time is precious, demands upon it should be minimized. This often means eliminating content and providing only what is required for the consumer to receive and understand the intended communication.

Provide for Feedback

Provide for confirmation/feedback. Good communication requires that persons receiving messages be allowed to confirm their perceptions and understanding. Too often, as is true in interpersonal communications, messages received are quite different from messages sent, or intended to be sent. In reports where dialogue is available (as in presentations, oral reports, etc.), provision for questions and discussion can meet these needs. In written or other "one-way" reporting (as in a public media report), provisions should be made in the report for consumers to check their understanding and interpretation. There can be summaries, reviews, comprehension checks (e.g., a quiz) or other devices that enable the consumer to interact with the content of the report.

Overview

A general structure applies to virtually any report type or medium. Any report should be preceded by an overview—an introductory summary in which the reader is informed briefly as to what is coming. This guideline derives from principles of education and communication, In order for report receivers ("learners") to properly assimilate and comprehend a report's content, they require a cognitive organizer: the "whole picture" into which the communication to follow is intended to fit. This front-end overview is a courtesy to an audience, for it tells them what is coming and lets them choose to participate based on this information. More than courtesy, however, a nutshell overview makes good educational and communications sense.

Summarize

The report should close with a summary. This reminds readers (participants, etc.) of the report's main features and may suggest next steps or provide for interaction.

Guide

In journalism, an excellent guideline is offered to assist reports in their copy writing: "Tell them what you're going to tell them, then tell them, then tell them what you told them." This makes a good report structure also.

HOW CAN YOU HELP AUDIENCES INTERPRET AND USE YOUR REPORTS?

Recent research by Alkin (1978) indicates that evaluation reports have the most impact when reporting is construed as a "dialogue" between evaluators and the audiences. Reviewers of reports must interact with the report, rather than simply receive it in a one-way transmission.

SOME OPTIONS
FOR INVOLVING
AUDIENCES

1. Discuss the reports with key audience members.
2. Make oral presentations.
3. Submit a rough draft of a report to some audience members for an edit and critique.
4. Distribute preliminary summary reports.
5. Have audience members make reports, write reviews, conduct meetings, etc.
6. Conduct panel meetings, hearings, open forums, etc.
7. Incorporate reports into training workshops in which audience members are involved.
8. Present reports at professional associations and meetings.
9. Invite commentary and reaction through publishing report summaries in journals and newsletters.
10. Make yourself or others available to attend meetings where reports can, or may not, be used and discussed.
11. Commission reviews, partisan papers, or other critiques and commentaries by persons influential with key audiences.
12. Present reports at faculty meetings.
13. Conduct a "conference" around a report (e.g., invite past graduates, some employers, and other faculty to a one-day conference on your graduate follow-up).
14. Solicit questions, concerns and related issues (e.g., via mail back forms, 3 × 5 cards).

BALANCING AN
EVALUATION
REPORT

Evaluation reports, and especially those that are to be widely disseminated, should be balanced in their perspectives. The balance of a report (whether it is oral, written, or graphic displays) can be easily assessed by an audience. Forgotten perspectives or uneven emphases are inevitably spotted.

AREAS TO BALANCE	PITFALLS
AUDIENCE PERSPECTIVES	One audience has been over-represented or their perspective over-emphasized in a report.
RESOURCE ALLOCATION	One aspect of the evaluation (e.g., data analysis or front-end planning) receives a disproportionate amount of funds, time, personnel, and reporting space.

BALANCING AN EVALUATION REPORT (continued)	AREAS TO BALANCE	PITFALLS
	OBJECT DESCRIPTION	The strengths (or weaknesses) of the object become the focus of the evaluation—leaving audiences to search for what was bad (or good).
	ISSUES DISCUSSED	Discussions of one particularly "hot" issue begin to monopolize the evaluation and its formal and informal reports.
	STAFF INFLUENCE	One staff person (or small group of staff) begins to have increasingly greater responsibility for and influence on evaluation reporting—both formal and informal.

GUIDELINES AND CRITERIA FOR PROMOTING IMPACT

Know and understand your audience
relate findings to their problems and concerns
use examples familiar to them
speak their language (i.e., not over their heads, not beneath them)

Incorporate audience members into report activities where possible (e.g., as co-presenters, reactors, reviewers)

Provide minority viewpoints, alternative explanations, rationales, explanations

Provide references and ascribe sources to opinions, interpretations and judgments so that audiences can identify and weigh them

WHEN SHOULD REPORTS BE SCHEDULED?

Audiences have to get reports *on time* (e.g., to coincide with a decision point) or, in many cases, they might as well not get a particular report. The reporting schedule shows:

Who gets the report
What report
When, and
How (oral, written, summary)

When you report to your intended audiences is not truly "optional." Your schedule is pretty well fixed by your purposes. If a purpose is, for example, to help administrators decide whether to continue a workshop series, they'll need your report just before they make the decision. But, you still need to consider how long before you should report, and how often (e.g., should you report in stages).

OPTIONAL STRATEGIES FOR SCHEDULING REPORTING

1. Determine report schedule by major audience decision/consideration events. This entails scheduling reports to coincide with or immediately precede events such as:
   · board meetings
   · formal reviews and hearings
   · internal decision sessions (e.g., staff meetings)
   · public hearings
   · elections and referendums
   · budget determination hearings or meetings
   · caucuses
   · etc.
2. Schedule by major events and stages in the "life" of the evaluation object, e.g.:
   · program design completion
   · completion of pilot workshops, trial classes, etc.
   · completion of phases
   · completion of project
3. Schedule according to commonly accepted time intervals, e.g.:
   · quarterly, semi-annual, bi-annual, annual, etc.
   · semesters, quarters
   · fiscal years
4. Schedule reports by major events in the course of the evaluation, e.g.:
   · completion of the evaluation design
   · draft of tentative purposes and criteria
   · completion of preliminary analysis
   · signing of evaluation contract
   · end-of-year report
5. Schedule opportunistically, e.g.:
   · major problems discovered

OPTIONAL STRATEGIES FOR SCHEDULING REPORTING *(continued)*

- · delays in schedule
- · early success, rare occurrences
- · unexpected findings
- · ad-hoc meetings, councils, boards, etc.

6. Schedule incrementally, e.g.:
- · news release, followed by
- · draft report for edit and review, followed by
- · preliminary report, followed by
- · final report, followed by
- · hearings and public discussion of result

EXAMPLE OF A REPORT SCHEDULE

Here is an example of a report schedule for a school district needs assessment.

Event	Date/Frequency	Format	Nature/Scope of Content	Audience
1. Monthly Progress Updates	end of month	memorandum	work accomplished, projected; problems, revisions to design; important future events	program staff
2. Preliminary News Release	1st month of study	news story	purpose, budget, organization, schedule, staff involved	general public
3. Interim Media Report	near end of study—after all data collected	television interview w/ NA Director	progress, preliminary findings, next steps, possible consequences	general public
4. Quarterly Report	end of each quarter (90 days)	written report	progress, resources consumed, problems encountered, next step, revisions to plan	school board administration advisory committee
5. Final Report: Summary Revision	30 days after end of study	written report w/no appendices	review of study, present data, conclusions, interpretations, recommendations	school board advisory committee administration others
6. Final Report: Technical	90 days after end of study	written report w/appendices (instruments, etc.)	same as above, w/fuller data reports included	administration SEA
7. Final Report: Hearing	90 days after study	Panel review and public hearings w/ audio/visual presentation by NA Director	data summaries, conclusion summaries, recommendations, implications	general public school staff

GUIDELINES
AND CRITERIA
FOR ASSESSING
REPORT
SCHEDULES

Be timely: get information to audiences when they can best make use of it.

Don't be too early: In an effort to get reports on time, you can be too early, such that your reports are not important to audiences, will be forgotten, or otherwise dealt with superficially.

Be economical: reporting too frequently for the sake of "keeping in touch" could threaten the primacy of your more important reports. You don't want to generate so much background noise that your important signals get lost.

Be specific: schedule reports for particular audiences at particular times. You are often better off to divide a report into two events when two audiences have differing time demands.

Be flexible: revise your schedule and remain open to opportunities for ad-hoc reports.

Evaluate your schedule against your evaluation purposes, audience needs and resources. Check for:

sufficiency to meet purposes and audience needs
sufficiency to meet internal communication needs
compatibility with purposes of the evaluation
coincidence with other major supporting or possibly conflicting events
feasibility relative to your resources

CHECKLIST FOR
REPORTS

Here's a checklist to guide and review the report function.

Identification of Purposes and Audiences

1. Review and clarify the *purposes* for the evaluation
2. Review and clarify the *audiences* for the evaluation
3. Identify report *purposes* and report *audiences*. Check to see that:

purposes are realistic; e.g., can meet audience needs and purposes
audiences account for all stakeholders in the program and its evaluation
external mandates (e.g., funders)
internal audiences (e.g., staff)
public
others
purposes are comprehensive; will meet audiences' information needs and interests (e.g., decision making, garnering support, soliciting involvement)

Report Planning
1. *Content* planned for reports is consistent with (a) report purposes and (b) audience's information *needs, rights* and *interests*
2. *Types* of reports (e.g., interim, summary, technical) are consistent with:

program operations and phases
evaluation stages
audience information demands

3. *Formats* (e.g., written, media announcements, hearings, conferences, meetings) are consistent with:

    purposes for reporting
    audiences
    principles of multiple media, dynamism, interest and education

4. *Formats* provide for follow-up, interaction and confirmation of receipt and understanding

Conducting Reporting Events

1. Each report (written, oral, other) is:

    clear
    simple and concise
    comprehensive
    balanced (i.e., not negatively or positively biased)

2. Conclusions are justified with defensible information and evidence
3. Value perspectives and viewpoints are clarified
4. Feedback, clarification, discussion, exploration and confirmation occur where provided for
5. Audiences are provided opportunities to refute, explain and justify negative findings
6. Human rights and privacy are protected
7. Report activities follow sound educational designs (e.g., overviews and summaries are provided, support documents are included)

REFERENCES

Alkin, M.C., Daillak, R. & White, P. *Using Evaluations: Does Evaluation Make a Difference?* Beverly Hills: Sage, 1979.

Braskamp, L.A., Brown, R.D. & Newman, D.L. *Studying Evaluation Utilization Through Simulations.* Unpublished paper, University of Illinois at Urbana, Champaign and University of Nebraska-Lincoln, undated.

Flesch, R. *On Business Communication: How to Say What You Mean in Plain English.* New York: Harper & Row, 1972.

Hawkridge, D.G., Campeau, P.L. & Trickett, P.K. *Preparing Evaluation Reports: A Guide for Authors. AIR Monograph.* Pittsburgh: American Institutes for Research, 6, 1970.

Kearney, C.P. & Harper, R.J. The Politics of Reporting Results. In E.R. House (ed.), *School Evaluation: The Politics and Process.* Berkeley: McCutchan, 1973.

Lanham, R.A. *Revising Prose.* New York: Scribners, 1978.

Office of Program Evaluation and Research. *Handbook for Reporting and Using Test Results.* Sacramento, CA: Bureau of Publication Sales, California State Department of Education.

Patton, M.Q. *Utilization-Focused Evaluation.* Beverly Hills: Sage, 1978.

Popham, W.J. *Educational Evaluation.* Englewood Cliffs, N.J.: Prentice Hall, 1975.

Smith, D.M. & Smith, N.L. *Writing Effective Evaluation Reports.* Portland, OR: Northwest Regional Educational Laboratory, March, 1980.

Managing Evaluation

Managing an evaluation involves orchestrating or supervising the conduct of all evaluation functions—focusing, designing, information collection and analysis, reporting, and meta-evaluation.

Evaluation management is similar enough to the management of most systems that it can be judged according to some similar standards. Management of a department, program, or an evaluation, for example, should be efficient, equitable, and effective. It should not over-consume staff time, precious dollars and materials, and the goodwill of those it involves and affects.

While management of evaluation is important, if it is effective it can go almost unnoticed. Good evaluation management helps rather than hinders audiences, it shortens rather than lengthens the time necessary to run an evaluation, it reduces potentially controversial issues, and it serves well all those involved in an evaluation.

WHEN YOU MAKE MANAGEMENT DECISIONS

Management bridges all other evaluation functions. Management responsibilities begin before the evaluation is implemented, they run through the entire evaluation, and they are typically the last events to be concluded after the evaluation. While management activities permeate the evaluation process, the most efficient evaluation management is unobtrusive.

WHO WILL BE IN CHARGE OF THE EVALUATION?

An evaluation may falter or fail because the evaluator isn't competent or isn't perceived as being competent by others. This makes the selection of an evaluator crucial even though a number of practical and political constraints can effectively limit that selection. To provide the best possible leadership for evaluation, it is important to be aware of alternative means to staff evaluation and to identify the skills that are important to see an evaluation through successfully.

Whether there is one evaluator or a team, a part-time consultant or a full-time manager/evaluator, the responsibilities the evaluator will have must be defined. For example, will the evaluator:

· conceptualize the evaluation
· design the evaluation
· construct instruments
· collect the data
· analyze the data
· devise methods to code, store and access the data
· negotiate with the audiences
· prepare contracts
· write the reports
· deliver reports
· interpret and recommend
· manage and interact with personnel

These responsibilities will be based upon the evaluation design which, in turn, reflects the evaluation questions and the evaluation purpose generated by stakeholders. Based upon the complexity of the evaluation design, the job description or a list of responsibilities such as those listed above should be drawn up. This list of responsibilities will allow you to make decisions.

There are presently a number of national professional evaluation organizations including the *Evaluation Network*, the *Evaluation & Research Society* (ERS), and *Division H* of the *American Educational Research Association*. Additionally, there are state-wide branches of evaluation organizations, offices of planning and evaluation within school districts, evaluation centers at universities, and national and regional evaluation laboratories. In short, it is possible to hire persons who have studied program evaluation, who are members of evaluation organizations, who have been involved in a number of evaluations, and who have reports and recommendations to verify their competence.

Use of such professionals can be on a consulting basis for internally run evaluations or on a short-term, full-time basis for entire evaluations. Often the cost of one or two days' time from an experienced evaluator brought in at the design stage will save time and resources in the long run.

When persons with a complete set of evaluation skills are not available, an option is to train existing personnel so that they can do evaluation tasks.

One way to accomplish this is by providing inservice training for staff—either on-site training or training offered through workshops and course work elsewhere.

Whatever the strategy used to staff the evaluation, the criterion for success is the provision of an evaluator or an evaluation team that is seen as credible and is capable of competently running the evaluation. Even the most competent evaluator can be seen, for political or theoretical reasons, as inappropriate for some evaluation jobs. If the evaluation is to have any chance of being useful, it must be produced by persons with believable independence, political viability, and competence.

ALTERNATIVE MEANS TO STAFF EVALUATION

Staff vs. External

Person already on the staff		vs.	Individual hired from outside especially for evaluation work	
Pros	Cons		Pros	Cons
knows the organization has known reputation, status, credibility	bias because of conflict of interest in evaluating a program in which there is a personal investment		comes without preconceived notion about the program is seen as independent observer by staff	unfamiliar with known traditions, camps, and protocol, and might antagonize selection sometimes based only upon recom-mendation

Individual vs. Team

Individual solely responsible for the evaluation		vs.	Team including content and evaluation persons who, together, have necessary skills	
Pros	Cons		Pros	Cons
responsibilities for the evaluation clear	success or failure heavily dependent upon a single individual		diffusion of responsibilities composite of multiple skills & perspectives	time spent on team building, logistics, & political considerations expenses involved

ALTERNATIVE
MEANS TO STAFF
EVALUATION
(continued)

Full-time vs. Part-time

Individual or team with full-time evaluation responsibilities		vs.	Individual or team with part-time evaluation responsibilities	
Pros	Cons		Pros	Cons
organized & coherent evaluation timely & ongoing information independence of evaluator(s)	cost involved discourages participation in evaluation evaluator(s) seen as outsider		multiple authorities can be brought in for short periods of time effective use of outside expertise	brief visits don't allow for thorough study expense & logistics involved in scheduling

Amateur vs. Professional

Person(s) with primary & major training in content area, no formal evaluation training or experience		vs.	Person(s) with primary & major training in evaluation	
Pros	Cons		Pros	Cons
knows content and object well can "pick up" many evaluation skills through experience	knowledge of object decreases evaluation objectivity limited evaluation competencies leads to few design options		brings in experience & technical skills to run evaluation provides multiple options through experience	outsider not acceptable to program staff; evaluation skills not valued bias toward a certain method prevents multiple options design

---

SKILL AREAS
CONSIDERED
NECESSARY FOR
AN EVALUATOR
OR AN
EVALUATION
TEAM

Keep in mind that evaluators must not only *be* competent, they must be *perceived* as competent. Conflict of interest or nonindependence may have more negative effects in the long run than missing skill areas (such as, computer know-how or statistical skills). While consultants can be brought in for technical assistance, no one can help an evaluator who is not perceived as trustworthy and credible.

Management skills
supervision
political savvy
professional ethics
communication (public relations) skills
interpersonal skills
systems analysis
contracting
budgeting
goal setting

SKILL AREAS CONSIDERED NECESSARY FOR AN EVALUATOR OR AN EVALUATION TEAM *(continued)*

Technical skills
instruments selection/development
test administration
statistical analysis
survey methods
observation techniques
psychometrics
experimental/quasi-experimental design
quality control of data
computer application
case-study methodology
cost analysis
report writing

Conceptual skills
ability to invent options
conceiving initial plans
categorizing and analyzing problems
ability to see and express relationships

Content expertise
working experience in area being evaluated
knowledge of major literature sources
understanding of important constructs in relevant field
familiar with experts in the field

SELECTING THE EVALUATOR

Is someone on the staff or in the immediate organization qualified to handle the job?

What kind of team might be put together from existing staff to achieve a composite of needed competencies?

Is there a professional evaluator who might be brought in on a part-time basis to provide consultation or do some of the technical tasks (e.g., designing an instrument, drawing a difficult sample)?

Is it possible to train some program staff to take on necessary responsibilities? Will they be credible to other staff?

If no one is available who is competent (or perceived as competent) to carry out the evaluation, should the evaluation be aborted?

EXAMPLE JOB DESCRIPTIONS

The person hired to do the evaluation will have the following responsibilities:
a. Designing a major evaluation component for a $200,000 project
b. Constructing instruments for the evaluation
c. Analyzing and reporting data to audiences
d. Managing evaluation budget and staff
1. Necessary competencies:
   a. Design skills (especially in the area of quasi-experimental or causal designs)
   b. Measurement expertise in designing instruments
   c. Statistical expertise in analyzing data; knowledge and experiences with computer programs preferable
   d. Past experience in handling budgets and managing other personnel

EXAMPLE JOB DESCRIPTIONS
(continued)

The person hired to do the evaluation will have the following responsibilities:
a. Interviewing audiences to identify key evaluation questions related to curriculum revision
b. Designing an evaluation to answer key questions
c. Collecting ongoing information and reporting it to audiences
d. Managing the evaluation budget and staff

2. Necessary competencies:
   a. Interviewing and writing skills and sensitivity to multiple perspectives
   b. Design experience, especially in developing emergent designs
   c. Experience in synthesizing, sorting, and cataloging qualitative data (interviews, case studies) and reporting such data to multiple audiences
   d. Experience with managing budgets and coordinating staff

The project director will be responsible for evaluation tasks including:
a. Specifying evaluation questions and negotiating them with key audiences (e.g., chairperson, sponsor, trainees)
b. Determining information sources and drafting instruments to answer questions
c. Reporting results to key audiences in written form
d. Specifying a management plan for the evaluation activities
3. Preferred competencies:
   a. Experience with evaluation activities (training or actual evaluation experience)
   b. Background in drafting and analyzing surveys, attitudinal instruments, or interview data
   c. Credibility and interpersonal skills with fellow co-workers and trainees
   d. Ability to specify and maintain a management plan

PROVIDING SAFEGUARDS FOR EVALUATOR OBJECTIVITY

1. Recruit or train staff with evaluation skills.
2. Bring in a "meta-evaluator" at certain phases such as design, analysis, or reporting.
3. Use an "independent" observer or multiple observers.
4. Plan at the outset for an ongoing or summative "audit."
5. Provide for public or staff reviews at various times throughout the evaluation.

(See also *Meta Evaluation*, the last chapter in the Sourcebook).

HOW SHOULD EVALUATION RESPONSIBILITIES BE FORMALIZED?

The evaluation agreement or contract specifies what will be done, how, when, and by whom. It is better if the contract or agreement is written before it becomes necessary to have it—usually after the evaluation has been focused and initial design decisions have been made. Even in the most informal of settings, it is smart to specify and document in advance the conditions that will guide these procedures and uses. The process of contracting provides an opportunity for the evaluator and stakeholders to review the services that will be provided by the evaluator and evaluation.

Remember that a management plan is not a legally binding contract and cannot be substituted for one. If you are unsure about the contents of a contract or what would constitute a breach of it, have it reviewed by an outsider or attorney.

CHECKLIST OF POSSIBLE ISSUES TO BE CONSIDERED IN AN EVALUATION CONTRACT OR AGREEMENT

1. Purpose of the evaluation
2. Major evaluation questions
3. Strategy for collecting information
   a. information sources
   b. sampling strategy or protocol to be used
   c. instruments/protocol
   d. schedule
4. Procedures that will be used to analyze the information
   a. the kind of information you will have (e.g., test scores, case studies, interviews, questionnaires)
   b. the appropriate ways to analyze it (e.g., content analysis, descriptive statistics, inferential statistics)
5. The reporting plan
   a. who will get reports
   b. what will the reports look like
   c. what is the reporting schedule
   d. how can people express reactions to the reports
6. Bias concerns
   a. what is likely to bias collection, analyses and reporting, and how will it be controlled
7. Client services
   a. what services are the client, program staff, or the housing organization providing to the evaluation (e.g., services, data, personnel, information, facilities, materials)
8. Timeline
   a. on what schedule will work be completed
*9. Revisions
   a. how, when and under what circumstances can the contract be amended or terminated

* Remember that it will probably be necessary to amend the contract or memorandum of agreement if the evaluation design is readjusted. Make sure that the agreement can be revised to accommodate changes, especially in a responsive evaluation that has an emerging design.

CHECKLIST
(continued)

10. Meta Evaluation
    a. who will be brought in to review evaluation progress and outcomes and at what points
11. Budget
    a. how will the evaluation be financed
    b. what amounts will be paid, at what point, for which tasks

---

USING A
PROPOSAL FOR
THE FORMAL
AGREEMENT

1. The CONTRACTOR agrees to undertake, perform and complete the services more specifically described in "A Proposal for the Development and Implementation of an Educational Assessment Program," prepared jointly by the CONTRACTOR and SPONSOR and submitted on July 6, 1980, which Proposal is incorporated herein by reference.
2. The CONTRACTOR shall commence performance of this contract on the 6th day of July, 1981, and shall complete performance no later than the 31st day of December, 1982.
3. The SPONSOR agrees to pay the CONTRACTOR according to the following payment schedule:

December 1, 1980	$16,248.60
June 1, 1981	8,624.30
December 31, 1982	2,208.10

SAMPLE
CONTRACT
SPECIFYING
RESPONSIBILITIES
OF BOTH PARTIES
IN THE
EVALUATION

The Pokomo Heights School District, hereinafter referred to as the District, has requested technical research services for a curriculum study by Dakota University through its Service Center, hereinafter referred to as DU-SC. This agreement between the District and DU-SC specifies the responsibilities, schedule of events, costs, and payment schedule for the services. This agreement is in effect during the period of the project July 17, 1982, until January 31, 1982. It may be modified only by mutual agreement of the two parties.

In order to achieve the objectives of the research project, the District agrees to:

1. Meet with DU-SC staff to supply information about the capabilities, current practices, and constraints of the school system.
2. Collect documents as requested by DU-SC staff.
3. Specify needs to be addressed in the final technical report.
4. Identify criteria for evaluating plans for curriculum change.
5. Identify, and obtain the services of, people to serve on advocate and design teams.
6. Provide resource people for three advocate teams and one design team.
7. Provide for facilities, materials, duplication, and refreshments for advocate team and design team sessions.
8. Assist in data collection activities to support the work of advocate and design teams.
9. Provide secretarial support for three advocate teams and one design team.
10. Respond to any questions which DU-SC staff may have regarding this project.

SAMPLE
CONTRACT
SPECIFYING
RESPONSIBILITIES
OF BOTH PARTIES
IN THE
EVALUATION
(continued)

11. Submit a total payment of $59,605 for the services provided to the District by DU-SC upon completion of the project.

Dakota University Service Center agrees to:

1. Conduct an organizational meeting for the project between DU-SC and District staff.
2. Develop resource notebooks for advocate team use.
3. Develop a profile of students to be served by curriculum changes.
4. Coordinate project work with the District's Study Committee on Improving Student Achievement.
5. Identify promising strategies for curriculum change.
6. Design and implement an advocate team study.
7. Prepare a technical report for curriculum changes with operational details, budget, and special considerations.
8. Present a draft report to the District's administrative team.
9. Make revisions in the technical report as needed.

Signed on behalf of

Dakota University   Pokomo Heights School District

BUDGET

Personnel	$32,000
Fringe (25% of Personnel, excluding research assistants)	7,000
Travel and per diem	8,680
Materials and duplication	1,126
Communications	150
TOTAL DIRECT	$48,956
INDIRECT*	$10,649
TOTAL	$59,605

MEMORANDUM OF
AGREEMENT
BETWEEN A
PROJECT
DIRECTOR AND
EVALUATOR

October 12, 1979

Dr. Robert Brinkerhoff
The Evaluation Center
Western Michigan University
Kalamazoo, MI 49008

Dear Bob:

This letter is to confirm the various arrangements that Janet Tremain (of the University of Kansas) and I discussed with you by telephone on October 11 regarding three site visits that we would make on behalf of the Evaluation Training Consortium. We understand that the following conditions and stipulations will hold:

1. *Site selection.* You will select three project sites which we will visit for two days each. The projects should be chosen so as to be within reasonable travel distance of our two home bases: Lawrence, Kansas, and Blooming-ton, Indiana. Further, at least two of the sites should be representative of

MEMORANDUM OF
AGREEMENT
BETWEEN A
PROJECT
DIRECTOR AND
EVALUATOR
(continued)

sites at which you believe useful and constructive evaluation applications have been made. The third site may be either like the first two or chosen to represent sites at which little progress has been made in evaluation applications.

2. *Purpose of site visits.* Our inquiry at each site will be directed toward the following matters:

   a. Eliciting an adequate description of site activities primarily by asking various respondents what they believe, from their perspective, that we ought to know about their projects. These perspectives will be checked through document examination and actual site observation.

   b. Discovering what evaluation activities have taken place at the project site and determining what impact, if any, such evaluation has had on improving or refining the projects.

   c. Discovering what problems, if any, confront the project directors and/or evaluators in applying the results of evaluation studies. Their responses will furnish primary data for your task of designing a level III workshop.

   d. Discovering what residues exist at each site that are the result of participation in either a Level I and/or Level II workshop.

We shall of course not assert that whatever we discover at one or more of these sites holds for all sites or from some sub-set of them; our interest is not in what is happening universally but what *can* happen when conditions are right.

3. *Schedule.*

   a. *Advance materials.* Project directors should be asked to furnish copies of documents from their files in duplicate to both Dr. Tremain and me as much in advance of the actual site visit as possible. Such documents might include but not be limited to: project proposals, evaluation reports, reports to BEH, think pieces, mission statements, staffing documents, personnel vitas, and the like. We would like both current and existing historical versions of such documents to assess changes that may have occurred.

   b. *Site visits.* The following schedule of site visits and related analysis/reporting activity is proposed:

   1) Institution A .... November 29–30, 1979
   2) Preliminary analysis of Institution A
      data and development of interim
      report (probably oral)............. December 1, 1979
   3) Institution B:....................... January 17–18, 1980
   4) Institution C:....................... January 24–25, 1980
   5) Final analysis and reporting work
      session.......................... February 1–3, 1980*
   6) Final report .... February 15, 1980
      *Two of these three days.

---

* It is impossible at this time to be more definitive about just who will be interviewed. It seems likely that, in a University setting, such other interview subjects may include, say, the chairpersons of special, elementary, and secondary education; professors teaching special courses or new courses stimulated by 94-142 provisions or specific project activities; teachers and other program products that might be expected to have profited from project activities; project clientele such as administrators who hire teachers, special students exposed to them; and so on. Selections will be made in part after reading advance documents as in (a) above and partly on site as interviews unfold.

MEMORANDUM OF
AGREEMENT
BETWEEN A
PROJECT
DIRECTOR AND
EVALUATOR
(continued)

c. *Site activities*:

Day 1:

9:00–10:30	Interview with project director.
10:30–12:00	Interview with project evaluator.
12:00– 3:00	Reanalysis of documents based on inputs from first two interviews.
3:00– 5:00	Further interviews as unfolding information dictates.*

Day 2

9:00– 3:00	Further interviews as above.
3:00– 4:00	Development of staff feedback report.
4:00– 5:00	Staff debriefing and credibility check on our perceptions.

4. *Budget*. Note: except for honoraria all figures below are estimates. It is our expectation that this is a cost reimbursable proposal, so that our actual expenses will be reimbursed rather than being limited to the amounts shown. Of course should our expenses be less than the estimated amounts savings would accrue to ETC. We understand that since the ETC budget is not entirely firm you may wish to exercise the option of dropping one or all of the visits proposed. We expect the earliest possible notice from you in such a contingency.

a. *Honoraria*:

Howard Schmidt, 9 days @ $200/day..................	$ 1,800
Janet Tremain, 9 days @ $150/day....................	1,350

b. *Travel expenses*:

Travel to three sites, estimated @ $175, for two persons..	1,050
Travel from Lawrence to Bloomington (or vice-versa) for final analysis and report preparation, February 1–3, 1980...	175
Per diem, 14 person-days at sites plus 2 person-days for final analysis/reporting activity, 16 days @ $45/day ...	720
Local extras (e.g., mileage to airport, airport parking, taxis and limousines, etc., estimated at $30/trip/person (3 site trips × 2 persons plus trip for one person for final analysis)	210

c.	*Clerical funds* (type and produce up to ten final reports)...	150
d.	Miscellaneous (site long distance calls, postage ,etc.)....	100

TOTAL $ 5,555

It is our understanding that honoraria and expenses will be payable as services are provided and expenses are incurred. If there are aspects of this proposal which do not coincide with your understanding of our telephone conversation, will you please advise us at once?

We are excited about this task and look forward to working with you on it. We await your designation of the site for November 29–30 visit and receipt of advance documents from the project personnel.

Cordially,

Howard Schmidt
Professor of Education

HS:tl
cc: Janet Tremain

PITFALLS
AFFECTING THE
ADEQUACY OF AN
EVALUATION
AGREEMENT

1. Conflict with Overlapping Regulations
   failure to consider organizational guidelines
   union policies
   human rights guidelines & laws
   professional standards

2. Internal Inconsistencies
   budget, timeline & tasks aren't realistically integrated
   responsible personnel change throughout

3. Unrealistic Budget & Timeline
   budget is general, not tied to tasks, and is underestimated
   timeline is unrealistic & doesn't link tasks to a schedule

4. Failure to Negotiate Contract with Significant Audiences
   uncovering significant audiences who were not considered in the contract

5. Failure to Review
   contract initially responsive, but not amended when circumstances & goals changed
   contract not reviewed & hence inadvertently omitted facts

6. Failure to Indicate Report Responsibilities
   failure to indicate who is finally responsible for the evaluation report, its editing, and its release. Plans for the review, reaction & final release should be clear.

The final measure of an agreement's adequacy is the number of times throughout the evaluation that conflicts arise that had to be resolved without guidance from and outside the boundaries of the contract.

HOW MUCH SHOULD THE EVALUATION COST?

The budget for an evaluation is the plan for acquiring and using financial resources to conduct the evaluation. Budgeting, like contracting, provides another opportunity to review the evaluation design. Generally, an evaluation budget includes the following major categories:

1. Personnel (salaries and fringe benefits)
2. Consultants
3. Travel and per diem
4. Printing and shipping (postage)
5. Conferences and meetings
6. Data processing
7. Supplies and materials
8. Overhead (rent, utilities, telephone)

A rule of thumb is that an evaluation budget should be approximately 10% of the program or project budget. Like all rules of thumb, this is just a way of providing an estimate—a beginning point for you to figure. Evaluation also can be budgeted at only 5% of the budget or at 15–25%. There are good reasons for varying the budget percentage.

In general, the larger the percentage you budget, the more evaluation residue you should be expecting. Leftovers from a single-shot evaluation budget, for instance, might include a formalized information system, data bank, evaluation guidelines and workbooks, evaluation policies, trained staff, or even the plans for an office of evaluation. When a one-shot evaluation will serve short range and focused programmatic needs only, the budget probably should not extend over the 10% rule of thumb.

It's important that the expenses associated with various evaluation tasks be accurately estimated so you can plan for the needed resources. Of particular concern in costing out evaluation are: (1) the type of information collected; (2) the amount of information needed; (3) the location of information sources; (4) the timeline; and (5) the cost of personnel involved in collection, analysis, and reporting.

EXAMPLE 1–
PROJECTING THE
BALANCE FOR
THE END OF A
PROJECT YEAR

A cumulative report through the end of the second month for a 12 month project budget at $30,000*

A	B	C	D	E	F
Line Item	Total Budget	Total Expenses	Second Month Balance	Rate per Month	Projected Year End Balance
Salaries & Wages	18,000	3,800	14,200	1,900	(4,800)
Benefits	2,700	570	2,130	285	(720)
Consultants/ Expenses	5,500	300	5,200	150	3,700
Meeting Expenses	2,000	-0-	2,000	-0-	2,000
Duplicating/Printing	1,000	180	820	90	(80)
Office Supplies	300	250	50	125	(1,200)
Equipment	-0-	-0-	-0-	-0-	-0-
Communications	300	30	270	15	120
Audio-Visual	200	20	180	10	80
TOTAL	$30,000	$ 5,150	$24,850	$ 2,575	$(900)

A and B–Major categories and amounts of the line item budget for the project ($30,000)

C–Project director's accounting of his total expenses through the second month ($5,150)

D–Second Month Balance = Total Budget (B) less Expenses (C) = $24,850

E–Rate per month is the average amount being spent each month. To estimate this figure the director divided his 2-month total expenses (C) by two in order to determine the average amount being spent for one month. The total rate per month he averaged at $2,575.

F–To project the year end balance, the director multiplied his rate per month for each line item times 12 (12 months in his project year). Then he subtracted that projected amount from the total allocated for each line item (A). In the case of salaries and wages, for instance, this projected amount tells him that if he continues to spend at the same rate per month for 12 months, he will be in the red $4,800 at year's end. Parentheses indicate a minus or an amount which is in the red. In projecting budget amounts, most managers try to keep estimates of over-expenditures within 10%. This means that if a projected expenditure is over 10% action should be taken to bring it back in line. Notice, however, that when the project year end total is added, the director is anticipating a $900 over-expenditure.

* It is important to note that examples of budgets are included only to provide general information about budgeting and estimating costs. Time and economic changes quickly date sample budgets, and guidelines for estimating costs can change from institution to institution.

EXAMPLE 3
EVALUATION
COMPONENT FOR
A $216,000
PROGRAM

I. DIRECT COSTS		$11,440.00

A. *Personnel*
  Eric F. Schmidt, Ph.D. (23 days)
  Donald T. Trumper (14 days)
  Paul L. Simon (46 days)
  Donna T. Helbert (22 days)
  Eileen Feldt (28 days)
  Jane W. Newman (10 days)
  (in this budget, days as opposed to percentage of full
  responsibilities or FTE's are used. This is often the choice
  when many of the staff are not regularly on the payroll.
  See pp. 196 for corresponding management plan)

B. *Fringe* (16% of salaries)   1,830.00
  (notice that the fringe or payroll deduction established by
  housing institution varies over time and across institutions

C. *Supplies*   4,345.00

Keypunching	$385.00
Printing and duplicating (surveys, envelopes, cover letters and reports)	1,750.00
Stamps and Postage	950.00
Telephone	875.00
Office Supplies	385.00

  (See Budget 2 for a breakdown of
  these items; keypunching is another
  item on which to seek competitive
  bids.)

D. *Transportation and lodging for staff and consultants*   946.00
  (This item represents in-state mileage and per diem for
  meals. A subtotal without a breakdown, such as this one,
  invites investigation)

E. *Computer Time*   2,750.00
  (This is an item for which you should seek competitive
  bids. It is an estimate affected by time, personnel, &
  deadline)

F. *Consultants*   710.00
  5 days @ $100.00
  3 days @ 70.00
  (Consultant fees that vary usually indicate a formal
  educational training)

II. INDIRECT COSTS (8%)		1,762.00
III. TOTAL PRICE		$23,783.00

TIPS FOR PROMOTING FISCAL ACCOUNTABILITY

1. maintain accurate financial records with public access
2. reflect comparison shopping or contract bidding for goods and services
3. reflect and document changes in the design or environment which bring about budgetary adjustments
4. account for dollars spent on evaluation objectives and tasks
5. systematically review the budget in light of evaluation progress
6. include fiscal information in interim and final reports for the public record

HOW SHOULD EVALUATION TASKS BE ORGANIZED AND SCHEDULED?

The management plan begins when the evaluator and stakeholders are ready to sit down and ask, "What must be done, when, and by whom?" The plan that emerges provides a breakdown of tasks and a timeline for all those involved in the evaluation. Keep in mind that a management plan is not a contract; it is not legally binding nor does it address ethical issues regarding responsibilities. Nor is the management plan an evaluation design; it does not determine the evaluation purpose and questions. In fact, it is guided by them.

The management plan charts the activities needed to implement the evaluation design and so provides a system for keeping track of progress. Most importantly, the management plan is a tool which encourages planning and forecasting and, depending upon the type of plan used, it can also demonstrate the relationship of tasks and the sequence of activities.

To put together a management plan for an evaluation, you need the following information:

1. specific activities that must be accomplished
2. when each activity needs to be done
3. who will be responsible for activities
4. how the activity will be accomplished
5. what resources are available to do the evaluation
6. the evaluation design or a general plan specifying what is to be done
7. update on design changes to revise and/or refine the management plan as time goes by

Additionally, it is important to specify who will be responsible for drafting, monitoring, and supervising the formalized management plan. Regardless of how many people are involved in an evaluation or its management, one person needs to be designated as ultimately responsible for the management plan. If that person is not also the evaluator, he or she needs to work closely with the evaluator.

PERT (PROGRAM EVALUATION & REVIEW TECHNIQUE)

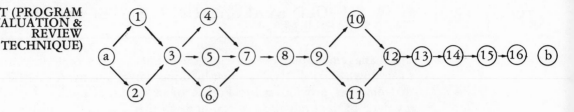

Activity or Procedure	Subgoal or Event
	a. Start scale development
1. Search literature for attitude scales	1. Complete search
2. Review attitude scaling procedures	2. Complete review
3. Select procedure to be used	3. Complete section
4. Construct scale items	4. Complete item construction
5. Assemble prototype scale	5. Complete scale assembly
6. Arrange field test of prototype scale	6. Complete arrangements
7. Field-test prototype scale	7. Complete field test
8. Score scale	8. Complete scoring
9. Item-analyze scale	9. ILLEGIBLE??
10. ILLEGIBLE??	

Pert is a set of time-related activities needed to accomplish an objective; it gives expected time for completing the work and probability for completing within that time. Many software programs at universities include PERT. They can be accessed easily and the PERT chart done efficiently from a computer terminal.

TIME/ACTIVITY ANALYSIS CHART

Time/Activity Analysis Chart

Activity	Personnel Responsible	Person Days	October 1 2 3 4	November 1 2 3 4	December 1 2 3 4
OBJECTIVE 1	Schmidt				
1. Develop research questions	Simon Trumper	14	├────────┤		
2. Determine data collection procedures (includes development of instrumentation)	Simon Schmidt	15		├────────────────────	────────┤
3. Develop analysis plan	Feldt Simon Schmidt	7			

Time/Activity Analysis Chart

Activity	Personnel Responsible	Person Days	October				November				December			
			1	2	3	4	1	2	3	4	1	2	3	4
4. Conduct study with appropriate respondents (develop sample)	Feldt Helbert	16					├─	──	──	──	─┤			
5A. Collect data	Simon Helbert Trumper Feldt	38							├─	──	──	──	──	─┤
B. Process data	Newman Helbert	13											├─	─┤
Objective 2:														
6. Analyze all data	Schmidt Simon Feldt	21												
Objective 3:														
7. Develop recommendations and produce final report	Schmidt Simon Trumper	19												

total = 143 days

The example above is a simple and easy way to break down evaluation tasks by objectives, person responsible, days allocated to task, and timeline for beginning, doing, and completing the task.

**ACTIVITY CHART
FROM MANAGING
A PROJECT
(EXCERPT)**

The evaluator put this chart
together initially by listing
tasks on 3 × 5 cards and
taping them to butcher
paper. Only a portion of the
chart is reproduced here.

1.1 Select content areas, general layout and criteria for handbook sections

1.2 Obtain, review and select existing materials for inclusion in parent handbook

1.2a Obtain approval or copyright permission for inclusion of existing materials

E. Obtain and analyze extant data to determine parent information needs

1.3 Select and consult with appropriate experts to assist in developing new materials

1.10 and 2.14 Draft evaluation formats and procedures for handbook and training sessions

START
· Obtain and orient stage
· Confirm space and equipment

2.4 Determine content of training sessions

2.5 Draft agenda for training sessions and establish criteria for facilities

2.12 Draft script for training sessions

E4. Conduct phone interviews with motel sales managers to evaluate facilities

A

2.1 Work with PTA office to identify pool of parents

2.7 Obtain list of parent invitees from PTA office

The Systems Network portrays each major management activity as an individual box. The arrows indicate what is needed to complete an activity and what the complete activity, in turn, feeds into. After the network is completed, activities can be linked to staff and timelines. This system is explained in the *Practitioner's Guide*, by Diane K. Yavorsky, Evaluation Research Center, University of Virginia, 1978.

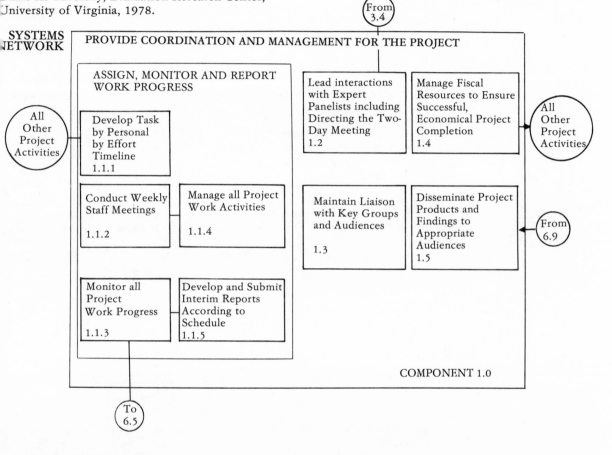

Activity by Staff Timeline

Activity Number	Primary Staff	Jan	Feb	Mar	Apr	May	Jun	Jul	Aug	Sep	Oct	Nov	Dec
1.1.1 Develop Timeline	Haladyna	├───────┤											
1.1.2 Conduct Staff Meetings	Staff		├───────┤		├─────────┤				├───────┤		├───────┤		
1.1.3 Monitor Progress	Haladyna	├──────────────────────────┤											
1.1.4 Manage Activities	Haladyna	├──────────────────────────────┤											
1.1.5 Develop Interim Reports	Haladyna			X			X			X			

EXAMPLE OF A MANAGEMENT PLAN FOR AN INSERVICE EVALUATION

This example illustrates how a very small and limited evaluation effort can be documented by activity and deadline.

Management Plan

Steps	Person Responsible	When
PHASE I		
1. Analyze documents for pertinent information (e.g., district needs assessment, building and district policies and procedures)		Jan. 5–Feb. 1
develop analysis procedure	Joyce	
analyze documents	Joyce; teacher volunteers	
summarize	Joyce	
2. Analyze/interpret all findings	Joyce and Jane	Feb. 1–15
3. Prepare report for teachers and distribute	Joyce	Feb. 1–15
4. Conduct teachers' meeting	Joyce	March 15
5. Revise report as needed	Joyce and Jane	March 15–30
PHASE II		
1. Review literature on in-service programs	Joyce (with assistance from University consultant)	April 1–30
2. Review evaluations of past inservices in building	Joyce and former inservice coordinator	April 1–30
3. Identify and talk to experts from successful programs	Joyce and Jane	May 1–15
4. Develop design and list of criteria	Joyce and Jane	May 15–30
5. Review design		
identify reviewers	Jane	Sept. 1–20
contact reviewers	Jane	
conduct reviews	Joyce	
summarize findings	Joyce	
6. Review design, as needed	Joyce and Jane	Sept. 21–30
7. Prepare report for teachers	Joyce	Oct. 1–10

WHAT KINDS OF PROBLEMS CAN BE EXPECTED?

Evaluation literature and experience tells us that there are certain problems that can be counted upon when implementing evaluation. In this section we try to forecast some of these problems, provide information about how to monitor to prevent them from occurring, and propose strategies to use to intervene when they occur.

The key issue in monitoring the evaluation is making sure the design is still intact and, more importantly, that it is still relevant and appropriate. Don't adhere to an evaluation design that because of programmatic or situational changes is no longer meaningful. Review the design with stakeholders regularly to find out if revisions are necessary.

Set up a *review schedule* for the design (consider other people besides yourself that might be consulted)
Review the design in light of the management plan and budget
Make necessary changes, document them, and share them with key stakeholders

PROBLEMS TO ANTICIPATE IN EVALUATION

FUNCTION	AREA OF CONCERN	SOME PROBLEMS TO ANTICIPATE	SOLUTION STRATEGY
Evaluation Focus	1. Purpose	1.1 purpose becomes invalid 1.2 additional purpose emerges	1. · revise or add purpose or abort evaluation
	2. Evaluation questions	2.1 questions become invalid 2.2 more questions need to be added 2.3 questions need to be refined	2. · refine, add, delete evaluation questions and check congruence with purpose
	3. Audiences	3.1 audiences change 3.2 important audiences were overlooked 3.3 audiences react negatively	3. · add audiences initially overlooked · provide debriefing, open discussions, public information
	4. Setting	4.1 setting changes dramatically	4. · readjust purpose and design to setting or, if setting is too hostile, abort evaluation
	5. Object	5.1 object changes so that descriptions, design, and even purpose are not appropriate	5. · change the purpose and questions as appropriate, continue only if "changed object" still can and should be evaluated

FUNCTION	AREA OF CONCERN	SOME PROBLEMS TO ANTICIPATE	SOLUTION STRATEGY
The Evaluation Design	1. Evaluation approach	1.1 existing evaluation technique forced on problem 1.2 no personnel to run selected evaluation approach 1.3 disagreement about best evaluation approach	1. · provide alternative and competing designs · change design or bring in consultant · assess approach in light of program, purpose
	2. Design issues	2.1 inability to address all relevant design issues 2.2 design issues change 2.3 design will not provide valid information	2. · select and justify issues to be dealt with · monitor design issues and refine to meet needs · abort evaluation or redesign
	3. Design construction	3.1 design doesn't answer questions 3.2 design doesn't include practical or credible information collection	3. · abort or redesign · anticipate reporting, analysis, and information collection in the evaluation design and review
	4. Design quality	4.1 lack of agreement about the quality of the design 4.2 evaluators unable to implement	4. · select standards by which design will be assessed and apply bring in consultant (meta-evaluator) or change staff
The Collection and Plan Process	1. Information sources	1.1 existing sources aren't tapped 1.2 desired information not available 1.3 limited information available	1. · carefully review what already exists and attempt to use and not to duplicate · use multiple or alternative information sources
	2. Procedures	2.1 appropriate procedures limited 2.2 procedures impractical 2.3 procedures not trustworthy according to audiences	2. · review alternatives with experts · simplify if too costly · use procedures that are credible to audiences
	3. Information scope	3.1 too much information available 3.2 too little information available 3.3 much information isn't very reliable	3. · sample using relevant criteria · use multiple information sources (tests, people, documents)
	4. Instrumentation	4.1 no instruments available 4.2 a number of instruments available 4.3 instrument developed doesn't work	4. · construct after reviewing others · select according to predetermined criteria · pilot to prevent failure
	5. Reliability and validity	5.1 nothing known about validity or reliability 5.2 instrument or procedure has low or no validity or reliability 5.3 no one capable of assessing these criteria	5. · find out; pilot · scrap instrument or refine · have a consultant review

FUNCTION	AREA OF CONCERN	SOME PROBLEMS TO ANTICIPATE	SOLUTION STRATEGY
	6. Collection plan	6.1 plan is too costly in terms of time and money 6.2 plan is not documented	6. · document and access plan to prevent · include this in management plan and disseminate
The Analysis Plan	1. Returned data	1.1 data unreliable, missing, messy 1.2 data cannot be synthesized 1.3 data are bulky	1. · monitor and design to prevent · design so categories or sorting are determined in advance · store and safeguard using an access system
	2. Data worth	2.1 data don't answer evaluation questions 2.2 data aren't believable	2. · establish appropriate and credible evidence in advance
	3. Analysis procedure	3.1 difficulty understanding data and what they indicate	3. · try a number of dependable analyses · use graphs and aides to help audiences · justify appropriateness of analyses
	4. Interpretation	4.1 disagreement exists about what information "means"	4. · provide audience alternative perspectives in report · include minority opinions · interpret information in light of several value stances
The Reporting Strategy	1. Report purpose(s)	1.1 different audiences want different information 1.2 one report wouldn't be readable for everyone 1.3 information is too technical	1. · plan for and provide multiple reports · append technical material, clarify in graphs, provide lay person summaries
	2. Audiences	2.1 new audiences become interested 2.2 audiences confused about how to use report	2. · include new audiences in written or oral report schedule · prepare reports with audiences in mind
	3. Content	3.1 disagreement exists about what should be in report 3.2 client wants to delete material	3. · outline proposed areas to be included at outset; guarantee balance
	4. Delivery	4.1 audiences want reports at different times	4. · specify schedule in advance and follow it. Provide ongoing communications and updates
	5. Style and structure	5.1 multiple reports become necessary along the way 5.2 reports serve a number of purposes	5. · coordinate all reports through one person (team) · select best alternative report structures for sequential and multiple reports

FUNCTION	AREA OF CONCERN	SOME PROBLEMS TO ANTICIPATE	SOLUTION STRATEGY
	6. Interpretation	6.1 strong differences exist about what the evaluation means 6.2 evaluators' recommendations are not in agreement with key audience	6. · report different interpretations or append a minority report · seek consensus or report differing interpretations
	7. Schedule	7.1 evaluation reports not ready on time	7. · plan and document the schedule for report; plan backwards so report deadline is met
Evaluating the Evaluation	1. Why evaluate	1.1 credibility of evaluation questioned 1.2 quality of design, information collection or analysis is poor 1.3 evaluator needs guidance or competence questioned	1. · bring in credible outsiders for independent observation · anticipate stage of evaluation procedure that needs review · select consultant to provide ongoing assistance
	2. Who	2.1 decision as to whom should be brought in to assess evaluation	2. · plan for meta evaluation and provide alternative choices for key audiences to select from
	3. Criteria	3.1 by what criteria or standards should the evaluation be evaluated	3. · determine criteria at the outset and share them with others · plan the evaluation to meet criteria

---

STOP PROBLEMS BEFORE THEY OCCUR

Ensure minimal disruption to the program (e.g., humane interactions and appropriate use of program personnel/resources)

Follow appropriate protocol (e.g., see and talk to supervisors first and then their staff)

Use discretion in discussing the evaluation or program progress

Respond to changes in the program or organization (crisis, changing goals) in light of the evaluation and not the program

Oversee staff and/or evaluation responsibilities (monitor design, management plan, and budget)

Absolutely adhere to final delivery date for the evaluation

Be alert to political factions as they emerge and assess them in light of their influence on the evaluation

Be full and frank in disclosures about the evaluation (when the evaluation is discussed, what is said should be such that it can be shared with all audiences)

Involve critics and skeptics through discussions, memoranda, hearings, requests for minority opinions, etc.

Consistently attend to key stakeholders and their views about the evaluation's progress and usefulness. (This will alert you to changes in purpose, questions, and object as well as refining your knowledge about "useful" information.)

REFERENCES

Anderson, S.B. & Ball, S. *The Profession and Practice of Program Evaluation*. San Francisco: Jossey-Bass, 1978.

Cook, Desmond L. *Educational Project Management*. Columbus, Ohio: Charles E. Merrill Publishing Co., 1971.

Joint Committee on Standards for Educational Evaluation. *Standards for Evaluation of Educational Programs, Projects & Materials*. New York: McGraw-Hill, 1981.

Scriven, Michael. Evaluation Bias and Its Control. *Occasional Paper Series*, No. 4, Evaluation Center, College of Education, Western Michigan University, Kalamazoo, Michigan, June, 1975.

Smith, Nick L. *Evaluation Contracting Checklist*. Northwest Regional Educational Laboratory, 300 S.W. Sixth Avenue, Portland, Oregon 97204.

Yavorsky, Diane K. *Discrepancy Evaluation: A Practitioner's Guide*. Evaluation Research Center, University of Virginia, 1978.

Meta-Evaluation

WHAT IT IS Just as you can evaluate a training project or a teacher training program, you can also evaluate your evaluations of those enterprises. In fact, if evaluators are going to "practice what they preach," this becomes mandatory. Meta-evaluation can often be done along with your "regular" evaluation activities to help make them better. It can also be done while you are evaluating or after you have finished the regular evaluation to give you and others an idea of how well things turned out.

Meta-evaluation (evaluating an evaluation) is based on the notion that evaluation ought to be a learning experience for all those involved in it, so that the evaluation can improve as it progresses and that future evaluations can be more successful. Meta-evaluation can serve many purposes. External meta-evaluation (e.g., using an expert evaluation consultant) can be used to certify and verify evaluation design, progress, and results for more certain and credible accountability. An internal evaluation report, for example, when accompanied by an external meta-evaluation report, will carry more authoritative credibility. Use of external meta-evaluation also provides an excellent basis on which to revise an evaluation design, its ongoing work, or evaluation reports. Or, if the evaluation's already concluded, a meta-evaluation can help you decide how seriously to take the results.

Less formal, internal meta-evaluation procedures are useful to revise an evaluation and also can help keep it on track. Likewise, meta-evaluation efforts help maintain commitment and involvement and raise the credibility and authority of the evaluation.

WHAT IT IS
(continued)   Meta-evaluation efforts can range from an extensive verification and replication study, to a brief consultant visit, to a short staff meeting to check over a survey instrument. (In fact, you do meta-evaluation whenever you ponder and investigate your evaluation design and functions.)

WHEN YOU META-EVALUATE

You can and should bring in a meta-evaluator whenever the evaluator or evaluation needs assistance. This might be at the planning stage or at any point during the evaluation. Often meta-evaluation is used to assess the evaluation after its completion. In these cases, key audiences are able to assess how seriously they should take the evaluation results, and evaluators can consider how the next evaluation might be made better.*

* Dick Frisbie, Western Michigan University, was a primary contributor to this chapter and wrote several draft versions.

WHAT ARE SOME GOOD USES OF META-EVALUATION?

Since your evaluation may quickly become a rather complicated activity, it is helpful to think of its quality in terms of each of the functions we have presented in the previous chapters. That way, you can more easily zero in on a particular problem, if one area seems to be giving you more trouble than the others.

The grid below is used to present some uses to which you could put meta-evaluation in terms of the categories we have just discussed. What's important to remember is that it's never too soon or too late to question the soundness and the worth of any part of your evaluation. Furthermore, if you don't question its quality, rest assured that someone else probably will.

SOME META-EVALUATION PURPOSES	Focus of Meta-Evaluation		
Evaluation Functions	Evaluating Evaluation Plans	Evaluating Evaluation in Progress	Evaluating Evaluation after its Completion
Focusing Evaluation	to assess and help refine the evaluation purpose and questions, investigate setting and identify audiences	to determine whether selected questions and purposes are being pursued; to evaluate how worthwhile they are	to evaluate the soundness and worth of the evaluation purpose and the questions addressed
Designing Evaluation	to evaluate and refine design strategies or to provide information about options and aid in designing	to evaluate the effectiveness of the design being implemented; to help monitor or revise if necessary	to determine whether the evaluation design was sound, implemented properly, and useful for audience(s)
Collecting Information	to evaluate or help design or select instruments and collection strategy	to observe and evaluate the collection of information	to assess the quality and relevance of information collected and methods used to collect it
Analyzing Information	to guide primary evaluator in selecting possible analysis strategies and consider who will interpret and how	to evaluate the analysis process and how effectively data are being aggregated, sorted and analyzed	to evaluate the adequacy and the accuracy of analyses and the interpretations of analyses

SOME META-EVALUATION PURPOSES *(continued)*	Focus of Meta-Evaluation			
	Evaluation Functions	Evaluating Evaluation Plans	Evaluating Evaluation in Progress	Evaluating Evaluation after its Completion
	Reporting Information	to evaluate report strategy and suggest format, audiences to consider, and report contents	to read and evaluate report drafts, discuss alternative reports, refine technical or lay people reports	to evaluate the evaluation reports, their balance, timeliness, adequacy and ensuing use
	Managing Evaluation	to evaluate and refine the management plan, budget, and contract	to evaluate how adequately the management plan is being monitored and the appropriateness of the contract and budget	to evaluate how well the evaluation was managed, and budgeted; to determine whether costs were reasonable and agreements upheld

SOME TYPICAL USES OF META-EVALUATION IN TRAINING PROGRAM EVALUATION*

Strategy for Meta-Evaluation

Have an external evaluation expert review the evaluation (its design, operation and findings), then write a summary meta-evaluation report for dissemination to key audiences.

Devote several (or even one) project staff meeting to a discussion of the evaluation's progress. Structure critical discussion around key criteria (e.g., utility, accuracy, propriety, feasibility).

Conduct reviews of all evaluation instruments with one or more of the following: measurement experts; staff members; potential respondents. Do this with analysis and other technical areas.

When It's Useful

Often, an internal evaluation may lack authority and credibility to outside audiences (e.g., a funding agent). The meta-evaluation can help increase the credibility of the evaluation. And, it helps the project staff weigh the significance of their findings.

When project staff are unfamiliar with evaluation, these meetings can do much to gain their greater understanding and commitment. Meetings like this help keep an evaluation on track and ensure greater flexibility and responsiveness when changes in the project occur rapidly.

"Home-made" instruments are notoriously susceptible to errors in content and structure. Reviews of instruments almost always result in revisions, and subsequently more reliable data.

* Most often, several of these are used in any one evaluation, and often in combinations not listed above.

**SOME TYPICAL
USES OF META-
EVALUATION IN
TRAINING
PROGRAM
EVALUATION***
(continued)

Strategy for Meta-Evaluation	When It's Useful
Have an expert review the evaluation design and prepare a report and/or conduct a summary discussion with evaluators and project staff. (See Case C-4 for an example.)	Evaluating an evaluation design before the evaluation is begun can help revise, verify and certify the design. The money spent on this will more than likely be recaptured in a better and more efficient evaluation.
Conduct panel reviews and hearings (e.g., at a conference) of your evaluation design, reports and findings. Disseminate your evaluation for critical reading and comment.	An especially important or otherwise significant evaluation ought to receive critical attention and dissemination.
Have an evaluation consultant work with you to review your plans and suggest revisions at several key points (e.g., design, data collection, interpretation, reporting).	When you do your own evaluation, an expert can help you make your work more effective, efficient and sound.

WHO SHOULD DO THE META-EVALUATION?

Even though the demands on evaluators are high, the demands on meta-evaluators are even higher. Not only should they be competent enough to *do* the original evaluation, but they also have to be able to tell if it was a good or bad one and be able to convince others that they know the difference. The types of staffing options mentioned in Managing Evaluation (pp. 177–178) are also available for meta-evaluation; but because of the additional expectations, some of the options will usually be preferred over others.

External meta-evaluators are usually preferred over insiders because they are likely to have more credibility to people outside of the project or organization. This is particularly important when you are concerned with an outsider's reaction to the evaluation. If you're doing the meta-evaluation mostly for people on the inside, having an external meta-evaluator (even if it's only someone from a different office of your own organization) also provides an excellent opportunity for you to get a fresh perspective, another point of view.

It is often preferable for a team to conduct the meta-evaluation, since it is difficult to get the necessary time and skills from a single individual. Of course, the more skilled the people are in relation to *all* of the content and evaluation areas, and the smaller your evaluation is, the fewer people you will need for the meta-evaluation.

If you're going for a fresh, outside perspective or for someone who has good credibility with outside audiences, it makes sense to have this kind of person around only for a short time. Have them do the job and be done with it. If you need them full time, maybe they should be running the evaluation outright.

Finally, if a choice *has* to be made between the two, we consider an expert in evaluation to be more crucial than an expert in the content area of interest. The reason for this is that meta-evaluation focuses on how good the *evaluation* is. If you don't have to choose between one or the other, you will do even better to include experts in both evaluation and content area.

Options	Reasons for Preference
Internal Meta-Evaluator(s) vs.	CONS bias (actual or perceived) because of conflict of interest in evaluating a program in which there is a personal investment
External Meta-Evaluator(s)	PROS comes without preconceived notion about the program is seen as independent observer by staff, outsiders

Options	Reasons for Preference
Individual Meta-Evaluation vs. Team Meta-Evaluation	**CONS** success or failure heavily dependent upon a single individual **PROS** composite of multiple skills and perspectives, especially regarding content area and evaluation expertise
Full-time Meta-Evaluator(s) vs. Part-time Meta-Evaluator(s)	**CONS** cost involved **PROS** multiple authorities can be brought in for short periods of time effective use of outside expertise
Content Expert vs. Evaluation Expert	**PROS** knows content and object well can "pick up" many evaluation skills through experience **PROS** brings in experience and technical skills to run evaluation provides multiple options through own background

WHAT CRITERIA SHOULD YOU USE TO EVALUATE THE EVALUATION?

If an evaluation is going to help improve a training program or be used to help decide if it should be continued, it's going to have to be a "good" evaluation. In order to decide what's good or bad about an evaluation you need a set of criteria or standards on which to base judgments. This is a different matter than deciding whether a program is good or bad. When you're looking at a training project, your evaluation question might be, "how can we tell if we have a good training project?" Your meta-evaluation question would then be, "How can we tell if we have a good evaluation of the training project?"

There are a number of sets of criteria and standards already available for judging evaluation. Some of them are listed below.

STANDARDS FOR EVALUATIONS OF EDUCATIONAL PROGRAMS, PROJECTS AND MATERIALS

Standards for Evaluations of Educational Programs, Projects, and Materials is by the Joint Committee on Standards for Educational Evaluation. These *Standards* are organized into thirty standards and four domains of evaluation which address utility (evaluations should be useful and practical), feasibility (evaluations should be realistic and prudent), propriety (evaluations should be conducted legally and ethically), and accuracy (evaluations should be technically adequate). A listing of the *Standards* follows:

A *Utility Standards*
The Utility Standards are intended to ensure that an evaluation will serve the practical information needs of given audiences. These standards are:

A1 *Audience Identification*
Audiences involved in or affected by the evaluation should be identified, so that their needs can be addressed.

A2 *Evaluator Credibility*
The persons conducting the evaluation should be both trustworthy and competent to perform the evaluation, so that their findings achieve maximum credibility and acceptance.

A3 *Information Scope and Selection*
Information collected should be of such scope and selected in such ways as to address pertinent questions about the object of the evaluation and be responsive to the needs and interests of specified audiences.

A4 *Valuational Interpretation*
The perspectives, procedures, and rationale used to interpret the findings should be carefully described, so that the bases for value judgments are clear.

A5 *Report Clarity*
The evaluation report should describe the object being evaluated and its context and the purposes, procedures, and findings of the evaluation, so that the audiences will readily understand what was done, why it was done, what information was obtained, what conclusions were drawn, and what recommendations were made.

STANDARDS FOR
EVALUATIONS OF
EDUCATIONAL
PROGRAMS,
PROJECTS AND
MATERIALS
(continued)

A6 *Report Dissemination*

Evaluation findings should be disseminated to clients and other right-to-know audiences, so that they can assess and use the findings.

A7 *Report Timeliness*

Release of reports should be timely, so that audiences can best use the reported information.

A8 *Evaluation Impact*

Evaluations should be planned and conducted in ways that encourage follow-through by members of the audiences.

B *Feasibility Standards*

The Feasibility Standards are intended to ensure that an evaluation will be realistic, prudent, diplomatic, and frugal; they are:

B1 *Practical Procedures*

The evaluation procedures should be practical, so that disruption is kept to a minimum and that needed information can be obtained.

B2 *Political Viability*

The evaluation should be planned and conducted with anticipation of the different positions of various interest groups, so that their cooperation may be obtained and so that possible attempts by any of these groups to curtail evaluation operations or to bias or misapply the results can be averted or counteracted.

B3 *Cost Effectiveness*

The evaluation should produce information of sufficient value to justify the resources extended.

C *Propriety Standards*

The Propriety Standards are intended to ensure that an evaluation will be conducted legally, ethically, and with due regard for the welfare of those involved in the evaluation, as well as those affected by its results. These standards are:

C1 *Formal Obligation*

Obligations of the formal parties to an evaluation (what is to be done, how, by whom, when) should be agreed to in writing, so that these parties are obligated to adhere to all conditions of the agreement or formally to renegotiate it.

C2 *Conflict of Interest*

Conflict of interest, frequently unavoidable, should be dealt with openly and honestly, so that it does not compromise the evaluation processes and results.

C3 *Full and Frank Disclosure*

Oral and written evaluation reports should be open, direct, and honest in their disclosure of pertinent findings, including limitations of the evaluation.

C4 *Public's Right to Know*

The formal parties to an evaluation should respect and assure the public's right to know, within the limits of other related principles and statutes, such as those dealing with public safety and the right to privacy.

STANDARDS FOR
EVALUATIONS OF
EDUCATIONAL
PROGRAMS,
PROJECTS AND
MATERIALS
(continued)

C5 *Rights of Human Subjects*

Evaluations should be designed and conducted so that the rights and welfare of the human subjects are respected and protected.

C6 *Human Interactions*

Evaluators should respect human dignity and worth in their interactions with other persons associated with an evaluation.

C7 *Balanced Reporting*

The evaluation should be complete and fair in its presentation of strengths and weaknesses of the object under investigation, so that strengths can be built upon and problem areas addressed.

C8 *Fiscal Responsibility*

The evaluator's allocation and expenditure of resources should reflect sound accountability procedures and otherwise be prudent and ethically responsible.

D *Accuracy Standards*

The Accuracy Standards are intended to ensure that an evaluation will reveal and convey technically adequate information about the features of the object being studied that determine its worth or merit. These standards are:

D1 *Object Identification*

The object of the evaluation (program, project, material) should be sufficiently examined, so that the form(s) of the object being considered in the evaluation can be clearly identified.

D2 *Context Analysis*

The context in which the program, project, or material exists should be examined in enough detail, so that its likely influences on the object can be identified.

D3 *Described Purposes and Procedures*

The purposes and procedures of the evaluation should be monitored and described in enough detail, so that they can be identified and assessed.

D4 *Defensible Information Sources*

The sources of information should be described in enough detail, so that the adequacy of the information can be assessed.

D5 *Valid Measurement*

The information-gathering instruments and procedures should be chosen or developed and then implemented in ways that will assure that the interpretation arrived at is valid for the given use.

D6 *Reliable Measurement*

The information-gathering instruments and procedures should be chosen or developed and then implemented in ways that will assure that the information obtained is sufficiently reliable for the intended use.

D7 *Systematic Data Control*

The data collected, processed, and reported in an evaluation should be reviewed and corrected, so that the results of the evaluation will not be flawed.

STANDARDS FOR EVALUATIONS OF EDUCATIONAL PROGRAMS, PROJECTS AND MATERIALS
(continued)

D8 *Analysis of Quantitative Information*

Quantitative information in an evaluation should be appropriately and systematically analyzed to ensure supportable interpretations.

D9 *Analysis of Qualitative Information*

Qualitative information in an evaluation should be appropriately and systematically analyzed to ensure supportable interpretations.

D10 *Justified Conclusions*

The conclusions reached in an evaluation should be explicitly justified, so that the audiences can assess them.

D11 *Objective Reporting*

The evaluation procedures should provide safeguards to protect the evaluation findings and reports against distortion by the personal feelings and biases of any party to the evaluation.

EVALUATION RESEARCH SOCIETY (ERS) STANDARDS FOR PROGRAM EVALUATION

Based on the 1980 ERS Exposure Draft, fifty-five professional standards are divided into six categories.

Phases of Evaluation
1. Formulation and Negotiation (12)
2. Structure and Design (6)
3. Data Collection and Preparation (12)
4. Data Analysis and Interpretation (9)
5. Communication and Disclosure (10)
6. Utilization (6)

JOINT DISSEMINATION AND REVIEW PANEL CRITERIA

The purpose of JDRP is to review the evidence of effectiveness submitted for a wide variety of educational products and practices. Only those submissions approved by JDRP may in any way be endorsed by the Department of Education or disseminated as exemplary using Federal Education Division funds.

According to JDRP, an adequate evaluation must be interpretable and credible, in terms of both the project and its evaluation. This means that: (1) the existence of an apparent effect must be established; (2) there must be evidence that the effect occurred as a result of the intervention in question; (3) there must be evidence that it would not have occurred without the intervention. Six criteria have been established to help determine if an evaluation has established these points. They are:

Criterion 1: Did a change occur?

Criterion 2: Was the effect consistent enough and observed often enough to be statistically significant?

Criterion 3: Was the effect educationally significant?

Criterion 4: Can the intervention be implemented in another location with a reasonable expectation of comparable impact?

Criterion 5: How likely is it that the observed effects resulted from the intervention?

Criterion 6: Is the presented evidence believable and interpretable?

STANDARDS FOR AUDITS OF GOVERNMENTAL ORGANIZATIONS, PROGRAMS, ACTIVITIES, AND FUNCTIONS

These standards must be followed for audits when federal dollars are involved, and they are recommended for use by the Comptroller General for state and local audits. These standards are divided into three main elements for the expanded scope of auditing a government organization, program, activity, or function.

Scope of Audit Work Using the GAO Standards

1. *Financial and compliance*—determines (a) whether the financial statements of an audited entity present fairly the financial position and the results of financial operations in accordance with generally accepted accounting principles and (b) whether the entity has complied with laws and regulations that may have a material effect upon the financial statements.
2. *Economy and efficiency*—determines (a) whether the entity is managing and utilizing its resources (such as personnel, property, space) economically and efficiently, (b) the causes of inefficiencies or uneconomical practices, and (c) whether the entity has complied with laws and regulations concerning matters of economy and efficiency.
3. *Program results*—determines (a) whether the desired results or benefits established by the legislature or other authorizing body are being achieved and (b) whether the agency has considered alternatives that might yield desired results at a lower cost.

In determining the scope for a particular audit, responsible audit and entity officials should consider the needs of the potential users of audit findings.

U.S. OFFICE OF SPECIAL EDUCATION AND REHABILITATION SERVICES, HANDICAPPED PERSONNEL PREPARATION PROGRAM: GUIDELINES FOR DEVELOPING/ RATING THE ADEQUACY OF PROGRAM EVALUATION DESIGNS INCLUDED WITH FUNDING PROPOSALS

These guidelines make up the specific criteria OSE uses to help select projects with sound evaluation designs. Here is a summary of the guidelines for the 1982 fiscal year (U.S. Department of Education, 1981).

Evaluation: Does the proposal describe an evaluation design which specifies:

1. An appropriate evaluation methodology used to judge the success of each project subcomponent?
2. The kinds of data to be collected for each subcomponent?
3. The criteria to be used to evaluate the result of the project?
4. Procedure for assessing the attainment of competence within the project?
5. A method to assess the contribution of project graduates
   a. toward meeting the needs of children INCLUDING the number of graduates prepared and placed by role;
   b. graduates' length of service; and
   c. graduates' proficiency as judged by employers?

U.S. OFFICE OF SPECIAL EDUCATION GUIDELINES *(continued)*

6. A method for assessing the effectiveness and efficiency of project resource usage?
7. A method for assessing the impact of this project on related projects within the institution and the community?
8. At least annual evaluation of progress in achieving project objectives?
9. At least annual evaluation of the effect of the project on persons being served by the project, including any persons who are members of groups that have been traditionally underrepresented such as members of racial or ethnic minority groups and handicapped persons, etc.?

CONSIDERATIONS WHEN CHOOSING A SET OF STANDARDS

Since there are alternative sets of standards from which to choose, you will have to select those that are right for your purpose and context. Below are some issues you might consider when selecting a set of standards or criteria.

I. Content of the Standards
  A. Authority
    1. What were the bases for generating the standards? e.g.:
      a. problems emerging in the field
      b. professional objectives
      c. conventional practice
      d. natural laws
      e. theory of logical framework
    2. What level of authority do the standards carry? e.g.:
      a. postulates
      b. principles
      c. rules
      d. guidelines
      e. research
      f. concepts
      g. suggested procedures
    3. What was used to verify that the standards are responsible and consistent? e.g.:
      a. research findings
      b. conceptual theories
      c. conventional practices
      d. professional votes
    4. Have the boundaries for professional judgment within the standards been determined? e.g.:
      a. standards provide for professional judgment
      b. standards provide a basis for judgment
      c. standards provide a frame of reference to promote predictable judgment
      d. standards delineate areas for professional judgment
      e. standards establish limitations of professional judgment
  B. Scope
    1. Have the standards' scope of relevant applicability been specified? e.g., regarding:
      a. professional activities and products
      b. professionals
      c. clients
      d. contexts

2. Have limitations and areas to which the standards are *not* applicable been identified? e.g., regarding:
   a. legal and professional jurisdiction
   b. contextual and functional exceptions
3. Under what conditions has it been decided to revise the standards? e.g.:
   a. based upon relevant new research findings
   b. in response to regulatory intervention
   c. in response to societal changes
   d. as a result of a change in the state of the art
   e. in lieu of enforcement problems

C. Support Documents
  1. Are relevant support documents available? e.g.:
    a. interpretations
    b. quotes
    c. bibliographies
    d. policy papers
    e. research

D. Renewal Strategies
  1. Have strategies to update or revise the standards been established? e.g.:
    a. close interaction with constituents and other agencies
    b. extensive exposure to pronouncements before their release
    c. research before and after release
    d. systematic attempts to anticipate emerging problems
    e. post-enactment review
    f. ongoing or ad hoc revision process
    g. formal appeals system

II. Use of the Standards
  A. Role of the Standards
    1. How will the standards be used for self-regulation?
    2. How will the standards be used for educating audiences? e.g.:
      a. open board meetings
      b. due process procedures
      c. discussion memoranda
      d. public hearings
      e. public files
      f. newsletters and news bulletins
      g. speaking engagements
      h. instructional campaigns
    3. How will the standards be used to educate and train professionals? e.g.:
      a. accreditation
      b. licensure
      c. education
      d. continuing education
      e. training

  B. Promotion, Monitoring, and Enforcement of the Standards
    1. How will the standards be used to define admission and the right to continue practicing in the field?
    2. How will the standards be used to establish ethical behavior of professionals?
    3. How will the standards be used to define sound and substandard practices?
    4. How will the standards be used in developing quality control measures? e.g.:

      a. as a basis to establish internal quality control policies
      b. as a tool for peer reviews
      c. as a tool for analyses of substandard evaluations
      d. as a basis to review voluntarily submitted reports
      e. as a basis to issue certificates of compliance
   5. How will substandard performance be penalized within the profession?
      e.g.:
      a. letters of constructive criticism
      b. letters of censure
      c. acceptance of resignation
      d. suspension or expulsion
C. Legal Use of the Standards
   1. How will substandard performance be established and penalized within the
      legal system? e.g.:
      a. use of standards by state boards to revoke, suspend, or refuse to renew a
         license has been anticipated
      b. use of standards by federal agencies responsible for professional services
         that are funded by or affect the public has been anticipated
      c. use of standards by courts in litigation involving real or alleged
         substandard conduct has been anticipated
D. Monitoring or Controlling Use of the Standards
   1. How will use of the standards by public-sector agencies, general audiences,
      and courts be monitored and controlled? e.g.:
      a. level of specificity in language of standard statements and attestation
         reports has been considered in light of litigation
      b. analyses of relevant court rulings resulting from failure to adhere to
         professional standards have been considered
      c. use of court-appointed masters has been explored
      d. extension of "safe harbor" concept when using new methodologies has
         been explored
      e. avenues of discouragement of "nuisance" suits have been considered

HOW DO YOU APPLY A SET OF META-EVALUATION CRITERIA?

Once you have selected a *set* of meta-evaluation criteria, it is quite likely that you will need to adapt it in some way to better fit your particular situation. This can be accomplished by deciding how important each criterion is in relation to each other and by specifying indicators of compliance or quality for *each* criterion used.

At one extreme, you may say (or imply by default) that each criterion is just as important as every other one. On the other extreme, you may decide that every criterion is of different importance to you, and you might devise a scale to weight them accordingly. For a number of reasons, such as an inability to get consensus from the people involved or a tendency to clump groups of criteria, you will probably wind up with something in between the two extremes, usually some kind of ranking.

When you know which criteria are actually going to be applied, you can go on to specify how you will distinguish or measure compliance. This activity involves: 1) determining how precisely you will define compliance (for example, you may distinguish compliance at a dichotomous level, "met or not met"; you may rank order quality—"poor, so-so, good, great"; or you may use a scale with equal intervals—"On a scale of 1 to 10, I'd give it a 7."); 2) giving concrete descriptions of when an evaluation would be judged to be at a particular level of compliance; and 3) identifying the likely sources of information you will use as evidence of compliance.

As always, when you're involved in a valuing process, you need to consider who has something to gain or lose from the activity and determine how their perspectives should be represented. (Some perspectives that may be relevant to you have been listed in Chapter 4.) Also keep in mind under what conditions you intend to apply criteria. For instance, do they apply to *any* evaluation, or only evaluations of training and development projects, or only to your particular project? Do they apply to any *phase* of an evaluation, or only to evaluation designs?

Finally, to determine compliance indicators, you should consider the amount of information available, the level of precision needed, and the level of agreement possible.

If everybody agrees on how important the standards or criteria are and agrees on how clearly you can distinguish between them, coming to an agreement about the quality of an evaluation should not be much of a problem. On the other hand, if people cannot agree on what's important or how you can tell when you have a good evaluation, then you risk settling on the least common denominator, a watered down set of criteria on which everyone can agree. The following tables are used to summarize how you can adapt an existing set of meta-evaluation criteria for your own context.

WAYS TO ESTABLISH THE RELATIVE STANDING BETWEEN META-EVALUATION CRITERIA

All items are of equal standing (e.g., professional standards)

Items are ranked by key audiences (This technique is used in the American Psychological Association's testing standards)

   e.g., Use, Don't Use

       Priority A, Priority B, Priority C

       Essential, Useful, Supplemental, Not Needed

Items are weighted

   e.g., #1 = 20, #2 = 0, #3 = 30, #4 = 10, #5 = 30

       Category 1 = 100, Category 2 = 50, Category 3 = 25, Category 4 = 0

CONSIDERATIONS WHEN ESTABLISHING RELATIVE STANDINGS OF META-EVALUATION CRITERIA

Talk to the groups involved and explore their position for deciding what's important

   e.g., parents of deaf children wanting "Total Communication" vs. a funder who wants a randomized experimental design

   e.g., evaluation designs in proposals for innovative training projects

       evaluations of field placements for student teachers

       evaluations to decide which programs stay and which go

Determine the existing requirements for the evaluation

   e.g., since JDRP approval is desired, a premium is placed on demonstrating that any beneficial changes can be linked to the project itself

       it is known that the evaluation report *must* be completed by May 15, with specific recommendations, if the School Board is going to use it in deciding whether to fund the Teacher Center another year

Indicate the level of precision needed

   e.g. only general verbal feedback is desired on the first draft of an evaluation design

       since Grant funds are limited and the number of proposals is high, a two-stage cut will be made, first on general considerations related to the Grant purposes, second on relative rankings of project designs, evaluation designs, and budgets

Anticipate the level of agreement possible

   e.g., in the above parent/funder example, a conflict exists between the right to treatment and the generalizability of results

       everyone agrees that the evaluation should take no more than 2% of the project budget, so a "bare bones" approach is needed

---

SOME EXAMPLE INDICATIONS OF COMPLIANCE FOR DIFFERENT MEASUREMENT APPROACHES

KIND OF MEASUREMENT	DESCRIPTOR	INDICATOR	SOURCES OF INFORMATION
		"Report Timeliness" Standard	
Dichotomous	Met	The Model Training Program Final Report was delivered on time.	The report itself.
	Not Met	The Model Training Program Final Report was not delivered on time.	Recipients of the report.
		"Described Purposes and Procedures" Standard	
Ranking	Low	The purposes for evaluating the Model Training Program evaluation were ill-defined.	Evaluation design.
	Medium	General uses for the Model Training Program evaluation were described.	Preceeding needs assessment.
	High	A clear listing of the types of decisions to be made and when, which was to come out of the Model Training Program evaluation, had been identified.	Management plan.
		"Valuational Interpretation" Standard	
Weighting	Completely Unacceptable (−1.00)	No one directly involved in or affected by the evaluation of the Model Training program had input into deciding how the project would be judged.	Sources listed above.
	Minimally Acceptable (0.00)	The project staff cooperated with the evaluator to decide what makes a "good" Model Training Program	Key informants. News media reports
	Expected (+0.75)	A group of administrators, Model Training Program staff, faculty, and students got together to decide what makes a "good" Model Training Program.	
	Most Desirable (+1.00)	A group of people representing all major university, school and community groups jointly established the criteria to determine what makes a "good" Model Training Program.	

WHAT PROCEDURES ARE USED IN META-EVALUATION?

Up until now, we have presented some general uses of meta-evaluation, suggested what types of people should conduct a meta-evaluation, and offered a number of possible ways to develop meta-evaluation activities. For the most part, these ideas would help you primarily to focus your meta-evaluation. What comes next can be thought of just like any other evaluation. You are now going to have to carefully consider the various aspects of designing, collecting, analyzing, reporting and managing the meta-evaluation. If you want to use the *Sourcebook* as a guide, you will need to recycle through the chapters again, this time using your *evaluation* of the training project (or whatever) as the object of interest.

As your meta evaluation begins to take shape and you clarify some of the uses to which you intend to put it (e.g., evaluating evaluation plans, activities, or results), you will also have a better idea of what types of procedures would be most appropriate, such as hiring consultants, putting together a review panel, getting a funding continuation decision from your funder, and the like. The list below includes some of your options.

	Focus of the Meta-Evaluation		
	Formative Uses		Summative Uses
	Evaluating Evaluation Plans	Evaluating Evaluation in Progress	Evaluating Evaluation After Its Completion
Procedures for Doing the Meta-Evaluation	hire consultant, e.g., evaluator, measurement specialist, or content specialist	independent observers, e.g., meta-evaluator, evaluation team, review panel	review of final reports, e.g., send reports to evaluator, consultant, advisory group
	review panel, e.g., advisory group	review of progress reports, e.g., logs, interim reports, budget update, management plan, collection schedule	meta-evaluator, e.g., sponsors or funding agent, advisory panel, professional evaluator(s)
	review of evaluation plans, e.g., design, contract management plan		

By attending to the advice and warnings about evaluation presented in this *Sourcebook*, we hope that you will be able to develop, conduct, and apply an evaluation of your training efforts which reflects sound and just practices in light of the current developmental state of the field of evaluation. At a minimum, we feel that this means that your evaluation should provide technically adequate information, which is realistically obtainable at a reasonable cost, for clearly useful purposes, which safeguard the rights and dignity of the people involved. If you can do this, you have done well.

For an example of a meta-evaluation, read Case C-4 in the *Casebook*. This case illustrates the use of the Joint Committee *Standards* to evaluate the evaluation design for a model training program at a university.

REFERENCES

American Psychological Association. *Standards for Educational and Psychological Tests and Manuals*. Washington, D.C.: APA, 1966.

Boros, O.K. *The Mental Measurements Yearbooks*. Highland Park, New Jersey: Gryphon Press, 1941–1965 (irregular).

Campbell, D.T., & Stanley, J.C. *Experimental and Quasi-Experimental Designs for Research*. Chicago: Rand McNally, 1966.

Comptroller General of the United States. *Standards for Audit of Governmental Organizations, Programs, Activities, and Functions*. Washington, D.C.: U.S. Government Printing Office, 1981.

Cook, T.D., & Campbell, D.T. *Quasi-Experimentation: Design and Analysis Issues for Field Settings*. Chicago: Rand McNally, 1979.

Evaluation Research Society. *Standards for Program Evaluation*. Exposure Draft, 1980.

Joint Committee on Standards for Educational Evaluation. *Standards for Evaluations of Educational Programs, Projects, and Materials*. New York: McGraw-Hill, 1981.

Tallmadse, G.K. *Joint Dissemination Review Panel Ideabook*. Washington, D.C.: U.S. Government Printing Office, 1977.

Ridings, J.M. *Standard Setting in Accounting and Auditing: Considerations for Education Evaluation*. Unpublished doctoral dissertation, Western Michigan University, 1980.

Stufflebeam, D.L. *Meta-Evaluation*. Occasional Paper Series, No. 3, The Evaluation Center, Western Michigan University, 1974.

U.S. Department of Education. *Application of Grants Under Handicapped Personnel Preparation Program*. Washington, D.C.: Author, 1981.